The iconic female

The iconic female

Goddesses of India, Nepal and Tibet

edited by Jayant Bhalchandra Bapat
and Ian Mabbett

Monash University Press
Clayton

Monash University Press
Building 11
Monash University
Victoria 3800, Australia
www.monash.edu.au/mai

All Monash University Press publications are subject to double blind peer review

National Library of Australia Cataloguing-in-Publication entry

Title: The iconic female : goddesses of India, Nepal and Tibet / editor Jayant Bhalchandra Bapat, Ian Mabbett.

ISBN: 9781876924669 (pbk.)

Notes: Bibliography.

Subjects: Goddesses--India.

Goddesses--China--Tibet.

Goddesses--Nepal.

Women and religion.

Other Authors/Contributors:

Bapat, Jayant Bhalchandra, 1938-

Mabbett, I. W. (Ian William), 1939-

Monash University. Monash Asia Institute.

Dewey Number: 202.114

Maps©Monash Asia Institute

Cover image by Sanjay Pande. Cover design by Jenny Hall.

Printed by BPA Print Group, Melbourne, Australia - www.bpabooks.com

We dedicate this volume to a great colleague, friend and mentor to many of us, Dr Rashmikant Desai.

Rashmi has put the welfare and research of his postgraduate students in fields as diverse as anthropology, sociology, politics, economics, music and Indology, who numbered more than forty, before his own academic advancement, and continues to do so.

contents

	Contributors	ix
	Preface	xi
	Acknowledgments	xiii
Chapter one	Contextualising the goddess *Ian Mabbett and Jayant Bhalchandra Bapat*	1
Chapter two	Archaeology of the goddess: an Indian paradox *Angelo Andrea Di Castro*	21
Chapter three	Pārvatī as creator of *māyā* or victim of *māyā*: the role of Gaṇeśa's mother in the *Gaṇeśapurāṇa* *Greg Bailey*	43
Chapter four	When Reṇukā was not a goddess *Rashmi Desai*	65
Chapter five	The Lajjāgaurī: mother, wife or *yoginī* *Jayant Bhalchandra Bapat*	79
Chapter six	Devī and tantric practice *John R Dupuche*	113
Chapter seven	The *ḍākinī* in Tibetan hagiography *David Templeman*	133
Chapter eight	Devī's lion herders: bards and bardic goddesses and the moral regulation of power in late-medieval Rajasthan *Max Harcourt*	149
Chapter nine	Songs in the presence of Mammai Mātājī *Effy George*	163
Chapter ten	The Khāḍādevī Temple of modern Mumbai: communal harmony and the Koḷī goddess *Marika Vicziany and Jayant Bhalchandra Bapat*	189
	Bibliography	209
	Index	225

contributors

Greg Bailey is a reader in Sanskrit at La Trobe University. He works on Sanskrit epic literature, Purāṇas and early Buddhist literature. He is also interested in medieval Tamil literature.

Jayant Bapat holds doctorates in Organic Chemistry and Social Anthropology and is a research fellow at the Monash Asia Institute. His current research interests include Hindu temple architecture, temple priests, the Purāṇas, goddess cults and gods and goddesses of the Koḷī fisher folk of Mumbai.

Rashmi Desai retired as a senior lecturer in Anthropology from Monash University and he is currently a research fellow at the Monash Asia Institute. Rashmi has a long-term research interest in the *Rāmāyaṇa*.

Angelo Andrea Di Castro is a lecturer and research associate at the Monash Asia Institute. He is a specialist in the archaeology of South Asia, in particular India, Gandhara, and the Himalayan regions. Angelo's current research interests include Asian religions from an archaeological perspective and the history of cultural exchange between the Indian world and the West.

John R Dupuche is a Catholic priest of the Archdiocese of Melbourne. He is an honorary visiting research fellow in the Institute for the Advancement of Research at the Australian Catholic University, chair of the Catholic Interfaith Committee and a member of the Premier's Multifaith Advisory Board.

Effy George obtained her PhD from La Trobe University, Melbourne, in 2006. She is currently with the Liberal Arts department at Victoria University. Her present anthropological research concerns the impact of modernity on South Asian women's art and culture. She is also an honorary fellow of the Monash Asia Institute.

Max Harcourt was a senior lecturer in the School of History at the University of NSW until his retirement in 2003. His current research interests are the treatment of modern Indian history in recent popular Indian cinema—particularly with regard to revolutionary politics in the Hindi and Punjabi regions in the period 1907–1934, and to the Quit India movement of 1942—and the role of the bard caste and bardic goddesses in pre-colonial era Rajasthan.

Ian Mabbett is a research fellow at the Monash Asia Institute. As a member of the Monash School of Historical Studies, he has taught subjects dealing with South Asian and Southeast Asian history and religion. His research interests are in ancient Indian history and religion, especially the history and philosophy of Buddhism. He is co-author of *The sociology of Indian Buddhism,* with Greg Bailey.

David Templeman worked with Tibetan refugees in the 1960's and early 1970's and became interested in Tibetan culture, history and religion. He published his first translation from Tibetan in 1981, followed by other books in 1983 and 1989. David is at present completing a doctorate on the 16–17th century Tibetan historian Tāranātha at Monash Asia Institute.

Marika Vicziany is Professor of Asian Political Economy at Monash University and Director of the Monash Asia Institute, a research institute with a strong commitment to Indian studies. She is also Director of the National Centre for South Asian Studies (Monash Asia Institute) that hosts the internationally renowned journal *South Asia*.

Preface

This exuberant collection of ten essays about the Devī is the work of Australian scholars who have been engaged in extensive fieldwork in India over many decades—the youngest of us has worked in India for only 20 years and the oldest for 60 years. We have not attempted to systematise our work on the Devī because as the first chapter argues, such systematisation defies the complexity of Indian goddesses. Rather this book reflects the celebrated diversity of India over time, regions, beliefs, ethnicities and practices. The Devī is not a static entity—in her many manifestations she lives, dies and is reborn continuously and unpredictably. The naked, headless Goddess Lajjāgaurī may have only been worshipped up to the 7th century, but new goddesses are constantly appearing while hundreds of old goddesses continue to evolve in directions that ensure the enduring power of the Devī in a rapidly modernising India.

Five years ago, the Monash Asia Institute at Monash University in Melbourne (Australia) organised a one-day symposium to bring together Australian scholars working on Indian goddesses. Only a small selection of those present at that gathering have essays in this collection—further collections will be published in the coming years. Other symposia followed that initial meeting with the result that most of the authors contributing to the present volume are engaged in larger monographs about Indian goddesses.

This collection also represents the first book on Indian religions to be published by Monash University Press, a subdivision of the Monash Asia Institute. The Press adheres to a strict process of external peer review, as a result of which we thank the various referees who kindly read earlier versions of these chapters and gave us very useful feedback. We also thank Jenny Hall, Publications Officer of the Monash Asia Institute, for her editing of the text and design of the front cover. Her professional standards, creative instincts and good humour have made her into a delightful member of our team. I would also like to thank the editors—Ian Mabbett and Jayant Bapat—who have been wonderful and persistent colleagues, totally dedicated to the task of bringing this book out in time for the Diwali festival in October 2008.

Throughout the world Indology, or the study of Indian cultures, has been at a low ebb for two decades. Basham's wonderful work on India, a hallmark of Indological studies, appeared to have been eclipsed by doom and gloom. But the contributors to this volume are great optimists—the energy that drove Basham's work out of his base in Canberra, is re-emerging. In the last few years, India has suddenly re-appeared on the world stage as a rising global power. Business studies on India are booming, especially in Australia where the bilateral relationship has been reinvigorated. The energy that drives that relationship is spreading, and has given Australian scholars of Indian culture a new determination to increase the appreciation of Indian culture amongst all communities that seek to engage with India and the growing Indian diaspora. This collection of essays will, we hope, contribute to that cultural re-engagement.

Marika Vicziany

Director, Monash Asia Institute

Monash University, Melbourne, Australia

Acknowledgments

This book has experienced a gestation of well over five years since its original conception, and it gives us immense pleasure to see it in print after such a long period. It is particularly agreeable for us to thank all those individuals whose help has been invaluable. Professor Marika Vicziany, the director of Monash Asia Institute, deserves a special mention, as she inspired the project, and her constant involvement and encouragement have made our task easier and have been a major factor in the volume's eventual successful completion. It has benefited also from the work of Emma Hegarty, who as Publications Officer for the Monash Asia Institute was responsible for steering the work successfully through all its earlier stages with helpfulness and professionalism; in the later stages Jenny Hall combined the roles of artist, chief editor, proof-reader, secretary, receptionist and organiser, and her impressive range of talents has been of great help to us both. We warmly thank all the authors who met their deadlines and still produced excellent chapters. Thanks are also due to the Monash Asia Institute Publications Committee which supported our endeavour.

Jayant Bhalchandra Bapat and Ian Mabbett

chapter one

Contextualising the goddess

Ian Mabbett and Jayant Bhalchandra Bapat

In Indian religion, the figure of the goddess, Devī, admits of no simple definition. She is commonly spoken of in the singular, a transcendent divine power, and yet, encountered in innumerable concrete embodiments, she is not one but many. In folk tales she often figures as the deity concerned with affliction, sexuality, fecundity and motherhood, and frequently in such tales, problematic wives or mothers may die violently and be apotheosised into spirits that must be propitiated. In Brahmanical Hinduism, by contrast, humans are not apotheosised and the Devī often appears in a subordinate role as the consort of a male deity. Alternatively and paradoxically, she also appears as pure *śakti*—power. Goddess cults are addressed severally or simultaneously to deities that epitomise sweetness and beauty, or nurturance and loving care, or shamelessness, violence, horror and death. She has been and remains, despite the relatively modern top-dressing of monistic theology, a multitude of ultimately disparate images, aspirations, doctrines, stories and rituals. She is not to be pinned down by a neat definition; she slips through any net that is set to catch her. Her name is legion.

The Devī has therefore proved fascinating to scholars in many disciplines. Many publications on the subject of the Indian goddesses have appeared. They cannot be reviewed at all thoroughly here. One of them, though, can usefully be picked out for special attention as a springboard for discussion, particularly because of the issues raised by its editor in explaining and defending the principles governing its composition.

The volume in question, *Autour de la déesse hindoue*, was published in Paris in 1981, edited by Madeleine Biardeau (Biardeau 1981). In the years since this publication, to be sure, there has been time for much to happen and, indeed, much has happened; there has been a massive increase in the publication of works dealing in various ways with *la déesse*, a great wealth of empirical evidence has come into the public domain and many really excellent studies have contributed enormously to our knowledge of Indian goddess cults of all sorts. The abundance of excellent scholarship devoted to Indian goddesses since the appearance of Biardeau's book might be expected to consign it to a remote and little-visited past era. Nevertheless, it is worth pausing to observe how, in certain important ways, it is somehow still natural for the reader to think of it as a recent publication. Why is this so?

Essentially, the lesson to be drawn is that, although knowledge about Indian goddesses has advanced in important ways, the terrain of scholarship has not vastly altered. Similar questions, similar issues and some of the same answers still occupy those who explore past and present goddess cults. The effect of the sheer abundance and variety of detail now available has been to offer more intellectual nourishment than can quickly be digested; it defies any hasty attempt to encompass it all within a grand theory. Generalisations and abstractions run into exceptions at every point. We believe that for the foreseeable future progress lies not so much in wholly new theories; it lies rather in the advancing appreciation of the nuances, in recognition of the difficulties in making old theories fit. Although there are exceptions that will be noted below, scholars still work with long-familiar methods and perspectives, and long-familiar ideas are not altogether abandoned, but they have to be refined. This much can be recognised all the more clearly when we look at the issues mentioned by Biardeau in her introductory discussion (Biardeau 1981:9–16).

Her main concern was to emphasise the growing scholarly convergence represented by the contributions in the book she edited. This convergence was not the result of a theoretical programme imposed upon the contributors; on the contrary, they applied different disciplines, adopted different perspectives, tackled radically different problems, and in some cases disagreed with each other. Wisely, Biardeau sought no dogmatic uniformity, no new collaborative theory. The convergence of ideas she recognised demanded a subtler conceptual framework. What was emerging in the perceptions of scholarship, she wrote, was not an advance towards any single agreed interpretation of the history of the goddess in Indian religion. It was, rather, a growing recognition of the inadequacy of old glib master-theories, a recognition that was evidenced by the silence of the contributors about them. Biardeau mentioned several of these theories, which she regarded as obsolescent. Their obsolescence, she suggested, was the result of the richer knowledge and clearer vision now available.

Thus, much of her introduction to the collection was occupied by a review of ideas which appeared significant by virtue of their absence—obsolescent theories formerly taken seriously, but now being overtaken by richer knowledge and clearer vision. The first two of these notions form a pair of opposites, though both, Biardeau said, have flaws. One is the theory that the multiplicity and variety of Indian goddess cults have arisen from a sort of push from below—the idea that the local cults of innumerable low castes and tribes have sought to rise in status and stake a claim to orthodox legitimacy, obtaining the *droit de la cité*. The other is that the whole kaleidoscope was formed by devolution from the original pantheon of orthodox Vedic cults; as society became more hierarchical, some were degraded. The first of these theories, declares Biardeau, is implausible because of the exclusiveness of Brahmanical orthodoxy which could not allow the sacral validity of base practices, and the second is unconvincing, failing as it does to account for totally new post-Vedic developments such as devotional religion and temple worship.

Another sort of theory marginalised by Biardeau is the view that mother goddesses of perhaps Mediterranean origin presided in prehistoric times over agricultural rites in a matriarchal society. Traces of such cults have often been supposed to survive in the goddess cults of later centuries in India, sometimes seen as vestiges of a once widespread but now lost pattern of social organisation in which women had a much more important role.

More generally, Biardeau criticises various theoretical categorisations, which seek to pinpoint the essential character of religious cults by putting them into pairs of opposite classes. There are several such pairs—high (pure) and low (impure), male and female, Aryan and Dravidian, heaven and earth. Any of these theoretical distinctions may be useful for certain purposes, but they all run into trouble if too much explanatory power is demanded of them, because they cannot account for all the important features of the empirical evidence.

A special case is the stark theoretical opposition between the great and little traditions, in which the former is identified with a supposedly transcendent Brahmanical world view divorced from the particularism of localities with their unsophisticated oral traditions. Biardeau (quite rightly up to a point, no doubt) sees this as an oversimplification, violating the strong association of Brāhmans with village culture (Biardeau 1981:12).

She further offers doubts about the role of psychological explanations of goddess cults, explanations which have on occasion suffered by being confined to the application of global Jungian archetypes, or just 'la psychanalyse', in a not very historical way (Biardeau 1981:12f).

Biardeau's observations add up to a useful conspectus of our knowledge of the Indian goddess in 1981 and the ways in which scholarly approaches appeared to be changing. It is notable, though, that the issues identified by her then are still with us now; as suggested above, the contours of scholarly discussion have not by any means changed beyond recognition. Moreover today, as in 1981, the momentum of scholarship on the Indian Devī has focused on a pragmatic engagement with what meets the scholar on the ground—namely, the religious beliefs and practices of India, regardless of whether they fit elegantly or poorly into any predefined theoretical construct.

Earlier studies of Indian religion were often marred by oversimplifications which later research strove to rectify, and in more recent years the abundance of well-directed studies has made it possible for us to appreciate far better the variety and complexity of goddess cults across India, past and present, and ways in which they do *not* fall into neat categories that formerly seemed to be fundamental. That, perhaps, is the chief lesson to be drawn by looking at the situation addressed by *Autour de la déesse* and comparing it with the situation of scholarship today. But things have not changed radically; the ideas and approaches which Biardeau criticised have not, in the meantime, become totally irrelevant to the present state of scholarship. Further, although we might agree with her specific criticisms and accept the need for more refined analysis, there are certainly those who would disagree about the obsolescence of some of the ideas she described as moribund.

An example is the notion of a push from below—the theory that in the course of history cults burgeoned because local deities rose in status and gained acceptance as orthodox through the aspirations of their devotees. This sort of theory may need to be carefully formulated if it is not to be vulnerable, but the social mobility of the cults maintained by local communities continues to be well attested. Many a rustic local icon has come to be recognised as a manifestation of a great Brahmanical deity when the local community's participation in a wider society has enhanced its status. There continues to be considerable use for MN Srinivas' concept of 'Sanskritisation'—the notion that, in their historical evolution, the cults and customs of some social communities have asserted their rise in the world by taking on the characteristics (especially the use of refined Sanskrit) of practices associated with elite or dominant groups (Srinivas 1952). However much it may need to be qualified, this concept has proved very fruitful in accounting for the dynamics of religion within the locality. (This will be illustrated in the course of the discussion below.) The Brahmanical or Sanskritic world view and the religious manifestations of local folk culture do not, of course, have incommensurably dissimilar origins or inhabit separate worlds; they have interacted over millennia, producing a kaleidoscope of forms which defy easy categorisation and which in specific historical situations can readily change their places in the pattern.

Again, psychological approaches figure among the less favoured methods of scholarship mentioned by Biardeau, but they have in fact prospered since, guiding a multitude of studies that seek to account for the practical, concrete forms taken by Indian religion; some scholars have explored the special features of Indian society that predispose to particular aspects of culture and psychology (Kakar 1991, idem 1996), and others have sought to relate the features of religious practice to underlying emotional conditions (such as Obeyesekere 1984, idem 1990; Kurtz 1992:20–6). In this, as in other matters, we need not disagree with Biardeau that the particular sorts of over-simple theories and glib speculations she targeted have had their day. At the same time, more refined reincarnations of them, much more securely based upon detailed Indian fieldwork, continue to be born.

In this connection one might adduce the long popular theory of a widespread mother-goddess cult of remote prehistoric origin, from which Indian goddesses worshipped in more recent times have sometimes been thought to be directly descended.

We need to distinguish rigorously between this theory of a specific unified cult of a single over-arching mother goddess and a mere tendency, evident in myth and art, to impose the metaphor of a mother goddess upon the workings of nature and the sources of existence. Such a tendency is indeed prominent in much of Indian religious culture. The incredibly rich and multi-layered legacy of Indian myth throbs with resonances that echo down the centuries and from one culture to another. Implicit within this complex web of images and values is the figure of a supreme goddess, mother of all, which may be detected as a structural motif from the Vedas to tantras and from village cults of rough stones to great temples attracting pilgrims from all over the world. There are valuable insights to be won in research that discovers the veiled presence of a Mahādevī in a poetic allusion to Draupadī's hair (Hiltebeitel 1981), or in a tantric meditation upon the image of a serpent coiled at the base of one's spine. On all sides, there are hints and allusions that point towards the Devī as a permanent possibility within the Indian religious imagination.

However, an imaginative potentiality or an aspiration that stirs within the unconscious mind is not the same thing as an actual cult of a singular divinity. We are not entitled to speak of a Devī as the 'Great Goddess' unless we can identify a potentiality made actual, a specific cult with a more or less organised form of worship whose priests quite explicitly recognise the singular identity of their deity. This idea, often linked with the theory of a matriarchal society widespread in prehistoric times and particularly associated with the writings of M Gimbutas (1974, 1999), is among the theories discounted by Biardeau; it has retreated from the centre of historical and anthropological scholarship, though it persists in some quarters. For example, MR Dexter writes: 'More likely, later [ie post-Vedic] goddesses retrieved a more ancient prestige which they had lost when the Indo-Europeans entered India' (Dexter 1990:81). While the archaeological evidence may not support it, the theory is ambivalent upon some points, and a well-based account of what the evidence actually shows is still to enter common knowledge. The subject is addressed by Di Castro's chapter in this volume.

Biardeau perceptively identified a number of old ideas about the goddess as unsubstantiated by the progress of research; yet further research has not yet rejected them all utterly and completely, for some of them have gained life in new forms. Ironically perhaps, it may seem to some that, among the scholarly assumptions Biardeau mentions, the one most surely doomed to abeyance or moratorium is the one she most favours—the faith that contributions to the study of the goddess share a vision of 'l'intérieur de la culture indienne', an underlying sense that beneath all the transformations and diversities of history there is an India-wide common consciousness within which the goddess finds meaning and purpose. For Biardeau, it was more or less axiomatic that the goddess is a basic category of the Hindu consciousness as such: 'Le postulat ici est que la *Déesse* est une catégorie fondamentale de la conscience hindoue come telle' (Biardeau 1981:14). It is a consciousness with shape and structure, and the role of the goddess within that structure is a proper object of scholarly research.

The idea here espoused by Biardeau expresses the vision that attributes personality, purpose and destiny to a civilisation, and it was particularly active in shaping the assumptions and methods of a great deal of French orientalist scholarship through much of the 20th century. (The word 'orientalist' is intended here in its proper sense: pertaining to the study of the East through language and literature.) One of its most distinguished early proponents was Paul Mus, whose explicit methods of scholarship related the evidence of texts to just such a supposed underlying Indian consciousness (Mabbett 2006:117–28). Perhaps, however, in the present stage of advancing knowledge, most of the immediate problems in the study of Indian religions increasingly require attention to relatively contingent and local factors, rather than an encompassing vision with more or less structuralist assumptions. The concrete evidence thrown up by scholarly fieldwork increasingly demands to be understood within a more pragmatic framework of hypotheses with little use for the notion of an encompassing Hindu or Indian consciousness, a notion which was not obviously essential to the methods of many of the contributors to Biardeau's volume, and is not part of any programme adopted in the present volume. Nevertheless, this macroscopic frame of reference has in the past contributed enormously to a sound intuitive grasp of the ways in which Indian culture could work (although it requires something like the massive erudition of Mus or Biardeau if it is to succeed) and it would be sad if it were to be altogether discarded.

Nevertheless, it is precisely at this point that we need to take account of the exceptions to the general principle that the nature of scholarship on Devī has not changed much in recent years. Certain new approaches have gained ground considerably and their proponents are markedly unsympathetic to the concept of a generic Hindu consciousness; for them, the notion of an enduring essence of real Hinduism that can be studied through texts is likely to obstruct understanding of actual religious practices on the ground, in the life of ordinary Indians. They see this concept as *a priori* privileging a particular point of view, that of Brāhman dominance, which treats certain 'Sanskritic' traditions as a core or centre and, thereby, establishes arbitrarily a scale or criterion of authenticity which marginalises many of the cults which play an important part in religious life, and which can just as validly be described as cores or centres of local or regional cultures. Sarah Caldwell has offered a succinct and eloquent reconceptualisation of the relationship between margins and centres which would allow us to identify certain 'extreme' forms of Kālī worship not as deviations from a Hindu norm but as local orthodoxy. 'Nuanced, critical, ethnographically informed studies of Kālī can therefore serve as a corrective to received understandings of the goddess as "extreme" and "marginal"' (Caldwell 2005:257); in Kerala, the Kālī addressed by local cults 'represents the essential and central values of the nonelite traditions' (Caldwell 2005:258).

To the extent that, or as long as, scholars concentrate upon the crafting of 'nuanced, critical, ethnographically informed' publications, they are essentially continuing a tradition of empirical scholarship that has been nurtured by studies of Indian religions for a long time. Even when they criticise old concepts and priorities, they are not necessarily making a sharp break with the past. What may well create the perception of such a break, however, is that recent studies have often been undertaken formally under the banner of declared programmes of research that are explicitly dedicated to particular causes. For example, influential causes are feminism, postcolonialism and subaltern studies. Those who are most consciously dedicated to the service of these causes are likely to see a sharply demarcated frontier between their own work and all older scholarship on India, particularly scholarship paying respect to written texts.

Research carried out under such banners may often be salutary, though the revisions of conventional ideas which it promotes may sometimes be controversial; the dubbing of certain perceived attitudes as 'orientalism' and the redefinition of Hinduism as a 19th-century Western invention are conspicuous examples (see Humes 2005; Urban 2005). Much has been written and much more will be written about such issues, but these debates must be left on one side here. It will be enough to observe in passing that there are possible dangers as well as advantages in the deliberately sympathetic focus upon classes of people neglected by mainstream study. Our appreciation of the culture of an often marginalised group can benefit enormously from a study focused specifically upon it; on the other hand, when a bright light is shone upon what goes on in the dark corners of society, the erstwhile centre may lose all its definition and subtlety of texture. In the case of Hinduism, the cultural forms associated with Brahmanical traditions and the canonical scriptures may (in an extreme case) come to be seen as irrelevant, even in places where they have in fact had a considerable influence.

Here then, in taking *Autour de la déesse hindoue* as a cadastral reference point in contemplating scholarship on Devī, we can recognise that its contribution, like that of various other collections of articles before and since, was to bring together the enquiries of scholars working at the frontiers of knowledge in such a way as to refine inherited ideas, identify misconceptions and demonstrate the need for distinctions and new concepts which earlier students had not been able to see.

The point is, precisely, that the same sort of task lies before us now, but there are many more inherited ideas to be refined, many more categories and concepts to be properly distinguished. What is wanted in the study of Indian divinities today, then, is a process of consolidation and incremental advance. We still need batteries of studies representing a variety of assumptions, topics and purposes. With more and more evidence against which to test generalisations, research can show up cumulatively the blind spots and oversimplifications inherent in earlier conclusions based upon less abundant evidence. This is not the same thing as decisively eliminating old approaches that have turned out to be wrong, thereby coming closer to the one right approach—on the contrary, old approaches can often reappear in new and more subtle forms. What does change, slowly but eventually decisively, is the whole context of our knowledge. However distinctive a cult may be in certain ways, it must fit into a whole picture of the variegated cultural pattern, and the whole picture grows incrementally clearer.

This sort of stepwise progress can be seen clearly in the way that ideas about the categories of 'high' and 'low' (or 'Sanskritic' and 'non-Sanskritic') cults of gods and goddesses have advanced. Successive studies produced at intervals through the second half of the 20th century demonstrate how, with increasing access to a richer and richer array of published evidence based on fieldwork, the complexity of the characteristics of goddesses in local shrines defies the sort of simple categorisation that at first seemed adequate, and hypotheses must continually be refined or rejected.

At its simplest, the typology of cults might favour a binary typology; on the one hand there are 'Sanskritic' gods and goddesses known from texts claiming Brahmanical orthodoxy and associated with iconography and rituals that belong within this orthodoxy, and on the other there are 'non-Sanskritic' deities lacking such characteristics and showing the marks of a rougher and simpler sort of local culture embodied largely in oral tradition. Studies conducted in particular localities have introduced more and more complications to this twofold division. As a first step, the case of EB Harper's research at Totagadde in Karnataka may be cited, introducing a threefold scheme. The gods recognised as most elevated are benevolent, Sanskritic, deities whose cults involve vegetarian diet; they are somewhat remote and even impersonal. The gods of the second category do not belong to the universal Brahmanical pantheon; they are essentially local, and they have different characteristics, potentially either benign or harmful; they are not above animal sacrifice; chief among them is Mariamma, goddess of smallpox and other diseases. The third contains dangerous spirits belonging to the local environment which do not have images made of them. These three classes, said to be recognised as separate categories by local people, correspond to local caste distinctions, respectively Brāhmans and Lingayats, Śūdras, and untouchables (Harper 1959:227–34). This work has been discussed by L Foulston (2002:173f) who also cites an unpublished paper by Brenda Beck which uses Harper's taxonomy of local deities.

What goes for gods goes also, up to a point at least, for goddesses; but they also have characteristics of their own. LA Babb, in the course of work published in the 1970s, attributed to Sanskritic goddesses a longer list of characteristics: they have mild subservient natures; they embody the transcendent and the ethical values of the Great Tradition; they do not accept meat offerings; they are not responsible for diseases; they do not subject any of their devotees to possession, and they are served by Brāhman priests using orthodox scriptures. The non-Sanskritic goddesses are the opposite in all these respects. In the area where Babb conducted research, at Chhattisgarh, local goddesses are said to be associated with disease, particularly smallpox, both inflicting and healing it. The disjunction between the Sanskritic and non-Sanskritic realms is said to be conceptually very clear, but there is continuity between the two levels, and they complement each other within a cosmological scheme (Babb 1970, 1975). This notion of a local community absorbing contrasting elements within a single cosmological scheme may indeed be valuable in the interpretation of many local religious cultures.[1]

In 1986, a few years after *Autour de la déesse hindoue*, there appeared a relatively elaborate analysis of certain goddesses worshipped in Karnataka using Jungian concepts. This was by AK Ramanujan, who identified two categories of goddess—'Breast Mothers', who were consorts of gods, and 'Tooth Mothers', who were virgin goddesses. The former are clearly substantially equivalent to Sanskritic deities. They are married and subordinate to their divine partners, associated with auspicious occasions, worshipped in households or in temples inside the village, represented by well-sculpted images, universal, pure, benevolent (unless offended, a significant new qualification), beneficent, vegetarian, and served by priests in Brahmanical rites. The 'Tooth Mothers' are opposite in character. They can be dangerous, are worshipped with blood sacrifices, represented by only roughly sculpted images or miscellaneous objects, and so forth (Ramanujan 1986:58 table 1.1). This interpretation of goddess cults explicitly applies Jungian concepts (Jung 1938:75–110).

The work of Babb and of Ramanujan, among others, was commented upon in the 1990s by Kathleen Erndl in relation to the results of her study of three goddess cults in north-west India. Her work showed that broad categorisations cannot be neatly applied to cults all over India. The goddesses she studied had major characteristics which ought to have consigned them to the category of 'Tooth Mother' (all being independent of any male god, linked to the earth rather than transcendent and apt to possess human subjects), but they also displayed 'Breast Mother' characteristics to a very substantial degree (Erndl 1993:153–7).

Relevant here, incidentally, is the question why some forms of the goddess are meek and subservient and some independent, wild and in certain respects dangerous. With what conditions are these characteristics primarily correlated? At first it was often assumed that being married was the main condition for controlled behaviour—a goddess who figures in myth and iconography as the consort of a great god is reckoned within Hindu doctrine as conjoined with or 'part of' her spouse, and thus unlikely to show wilful or aggressive behaviour—though in fact tantric influences produce dramatic exceptions to this rule. Śiva's consort can sometimes be mad, bad and dangerous to know. The character of Śiva's consort, often wild and dangerous, has been much discussed (for example by Wadley (1977) and by Sax (1991)). DR Brooks writes: 'Throughout Hindu tradition, we observe that the feminine Śakti must be controlled by the masculine Śiva in order to be beneficent and prevent dangerous events' (Brooks 1990:65). David Shulman, investigating beliefs about Śiva and his consort in Tamil myths, emphasises the dual nature of the goddess, tame and subservient or virginal and dangerous. Śiva's bride is often divided into two—a dark, destructive 'sheath' (Kauśikī, Kālī) and a golden, gentle wife (Umā, Gaurī). Śiva's union with the dark Kālī lies at the heart of the Tamil myths of marriage, but the god's wedding to the benign goddess is most frequently celebrated in temple rituals today (Shulman 1980:267).

Thus the 'marriage control model' can be questioned. Some have favoured associating the axis of subservience/wilfulness not with being or not being the consort of a great god but with the axes of motherliness/unmotherliness, or order/disorder (Mackenzie Brown 1991:122–5; Kurtz 1992:20–6; Pintchman 1994:204f; Tambs-Lyche 1999:9–35 at 11f.).

The extent to which significance can be convincingly found in such correlations must depend upon the detail and abundance of evidence assembled by successive scholars. Much depends upon context and point of view. Tantric tradition often inverts the otherwise common association of active power with the god and passivity or subservience with the goddess, but the god/goddess relationship, in a cosmology where polar opposites are likely to change places, defies any simple conclusions about psychological, cultural or social implications. It seems best to suppose that maleness and femaleness in the tantric vision do not have fixed intrinsic natures that can be conclusively identified as active or passive.

In 2002 Lynn Foulston reviewed the work of her predecessors in order to focus upon the complexity of goddess characteristics which cannot be neatly compartmentalised. This approach thus extended some of Erndl's findings. Foulston brings together the many features which have been held to characterise either the exalted goddesses of pan-Indian Brahmanical tradition or the local goddesses, respectively, and examines how far they fit the various cults found in two places which she examined closely (one in

Orissa, one in Tamilnadu). If every goddess conformed to one of the two ideal types (Sanskritic and non-Sanskritic), all those in the first category would be (to simplify) universal, benign, embodied in sculpted images, vegetarian, married, served by a Brāhman priest, and never subjecting devotees to possession, while those in the other would have appropriate contrasting characteristics; but in fact the goddesses studied combine characteristics from both categories in all sorts of permutations and very few approximate closely to ideal types (Foulston 2002:172–90). Certainly, the characteristics tabulated may well serve as guides to the general features of the ideal of a Brahmanical goddess in the 'Great Tradition', but few cults exhibit them in pure form and very many other cults of local divinities possess features ideally reserved for their betters.

This is not, nowadays, really surprising, but it brings out very clearly how each new study, if it is clearly focused upon features that need to be rigorously distinguished, can enrich our understanding, strengthening or weakening old hypotheses. Successive studies in different places should not, of course, be treated as descriptions of a homogeneous Indian system; by that standard, each one would be vulnerable to the complaint that it left out most of the things mentioned by all the others. Any of the studies of which we dispose may in principle be a keenly insightful description of the actually important features of the unique social environment investigated by its author. But the accumulation of numerous studies provides us with an increasingly reliable sense of what is widespread and what is special to particular places and how the common features function in their environments.

Perhaps the most important lesson to draw from the literature on the characteristics of 'Sanskritic' and 'non-Sanskritic' goddesses is that we must beware of reading into the two concepts features of two separate and distinct cultural worlds, one high and one low. The dynamics of social and religious change throughout India's history have ensured that, in practice, we confront a kaleidoscope of multiform images in constant collision and transformation, continually adapting to changing contexts. The evolution of Indian goddesses from rough local icons to manifestations of the absolute beyond all duality should not be thought of as a single leap from the rustic world of the Little Tradition to the loftiest of Brahmanical conceptualisations. Throughout the process, Devī could combine a variety of higher and lower, or richly local and ethereally abstract, forms, and as great goddess she could give high status to those who served her in the performance of purely local traditions.

In the light of these considerations, the authors of the present volume expect to confront an atomised Devī, a multitude of subculture-specific forms, each deserving to be studied as a distinctive and in some ways unique conceptualisation of the divine. Yet, at the same time, we expect to discern some of the ways in which each fits into a broader picture with a connected history. In comparatively recent centuries, Indian religion has been marked by a trend to assimilate each manifestation of divinity to the more literary regional or pan-Indian cosmologies which order and explain the co-existence of gross and refined elements, and create stories to make sense of the often bizarre behaviour attributed by myth to deities. Thus, what began as multiple local beliefs have been worked upon subsequently, under the impact of Sanskritisation, to be reconceptualised in a larger theological framework. It is time for this trend to be brought into clearer focus. Too commonly cults are written of as if they belonged to a timeless Indian culture; in fact there is plenty of evidence available for a much more detailed and richly textured history of religious change than we have at present. This history has been marked, over several centuries, by the encroachment and the crystallisation of a core orthodoxy, a tradition which in some ways can be identified as a Brahmanical point of view. We need a diachronic perspective in order to see the trend clearly. In this book the diachronic dimension can be recognised in the distribution of attention given to the archaeological record, to the problems of interpreting Sanskrit texts, to a variety of written sources that belong to earlier history, and also to the data of observation in our own times. It is a dimension which permits us to recognise how the identification of Devī as a name for the absolute, beyond duality, belongs principally to comparatively recent times. Within this frame, the chapters below can be related, in different ways, to the evolution of the Indian goddess. This evolution has led to a layering of the identity of any goddess, capable of being interpreted within multiple frameworks; at some levels purely local traditions owing little to any overarching Hindu system supply the motifs for her biography, while at others she is a manifestation of the universal Mahādevī and deriving her energy from the pan-Indian Sanskrit *corpus* of sacred literature, into which she is plugged. Her cult may on these levels be claimed to be based on Vedānta and enframed by Brahmanical orthodoxy.

The processes of universalisation are familiar in the history of Hinduism. MN Srinivas' term 'Sanskritisation' is apt enough as a label, although of course we need to recognise that, sometimes, the cultural forms imitated do not necessarily contain more genuinely Sanskrit material than the former culture of the imitators (Raghavan 1956; Staal 1963:261–75). The social authority of the Brāhmans has, however, commonly determined that a set of core traditions, especially associated with Sanskrit lore, should come to permeate the local cultures of those groups which are then absorbed within the metropolitan high culture.

It is not always the case that the religious beliefs and practices of the group which is Sanskritised are abolished. On the contrary, they may continue in strength, but in a new guise; they may be declared to be manifestations of a fundamental universal power known best through the subtle exegesis of exalted Sanskrit scriptures.

> The village-deity who wants the sacrifice of animals and toddy is also one of the myriad manifestations of the formless Brahma whom the philosopher contemplates. The gods of the lower castes are not denied, but affirmed, and affirmed in such a way that their subsequent Sanskritisation is rendered easier—Once inside Sanskritic Hinduism the local rites and beliefs undergo Sanskritisation rapidly and in a thoroughgoing manner (Srinivas 1952:227).

Cosmopolitanism works in favour of the process. Local gods or goddesses become regional, and regional ones become pan-Indian as advancing wealth and technology promote wider and wider horizons. A pertinent example is that of the goddess Vindhyavāsinī, the increasing prominence of whose cult has been studied by Cynthia Ann Humes. The shrine of the goddess is visited by pilgrims who come from further and further afield, and have more and more sophisticated knowledge of core Hindu texts, and in consequence her priests have found it natural to identify her as a form of the great goddess known in texts such as the *Devībhāgavatapurāṇa* (Humes 1996:74f.). Possibly this sort of mechanism for cultural change offers a good model for the understanding of 'Sanskritisation' more generally—the process is one that involves initiatives taken by local agents; their self-perceptions are subtly transformed as changes take place in their environment. The opposite sort of process, in which local religious figures are subject to manipulation by representatives of hegemonic cosmopolitan Brahmanism, has been suggested in some cases, for example by T Pintchman (1994:17). In practice, no doubt, elements of both interpretations might apply; it is well recognised that both 'top-down' and 'bottom-up' processes promote acculturation.

Social mobility, though difficult for individuals, has never been impossible for groups, whose political and economic status has often permitted their local cults to become fully integrated within the Sanskritic 'Great Tradition'. This is made possible by the breadth of the devotees' horizons and the depth of their knowledge. During the process of assimilation, one of the mechanisms facilitating the process may be an enframing of the local material within whatever tradition is regarded as dominant or orthodox, representing the encompassing structure of high Sanskritic lore. What is enframed is given legitimacy instead of being destroyed, but is subjected to a higher authority. It loses its unique identity and is reconceptualised, being put in a new context as part of a Brahmanical narrative.

This idea of enframing is illustrated by cases of stories being put inside stories; the Brahmanical narrative is often a narrative in a straightforward sense. Texts tell stories and stories are often told within stories. The story that tells all the rest, at the highest analytical level, gives them meaning by imprinting upon them the authority of the god, often Śiva, who utters them. Subtly, it may be that Devī (or a particular *devī*) loses unique authority over her devotees at the same time that she gains in majesty and status, for, by being promoted to the status of cosmic *śakti*, supreme power in the universe, she accepts a position within a scheme of cosmic explanation that has been created by and belongs to the Brāhmans.

To understand the evolution of Indian goddesses in their proper historical context, we need to read sensitively the stories that tell of their exploits, and we need to learn how to recognise the likely resonances that they had for their early listeners. The stories told in Sanskrit literature have many frames within frames—none more so, perhaps, than that of the *Mahābhārata*, and it is wholly within the scheme of this volume that we have included a chapter by Rashmi Desai, which applies anthropological insights to the contextualisation of an episode of matricide in the great epic, the killing of Reṇukā. Raising questions about motherhood, the symbolism of decapitation, guilt, patriarchy, filial duty and competition between priests and lords, it supplies many of the elements needed for a reading of the cultural world in which Devī figured. It points, especially, to the contrast between the classical, literary versions in which Reṇukā is very definitely *not* a goddess and the various local cults in which she is apotheosised.

Desai points to an aspect of the Reṇukā myth to which little attention has yet been paid. By isolating the story in the *Mahābhārata* from other accounts, he argues that the tale is really styled as a mini epic with Paraśurāma as the hero. As befits the epical form, exemplified in the Rāmāyaṇa as it appears in the *Mahābhārata*, the Paraśurāma story also ranges from his birth to his ultimate withdrawal from the affairs of the world. Desai's argument is that we need to distinguish between the Bhṛgu/Brahmanic interpolation and the story of the Kṣatriya heroes, the Paṇdava brothers; the two themes stand in juxtaposition within the *Mahābhārata*.

Di Castro's chapter, as noted above, deals explicitly with the atomised and heterogeneous character of Devī in archaeological sources, before Sanskritisation or Brahmanisation. He discusses in detail the objections to taking for granted the notion of the continuous worship of a primeval goddess. He notes that archaeological evidence is often decontextualised by its removal from the place of the origin. Also literary sources only refer to a much later period. He concludes that, although attractive, the idea of a continuous transmission of a coherent goddess cult starting from the Palaeolithic period through to the Neolithic-Chalcolithic time and finally ending in the Early Historic period needs to be supported by much stronger evidence than what we have available today.

Bapat's essay illustrates the striking heterogeneity of early forms of goddess worship by focusing upon a highly distinctive cult that turned out to be a *cul-de-sac* of divine evolution—that of Lajjāgaurī, which lasted only until the seventh century CE. It was directed to the worship of a naked and headless female image found in several regions of the Indian subcontinent. The essay challenges the hypothesis by art historians that the Lajjāgaurī image evolved from a Kalaśa motif to a fully anthropomorphic figure. Although the idea of such an evolution is logical and hence tempting, the myths surrounding the image do not support it. This shows once again that mythology is far more complex than straightforward logical thought. Bapat concludes that Lajjāgaurī was worshipped mainly as the mother goddess responsible for creation and sustenance. It is also possible, however, that the large images installed in well-built shrines may have been used as vehicles for Cakrapūjā by left-handed tantrics. In the current contentious climate of redefining Hinduism, the author refutes the arguments of some that the image is obscene and pornographic and stresses that the creation and worship of this image run parallel to the worship of the Śivaliṅga which is still very much in vogue today.

Dupuche deals with the tantric aspects of goddess worship as elaborated in Kashmir Śaivism. This brings us to the period when goddesses were coming to be Sanskritised as universal deities. The goddess as the supreme mother gives rise to infinite transient forms and all the goddesses are derived from her. She is the one who constitutes the ultimate source of reality and, by coming into contact with the sexual fluid emitted by her, the practitioner is led back to the original consciousness: the state of being one with the supreme deity. Dupuche emphasises the importance of the physical substances, including bodily fluids, that are used to accomplish the goal of achieving this oneness.

Tantric religion, intimately concerned with female images, was shared by Hinduism with Buddhism, and Templeman describes, among other things, the tantric Buddhist aspect of Devī. He argues that, in travelling from India to

Tibet, the character of the *ḍākinī* changed from being a wrathful, malicious demoness to an ambivalent character, either wisdom-giving or threatening. In this migration of the *ḍākinī* from one culture to another, Templeman sees a symbolic and hidden message of the defeat of Buddhism in the area of Assam.

Harcourt's chapter concerns a local group that served the goddess in a demanding role. It has justly been observed that suffering is a form of *tapas* (ascetic austerities) and that the suffering of women can lead to the possession of special powers, such as *trāga*. Harcourt's chapter studies the role of the Cāraṇas, a community of bards or 'fame-spreaders' in pre-British Rajasthan (from the 15th century onwards), whose *trāga* was associated with the descent of their caste from a heavenly or divine condition. Underpinned by the authority of Devī, they played an important part in the maintenance of social stability during a period of insecurity and political turbulence. The Cāraṇas could promote social equilibrium by deliberately shaming those whose immoral assertions of power upset it—the status of the Cāraṇas was such that by acts of self-mutilation (and in extreme cases suicide) they could induce miscreants to repent, and this was the function which they were frequently engaged to perform in the service of a goddess, acknowledged by all, who wanted justice.

The core Sanskrit tradition of Hinduism absorbed into itself countless stories of unknown local origins and attached them to the gods and goddesses known throughout India; such stories came to be framed within the narratives of texts such as the Purāṇas. Bailey, in his chapter on the goddess Pārvatī in the *Gaṇeśapurāṇa*, also relates the problems of hermeneutic sensitivity to the contexts of episodes within Sanskrit texts. He describes the poignant struggle between motherhood and goddess-hood in Pārvatī's mind in dealing with her son, the child-god Gaṇeśa. The author analyses several myths in the *Gaṇeśapurāṇa* where the Goddess' maternal instincts override her divine qualities. He argues that the intention of the Purāṇa must be to treat the child first and foremost as a son rather than a god. Two observations can be made about Bailey's chapter. Firstly, the juxtaposition of the child and the god is a deliberate ploy on the part of the composer of the Purāṇa. Secondly, if Pārvatī is to be recognised as the mother of the world, then it is her motherly qualities that must take precedence in the elaboration of the myths. In both respects, she is given a clearly defined role within a Brahmanical theological frame.

Studies of modern cults tend to display the universalisation of the Devī as a name for the supreme and absolute divine. We include a chapter based upon fieldwork among the Rabari people who live on the Saurashtran Peninsula. George examines traditional women's songs in a caste neighbourhood close to the shore of the Arabian Sea. Worship is addressed to Mammai Mātājī as the supreme deity, a great goddess transcending space, time and duality. Her cult, though, is embodied in a distinctive local tradition, especially in a ten-day festival called Punj, which can unite as many as 100,000 Rabari people from all over the region. Men chant and women sing devotional songs; female religiosity is embodied in intensely personal forms, and their role in the ritual is integral to the spiritual experience engendered by it and to the generation of a profound intuitive encounter with the goddess that is fostered by dedication to her cult in a jealously guarded tradition.

Finally, the chapter by Vicziany and Bapat analyses the survival of the Koḷī goddesses of Mumbai despite the pressure-cooker dynamics of India's largest and most cosmopolitan city. These tribal goddesses have been surrounded by Brahmanical and other religious icons, but in contrast to Mumbādevī (the patron goddess of Mumbai) they have not been Sanskritised. Nor has *Hindutva* (India's Hindu fundamentalist movement) succeeded in replacing the Koḷī goddesses with Brahmanical favourites such as Gaṇeśa. Rather the two traditions co-exist in a world in which the Koḷī Devī's power remains undiminished amongst Koḷī and non-Koḷī devotees. The particular goddess that forms the focus of this chapter is Khāḍādevī, located in a temple that sits inside the Kolaba police station in the central business district of Bombay. Judging by the gifts given to her, Khāḍādevī has been very successful in answering the prayers of childless women by transferring her fertility to both the indigenous Koḷī fisherfolk and non-Koḷīs. At the same time, in a more muted way, oral traditions speak of the revenge of the Goddess—the last time an official came to the temple with the proposition that a new road be built through the temple grounds to connect up the Kolaba Causeway to another important, parallel road, he was struck down and died of a heart attack before he reached the front gate of the compound.

All these contributions come together to display (as indeed do other publications devoted to the Devī) her protean diversity. In folk Hinduism, she is the boon-giving goddess of fertility and plenitude. For the village folk, she appears in many ambiguously benevolent and malevolent forms. She was worshipped as Lajjāgaurī in her naked form. Devī is the symbol of the ideal mother who dotes upon her son Gaṇeśa, often forgetting that he himself is a god. She is the *śakti* that the gods created when they could not destroy demons like Mahiṣāsura and many others. As the dangerous goddess Kālī, she is the one who demands the extreme sacrifice of his life from a Cāraṇa devotee. She can also manifest herself as a terrifying *ḍākinī* who devours humans and feeds on blood. And she embodies powers that politicians from medieval Rajasthan to modern Mumbai have invoked to give energy and legitimacy to their contests. To adapt from Joseph Campbell, she is truly the 'heroine with a thousand faces'.

Yet, as this volume also chronicles, these multiple forms of the goddess have come progressively to converge upon a universal and abstract vision of her power. She is the ultimate mother who creates the universe. She is seen as the Supreme Being, the ultimate *brahman*. It is the milk from her breasts that sustains every living thing. Ultimately, in the most abstract reaches of *advaitin* philosophy, she becomes identical with all that exists, occupying a transcendent realm where all duality is dissolved.

Notes

1 Even among Dalit world views we find gods and goddesses ranked according to their vegetarianism and otherwise.

chapter two

Archaeology of the goddess: an Indian paradox

Angelo Andrea Di Castro

Archaeology has undergone radical redefinitions during the last 30 years. Formerly, the focus was on the formulation of models of adaptation and of subsistence economy, inferred on the basis of material data and eco-environmental analysis. Now, by contrast, archaeologists seek to describe and explain the processes underlying the change of cultures. They are concerned to identify the agency of change and adaptation of individuals and societies, reflecting on the symbolic aspects of material culture, and they reject the idea that the complexities of human behaviour can be reduced to universal generalisations (Trigger 1989:350).[1]

Previously, the role of religion and the study of ritual in archaeology have been generally overlooked and, at times, dismissed as epiphenomena of human behaviour, or used as trash-bin categories (Renfrew 1994:50; Trigger 1989:298–302; Townsend 1990:187; Verhoeven 2002:233). More attention is now paid to understanding how religious phenomena may alter societies and how underlying religious factors may have implications for social change and contribute to the determination of material culture (Trigger 1989:334, 341; Insoll 2004:22).

This shift has promoted new ideas about the role of goddess cults in the development of ancient Indian culture and it is important to assess the value of these ideas by matching them carefully against the specifically archaeological evidence. Following the theories of John Marshall on the Indus religion, the cult of the Devī is often considered the fountainhead of Indian religion (Marshall 1931:50–1; Banerjea 1966:110; Lalye 1973:12–3, 159; Srivastava 1979:2–3, 22ff, 30–3, 198; Agrawala 1984:23ff; Bhattacharyya 1996:16–7, 26–8, 53; 1999:19–20, 28, 114, 148–50, 273). The assumption of preconceived ahistorical categories such as 'Great Mother' or 'Earth Mother' derived from the concept of 'fertility' is reflecting an essentialist approach to the study of the goddess cult in India (Nelson 1997:151–68).[2] Many scholars fall into the trap of essentialism when they make extreme generalisations; for instance Hawley, discussing in a simplified manner the origin of the Devī's cult, draws a straight line from the Indus Civilisation to the Mauryan era, stating that, 'female sculptures from the Mauryan period…and even later often look very much like their Indus prototypes' (Hawley 1996:1–2).

Perhaps the only shared things connecting the Indus Valley, Maurya, Shunga and Kushan terracotta figurines are the clay and the representation of female figures (not always cult icons as Hawley implies). Similarly, cultural and chronological distances are obliterated by Dehejia to ascertain the continuity of ancient cultic traditions assumed by the presence of terracotta figurines from the Indus Valley to the Gangetic towns (Dehejia 1999:18). The temporal dimension is not totally suspended, but it is compressed to conceal the discontinuity of material evidence through the millennia. An essentialist notion also underlies the concepts of the goddess as described by Menzies, who seems to follow Dehejia and Gimbutas, assuming the existence of a Great Mother Goddess cult in the millennia BCE that reached the coast of the Indian Ocean from the Mediterranean regions (Menzies, 2006:13; Dehejia 1999:18; Gimbutas 2001a:316–7). The idea of primeval goddess-oriented religiosity is also associated with a certain feminist spirituality in which the 'creatrix' is at the origin of the earliest civilisations organised as matriarchal societies. This notion implies that a pre-Aryan goddess cult would have survived the process of Aryanisation and would have eventually re-emerged in South Asia in various tribal forms and in certain rural and urban rituals (Gimbutas 2001a:316–7; Jayakar 1989: passim; Bhattacharyya 1999:26–9, Appendix II; Dehejia 1999:18).

This line of thought is often nourished by literary theories; the main concern in this chapter, by contrast, is to reassert the importance of methods applied and tested in concrete archaeological contexts. Whatever is original in the present discussion lies not so much in its questioning of certain recently influential ideas as in its plea for rigour in exploring the questions to which such ideas are offered as answers. The exploration must deal scrupulously with the archaeological evidence. Hence this chapter will review some of the key archaeological theories and a range of secondary works on the Indian goddesses, focusing on the archaeology of Indian religion as such, rather than looking at the textual evidence, and will try to read particular aspects of the material culture from prehistory to the Early Historic period. This will also demonstrate that crafting a past out of fragmented evidence seems to accommodate particular kinds of ideological manipulations (for example the tendency in some feminist matriarchal theories to assume that the gender disparity was preceded by an idyllic past characterised by peaceful democratic matrilineal polities ruled by priestesses (Gimbutas 2001b:125)). More importantly I argue that reinventing a continuous religious tradition forms part of a process of assimilation that seeks to reduce the cultural complexity of Indian religions into an expanded Brahmanic hegemony.

Cognitive approaches and feminist spirituality

To study the way ancient people thought so as to understand the ideological aspect of ancient societies based on the material evidence is proper to the application of cognitive archaeology (Renfrew & Bahn 1991:339). We can follow Renfrew's method of detection of ritual indicators in the archaeological investigation (Renfrew 1994:51), although our basic ability to perceive a vision of the way a past social order was arranged is always challenged by the elusive nature of the real meaning assigned to it by the ancient people who gave significance to that order (Hodder 1999:77).

To see the value of such an alternative, we need a more specific idea of what the paradigm is. Verhoeven recently proposed an alternative to the paradigm elaborated by Renfrew for investigating ritual activities in ancient cultures. He considers Renfrew's method too limited in its static universal conception. In order to study ancient religious behaviour, Verhoeven proposes an open model based on five elementary tenets, defined as: ritual framing (association of particular places, times, activities, and materials, etc); syntax (structural aspects of time/space, contexts, culture, material, typology, etc); symbolism (direct, metaphorical and allusive); dimensions (the multidimensional aspects of rituals); analogy (an investigative method) (Renfrew 1994; Verhoeven 2002:235, 236).

Demarcating the boundaries of the religious and secular spheres might prove difficult because some artefacts could be used in sacred contexts as well as for utilitarian purposes. Verhoeven's ritual framing would facilitate the recognition of the religious sphere and bypass the problem of the mutual 'embeddedness' of religious and secular activities (Renfrew 1994:47). The personal ideas or cultural conditioning of the archaeologist can also bias the interpretation of artefacts. The way we organise our knowledge is one area of cognitive archaeology that must be taken into account (Hodder 1993:256). For instance, Piggott considered the terracotta figurines of the Zhob culture (fourth–third millennia BCE) as manifestations of the mother goddess related to both the world of the dead and the regenerative aspects of the vegetal cycle (Piggott 1950:127). He projected onto these figurines ideas of a gruesome goddess derived from Purāṇic Hinduism. His interpretation based on the peculiar design of the figurines' heads was curbed by relatively limited data.

Recent evidence demonstrates that the 'circular eye-holes' and the 'grim slit mouth' are stylistic features shared by both genders, not representing any mother goddess skull (Piggott 1950:126).[3] Such cases clearly show how a particular interpretation may be influenced by a preconceived notion and pass into received wisdom, even though not securely based upon the evidence.

In dealing with the Indus Civilisation we are faced with the paradox of an undeciphered script. Written evidence may disclose the meaning of artefacts, yet we have to take into account the discrepancy between what people say and what people do (Hodder 1999:72). Literary sources may help us measure an ancient society in a consistent way; however, we must be aware that it can also condition and bias an archaeological interpretation.[4] In considering religious texts as ideological expressions of a society, we must remember that such texts may reflect a vision of the world and the hegemonic ideology in which they were created. The early Iron Age society of the Indo-Aryan speaking people observed through the Vedic texts may reveal the way religious concepts, rituals and social boundaries operated in the higher sections of the society, although we risk not recognising rituals belonging to non-assimilated and subaltern traditions.

Much research on ancient Indian goddesses has been conditioned by later sources with an inclination towards a Purāṇic ideological framework. Undoubtedly the Purāṇas preserve part of the archaic tradition and mythology. It is the new ideology in which the Purāṇas are reformulated that changes the ethical and social values and the consequent interpretation of symbolic narrations, myths and divinities in the Hindu context.

> Students of Indian mythology, at times adhering acritically to the object of their study, seem to have been taken by the successful neo-Brahmanic attempt to bridge the distance between the Vedic and Purāṇic myths, complying with the Brahmans' will to abolish history—or at least...a history whose legitimacy they refuse to endorse (Verardi 2003:10).

Regarding the controversial possibility of harmonising textual and archaeological evidence, Chakrabarti's position is openly radical: because it is impossible to place chronologically the composition of the Veda we cannot discuss a Vedic Age, not to mention a Vedic archaeology (Chakrabarti 2001:35).[5] Once the Vedic problem has been removed Chakrabarti's concern is to demonstrate that various Hindu religious customs and ideas have prehistoric origins and that they seem to be present in Indus Valley finds (Chakrabarti 2004:20). His claim basically follows the theories of Marshall who sought in the Indus Valley the cradle of Hinduism.

One of the major issues concerning the prehistory of the subcontinent is the archaeologists' ability to identify the elements and assess the cultural changes which occurred beyond the Indo-Aryan linguistic milieu that characterise the Vedic texts. It is possible that groups of Indo-Aryan speaking people were in contact with the Indus people in the first half of the second millennium BCE (Allchin & Allchin 1982:300–1; Bryant 2001:195–6, 300; Possehl 2002:240–1). The difficulty is in understanding the processes underlying the absorption or adoption of language and of material and spiritual culture, which could justify the transmission of a 'pre-Aryan' goddess cult in post-Vedic Hinduism.[6] Interestingly Parpola believes that some sections of the Indo-Aryan speaking people already worshipped a major goddess before their migration into the Ganges Valley. He supposes that the Bronze Age Bactrian Indo-Iranians venerated a proto-Durgā and identifies them with the Dāsas, the people living in the fortified towns later conquered by the Ṛgvedic Aryans (Parpola 1994:149–52, 246–56; 1995:367–70; 2002).

The old notion of 'pre-Aryan' origins of the mother goddesses was associated with the old concept of the ancient matriarchate, using essentialist notions of generation, maternity, nourishment and protection as fundamental matriarchal societies' symbolic values. Primitive India would have been characterised by similar features, and comparisons with Western Asian archaeological material and allied mythologies are sometimes called for (Marshall 1931:51; Lalye 1973:389–91; Stutley 1985:46).[7] Furthermore, by taking the ethnographic record as a re-enactment of prehistoric behaviour, the prevailing worship of goddesses amongst tribal Indians is taken as a model for ancient religious activities. In this way an uninterrupted continuity in the cultic tradition of the Devī from prehistory to a later Purāṇic canonisation of the goddess as *śakti* has been assumed (Lalye 1973:12–3).[8] Nevertheless the association of deities, vegetal realm, fertility, and female energies can already be attested in the *Atharva Veda*, several centuries before the tantric traditions (*Atharva Veda* III, 20:3; VI, 20:2; V, 25:1–3; VII, 49; XII, 1:1,2, 17,25, 57, 61; Stutley 1985:120–1, Jayakar 1989:156–7).

Reformulations of gender studies and feminist archaeology have resulted in other perceptions of the 'goddess' (Nelson 1997; Eller 2000).[9] Many American feminists have invoked a return to a golden age inspired by the feminine, following Gimbutas' model of prehistoric Europe: a peaceful matriarchal society with monotheistic orientations towards a powerful all-encompassing goddess (Gimbutas 2001a:321; Sjöö & Mor 1991:13, 19, 433–4; Eisler 1992).[10] This would not simply signify a spiritual 'reappearance' of the goddess like medieval Śāktism, but rather a new social paradigm, virtually a restoration of a mythical matriarchy (Eisler 1992; Hamilton

1998). Such a reconstruction of a matriarchal past seems more political than historical (Meskell 1998:147). According to Hodder there is a clear conflict between certain approaches to the past, namely spiritual and scientific ones; archaeology, as envisioned by the feminist matriarchal tradition (Hodder 1998:165),[11] is lacking an open-ended, evidential and inclusive methodology (Hodder 1998:167). Similarly Meskell warns against the dangers of rewriting the past by presenting some archaeological data, rearranged in a deceitful fictional manner with a claim of scientific validation, heavily characterised by contemporary socio-cultural bias (Meskell 1998:147).

Cynthia Eller argues that feminist matriarchalists do not make consistent use of archaeological evidence and she considers the matriarchal myth as disadvantageous and unproductive to the feminist cause (Eller 2000:111–5, 175). To her the problem is how to investigate the origin of gender disparity, as well as the reasons and mechanism for the perpetuation of sexism that has resulted since, together with the way in which this could be eventually ended (Eller 2000:183–6). The assumption that goddess worship implies a matriarchal organisation, an egalitarian society, or a society in which women's position is higher than that of men does not find any substantiation in the historical or archaeological record. In effect Eller highlights the lack of evidence for a matriarchalist assumption and admits that:

> ...far from being a sign of special respect accorded to women, goddess worship would, in the absence of other evidence, be expected to correlate with a poor state of affairs for women (Eller 2000:106).

This agrees with the Indian paradox of a centuries old socio-economic disparity and degradation of women, mother sanctification, and the cult of mother goddesses.[12]

Early manifestations of goddesses

A significant example of a prehistoric cult comes from an Upper Palaeolithic site in Madhya Pradesh. The excavators identified an ancient altar at Baghor near a modern tribal cult site of the Mushars, a group of Dravidian hunter-gatherers, who worship the goddess Bansuri/Bansapati as personification of the forest (Kenoyer et al 1983). The site, dated 13,000 BCE, corresponds to a seasonal camp episodically occupied by hunter-gatherers. In a central area of the camp a rubble platform was found. On the platform a unique triangular stone with a concentric decoration of red ochre was standing upright. Kenoyer suggests parallels with similar ritual structures set up by contemporary hunter-gatherers in the same region, where tribal communities arrange on the top of platforms triangular stones representing the female principle. These stones smeared with red ochre on the occasion of specific rituals are now called *śakti* (Kenoyer 1993:243). Kenoyer believes that the use of the triangle as a fertility symbol continues to modern times from the Upper Palaeolithic period, having passed various stages through to the decoration of Chalcolithic pottery and on into more recent tribal symbols and tantric iconography (Kenoyer 1993:247).

Scholars have inferred the presence of a cult of the goddess in the Indus Valley from material evidence consisting of figurines, seals and a controversial class of objects known as Indus ringstones. The reconstruction of the religious background of the goddess suggested by Marshall is based on circumstantial evidence and comparisons with modern Hindu practices (Marshall 1931:49–50).[13] The only positive information we can gather from the terracotta images concerns gender, ethnic diversity, fashion, costumes, jewellery, and other aspects of social identity (see Kenoyer 2000:111, 132–5; Possehl 2002:117–20, 177–83; Clark 2003).

The iconographic study of the Indus seals might offer valuable information about the original mythologies despite the debatable identities of personages and their actual narratives. Significant similarities with contemporaneous Mesopotamian and Elamite themes have been pointed out (Parpola 1994:126–33, 179–97, 219, 246–56; Winkelmann 2000; Possehl 2002:146). Such similarities parallel the religious iconography of the Bactro-Margian tradition, as the Oxus Civilisation functioned as a mediator between the Indus Civilisation and the people of the Iranian plateau (Francfort 1992:179).[14] Winkelmann envisions a dominance of goddesses in the Indus pantheon: the lady of the beasts with felines or snakes; a fertility goddess associated with domesticated animals; a deity with birds; one within an enclosure; a composite figure of a bull-woman; and a nude figure protected by two men (Winkelmann 2000:360). Interestingly the Oxus parallels show female deities associated with felines, eagles, dragons, snakes, herbivores, and plants (Francfort 1992:chart 1; 1994). Parpola suggests the identification of a 'proto-Durgā' with a series of composite images of a tiger-woman and with those of a tree-deity. He compares symbolic aspects of war and fertility with Mesopotamian goddesses like Ishtar or Inanna seeking evidence from palaeo-astronomy, Near-Eastern archaeology, Vedic mythology, tantrism, and ethnography (Parpola 1994:240–72). Jayakar sees the association of tigers, trees, and female figures on the Indus seals as a powerful symbol of spiritual transformation. The metamorphosis of a tiger-woman and the epiphany of the tree-deity can be seen in relation either to archaic rituals connected with the alchemical tradition or to an adaptation of the tribal cults of the Purāṇic Ambā or Durgā (Jayakar 1989:64–76).[15] Others assign a special role to the composite tiger-woman figure, considered an ancestor of Huligammā, the Southern Indian Tiger-Mother (Allchin & Allchin 1982:215).

A famous Indus seal shows a ritual scene with a row of seven female figures at the bottom and a goat-like composite animal positioned next to a kneeling horned man who in turn seems to offer a severed head placed on a small altar to a naked female(?) deity amidst the branches of a fig tree. In this scene, resembling a depiction of a *yakṣa* ritual, an essential characteristic of a pre-Aryan tree-cult has been highlighted by Marshall (1931:63–5) and Kenoyer (2000:105–7) and a variety of associations have been claimed, such as: Durgā and the Seven Mothers (Srivastava 1979:28,136; Allchin & Allchin 1982:215; Chakrabarti 2001:42–4); the seven rivers of the *Ṛgveda* (Possehl 2002:145–6); astral calculations (Parpola 1994:256–61); or an amalgamation of the lesser tradition of the villages with the greater tradition of the Indus towns, as a paradigm for Indian religious life (Dani & Thapar 1999:295).

Marshall envisioned 'suggestive evidence of Śāktism' in the Indus religion, referring to a worship of the phallus associated with stone rings representing the vulva (Marshall 1931:57). These stone rings or *yoni* rings, supposedly symbolising the cosmic energy of the mother goddess, would have had the magical properties of protection and regeneration. To corroborate this view Marshall suggested an analogy with various ringstones found at Taxila, and elsewhere (see below).[16] The interpretation of the Indus ringstones, whose actual dimensions range from a few centimetres to about half a metre, is fairly controversial. Mackay considered the larger ones architectural elements, and the smaller as mace-heads (Mackay 1931:473; 1948:29–30, 101; Kenoyer 2000:53, 110, figs. 3.9–10; Possehl 2002:69, 202–3).[17]

Some of the earliest Chalcolithic manifestations of goddesses are from Navdatoli (Malwa Culture, circa 1700–1200 BCE) consisting of naked figures applied to handmade storage jars. In one case the goddess, depicted next to a shrine, a lizard (crocodile?) and a worshipping woman, is identified as a proto-*śakti*, since in later Hinduism Durgā and Pārvatī are also associated with reptiles (Sankalia et al 1971:pl. XXII.A–C; Dhavalikar 1985:77; Agrawal 1982:230; Banerjea 1956:172). Clay figurines of crude workmanship with small conical-bulbous heads, or headless figurines with short limbs sometimes with violin-shaped bodies are characteristic of the Chalcolithic culture (see for instance Banerji 1994:figs. XI, XIV, pls. 61–4, 66–7). Specific worship of a mother goddess and bull was inferred from the predominant number of bull figurines recorded in the discoveries (Dhavalikar 1985:76–7; Chakrabarti 2001:47–8). A significant find at Inamgaon might exemplify this particular cult. A headless figurine accompanied by a bull, both lying on top of a clay receptacle containing a second female figurine, was found in a small pit dug out of the corner of a house floor of the early Jorwe period (around 1300 BCE). It appears that the bull and the figurine, seemingly riding on its back, were joined by means of a stick, suggesting an early representation of a *vāhana*, the divine mount (Dhavalikar 1977:49). The deposit, carefully placed in the floor, possibly indicates that some ritual was performed in the house, perhaps connected with childbirth.[18]

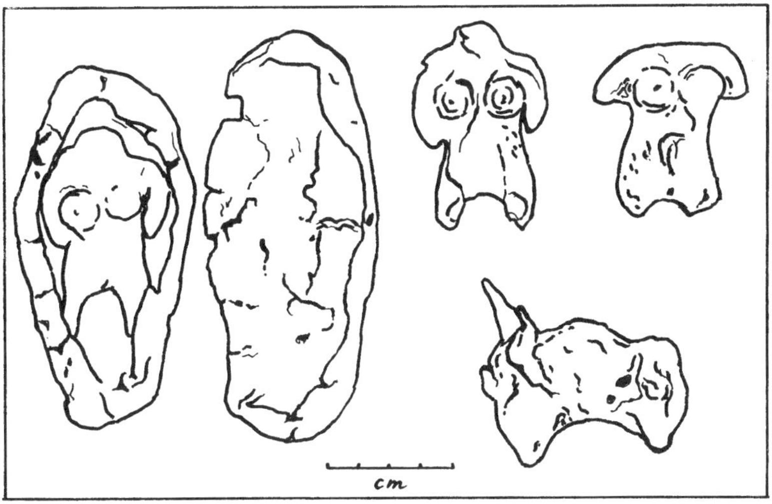

Figure 1: Terracotta figurines from Inamgaon (adaptation from Allchin & Allchin 1982 fig 10.18).

The Iron Age artefacts from Swat and neighbouring regions provide evidence of a transitional phase apparently corresponding to the emergence of the Indo-Aryan speaking people (Dani 1999:397). The terracotta figurines of the Gandhāra Graves represent a typical style discernible as a formal schematisation of the body in the form of flat tablets with rough-hewn anatomical details and incised decorations (Allchin & Allchin 1982:236–41, fig 9.10; Banerji 1994:144–52, pls. 71–5). Interesting cult objects have been discovered in the burials of the last period of Zarif Karuna (late second–early first millennium BCE) in the Peshawar Valley: bull figurines placed in various tombs, a remarkable female figurine with a fan-shaped head and the pubic area decorated with a series of concentric triangles, and an alabaster amulet of an eye-goddess associated by the excavator to Mesopotamian cultic traditions (Khan 1979:85, pl. XIX A). The main features of this amulet are two large eyes and circular designs on the rectangular portion (Dani 1999:416).

Rather than looking to Mesopotamian associations, we can find intriguing iconographic similarities in Neolithic-Chalcolithic antecedents, such as a polished bone amulet dated around the sixth millennium BCE discovered at Mehrgarh (Jarrige 2000:fig 8B). Although this connection with Sistan might be questionable because of the chronological distance, it would be instructive to examine additional ivory and bone eye-goddess amulets of the Early Historic period (second half of the first millennium BCE). These highly conventionalised anthropomorphic amulets, sometimes looking like crosses, show incised lines, circles and dots and usually a wide triangle, alluding to their feminine character. Judging from their wide distribution, from Madhya Pradesh and Saurāshtra and on through the Ganges Valley up to Gandhāra, we can imagine that around the Mauryan period this simple craft object was commonly produced (Gupta 1980:309). They are said to protect against smallpox, perhaps because of the dots evoking skin diseases like smallpox and measles. Although we cannot say for certain that these artefacts are ascribable to Śītalā, the Hindu goddess of smallpox and one of the Seven Mothers, it is quite possible that some protective aspects of these cult objects originated in the Neolithic-Chalcolithic tradition and were transmitted through to the third and second millennia BCE (Sankalia et al 1971:406; Ghosh 1989 vol. I:263, 268).[19]

Goddesses in a changing world

The Iron Age urbanisation of the Ganges plain during the first half of the first millennium BCE brought about dramatic changes; the transition from tribal chiefdoms (*janapadas*) to a centralised administration during the pre-Maurya and Mauryan periods resulted in settlement developments, demographic increase, urbanisation, and changing socio-economic conditions. In this context it is possible to trace distinctions that existed between mainstream urban and traditional rural cultures. Probably during the process of integration, some groups were marginalised and alienated from their original homelands and ancestral rituals. From this angle we might picture a widespread diffusion of the eye-goddess's amulets as manifestations of the religious tradition of the Neolithic-Chalcolithic agriculturists, merged within and between the new socio-cultural contexts of the urban centres. The anti-Brahmanic position of Buddhism and Jainism can also be related to this complex urban phenomenon of social integration/opposition. It appears that a sort of cultic amalgamation took place in both movements, with their inclusion and acceptance of popular cults connected to *yakṣa*s, local goddesses and *nāga*s.

Kosambi (1962:82–151), analysing old rituals offered to mother goddesses at crossroads, identifies associations between Neolithic tracks, archaic and contemporary mother goddesses' cult places, trade routes and Buddhist caves. By stressing analogies with ancient routes in the Gangetic regions, he takes Lumbinī, the birthplace of Buddha, as an archaic cult site of a local goddess. At the time of its discovery the site was known as *Rummindei* and the local people were worshipping the goddess 'Rummini' where the Māyādevī temple originally stood (Führer 1897:28; Mukherji 1901:34; Kosambi 1962:106; Mitra 1972:198). Kosambi argues that Māyā—Buddha's mother—went to Lumbinī in order to worship the goddess and gain protection for the imminent childbirth, rather than travelling on her way to the parental house as described in the *Mahāvastu*.[20]

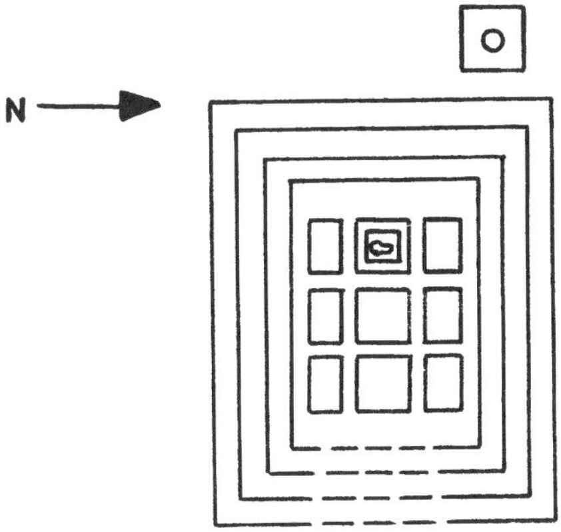

Figure 2: Early structural phase of the Mauryan period of the Māyādevī temple at Lumbinī. The conglomerate stone is in the middle top square pit (adaptation from Rijal 1996 plate II).

Excavations carried out at Lumbinī in the 1990s have yielded significant data from the Mauryan period, bringing to light important evidence regarding the foundation of the Māyādevī temple having a grid pattern. It is claimed that the exact place of the nativity of the Buddha was identified in one of the central cells of the grid, where a sandstone conglomeration was found placed on seven courses of Mauryan bricks (Rijal 1996:5). In a final report which is yet to appear,[21] it is expected that we will have definitive data regarding the stratigraphy and the general reconstruction of the pre-structural phase. At present we can surmise that during the Aśokan reorganisation of the area the conglomerate was placed on a brick plinth, and that before Aśoka, perhaps a simple railing, a *vedikā*, or a more articulated structure like the *bodhighara* of Bodh Gayā surrounded the sacred area (Rijal 1996; Mishra 1996; Tiwari 1996; Giri 2003:67–9, 232). Relevant information can be inferred from the Aśokan column at Lumbinī which records the visit of the Mauryan sovereign during the 20th year of his reign to the site which the tradition indicated as the Buddha's birthplace. The translation of the inscription is still controversial.[22] Agrawala proposes that, rather than a stone enclosure (*silāvigaḍābīcā),* the Lumbinī inscription could refer to a *pūjāśilā*, a stone slab for offerings; since no stone railing was discovered, a wall was probably made of earth which enclosed the offering stone (Agrawala 1970:141). Could the conglomerate excavated in the Māyādevī temple be interpreted as a kind of *pūjāśilā*? Epigraphists and philologists could answer this question. The discovery of the conglomerate however can shed light on the process of assimilation of rituals of local traditions into Buddhism. We suggested elsewhere that the sandstone conglomerate, probably considered by the early Buddhist tradition as the actual place where the new-born Buddha was placed and anointed, was most likely the stone next to the tree where the local goddess of Lumbinī had received votive offerings (Di Castro 1998:73).

Figure 3: Drawing showing the middle top square pit of the Mauryan phase of the Māyādevī temple at Lumbinī. The conglomerate stone is rendered by hatching (from a photo of the Lumbinī Development Trust).

In tackling the difficulty of identifying factual events distorted in the traditional narratives, we need to distinguish between diverse kinds of evidence; the story of Buddha's miraculous birth had been written down some centuries after it happened, and the earliest references, the *Suttanipāta* and the Aśokan pillar, only mention the place of the nativity. Following the initial line of Kosambi's reasoning concerning Māyādevī's visit to Lumbinī to ask for protection for the childbirth, we can make a cursory summary of various clues when considering the adaptation of local cults into Buddhism and the deification of Māyādevī associated with the presumed goddess worshipped at Lumbinī. After the childbirth the tradition states that Māyādevī's death occurred on the fatal 'sixth night', establishing accordingly another association with mother goddesses worshipped for childbirth (Kosambi 1962:91, 102).[23] In the *Divyāvadāna*, a later Buddhist text, mention is made of a tree-deity that witnessed the birth of the Buddha (Coomaraswamy 1971, part 1:34). Later Buddhist iconography represents Māyādevī in the classical *śālabhañjikā* pose grasping the *śāl* tree as a *yakṣiṇī*, or as a *vṛkṣadevatā,* a dryad. Recent archaeological investigations demonstrate that particular attention was given to a conglomerate stone in the Māyādevī temple. Offerings for *grāmadevatās*, mother goddesses and *yakṣas*/*yakṣiṇīs*, are often placed on or before natural stones that sometimes are the aniconic representations of the same deities. Stone tables/altars and sacred trees, basic elements of a *yakṣa* cult-place, are associated with various episodes of the Buddha's life. For example, when he was absorbed in meditation under the *bodhi* tree, one of Sujātā's maidservants regarded him as a tree-spirit. In other episodes Buddha is linked to *yakṣa* shrines such as in Vaiśālī or during his Parinirvāṇa in the Mallas' grove, while he was lying on a couch that presumably was an altar for offerings (Coomaraswamy 1971 part 1:17, 23). Eventually, once all Buddhist memories had vanished in the region, a local goddess cult took over in Lumbinī where people paid respect up until the beginning of the 20th century.

Other relevant elements of a goddess cult in the Ganges civilisation can be obtained from the so-called Mauryan and Shungan ringstones. These objects, already described as earrings or moulds for gold repoussé, can be either flat, round or pierced stone rings bearing in each case elaborate decoration (Lohuizen-de Leeuw 1972:29; Allchin 1995:268).[24] Besides all functional interpretation, it is the striking appearance of these objects that makes them fascinating and mysterious, as they display naked female figures interpreted as goddesses, alternating palm trees, or honeysuckle and lotus vines, and a variety of animals. Ritual scenes and symbols are clearly depicted on them: for instance a fragmentary ringstone from Rupar shows a man approaching a naked goddess beside a hut (a 'shrine'?) in front of which a seated man offers a piece of fruit (?) to a woman, perhaps alluding to a fertility ritual (Gupta 1980:fig 23a; Agrawala 1993:fig 23). Elsewhere male and female figures are handing small animals to a naked goddess (Gupta 1980:pl. 31; Agrawala 1993:fig 45). Another fragment shows a woman dancing next to a man who is playing a harp, and near a water tank a kneeling woman worships a small heap with a cross-like object on the top (Agrawala 1993:fig 79). The lunar aspect of the goddess is made explicit by moon crescents often depicted on the side of naked figures or alternating with a taurine symbol, or *nandipada* (Gupta 1980:figs 19a–b, 33, 117a; Agrawala 1993:figs. 37–9, 62, 63). The latter symbol can also be read as the Brāhmī letter *ma* which may allude to the maternal aspect and perhaps the name of the deity (Agrawala 1993:66).

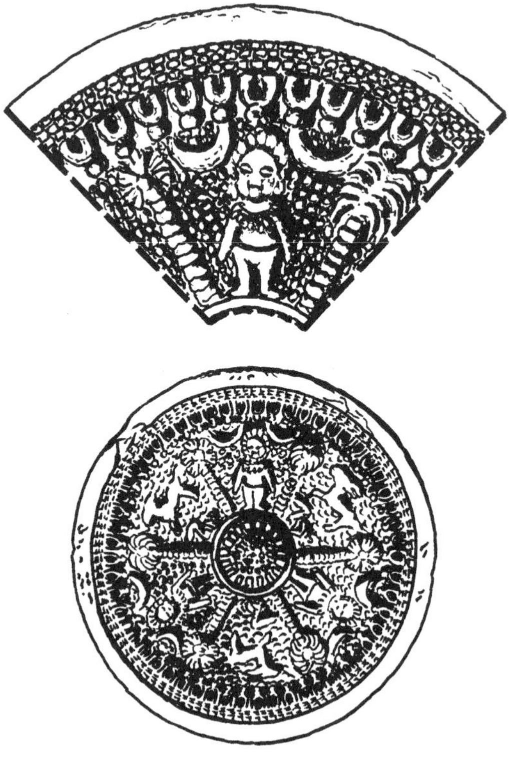

Figure 4: Stone disc from Murtaziganj showing nude goddesses with crescents and taurine sumbols (adaptation from Agrawala 1993, fig 38).

Marshall, who associated these artefacts with the Indus ringstones, suggests connections with Śāktism (Marshall 1931:62–3). Banerjea relates the Mauryan ringstones to Śāktism, because of the presence of bordering bands decorated with lizards (or alligators) comparable to medieval images of Pārvatī (Banerjea 1956:172). Some scholars have attempted to identify the figures of the ringstones with Śrī Lakṣmī, seeking correlations with the late Vedic texts and epics (Chandra 1971; Agrawala 1993:66–9). Likewise, others have sought in these artefacts the symbolism of death and rebirth (Gupta 1980:71). To establish the identity of these deities is highly problematical. The ritual scenes on the ringstones are possibly connected to non-Vedic, perhaps rural or tribal practices, and the Vedic and Brahmanic texts in general record neither these practices nor more rarefied esoteric ones. It seems that these esoteric rituals were performed in the forest far from towns and villages, perhaps in conjunction with animal sacrifices (Gupta 1980:70, 72).

In considering Gupta's model, Raymond Allchin wonders whether the people who produced such artefacts belonged to a particular professional group involved in jewel-making over an extended area stretching from Gandhāra to Pāṭaliputra (Allchin 1995:268). Iconographic parallels to the ringstone goddess have been indicated with gold leaves from the stupas of Lauriyā Nandangarh and with a steatite plaque from Rājgir (Gupta 1980:71, 60; Agrawala 1993:58, 15; Allchin 1993:268, 265). The latter shows three couples in three distinct compartments: on the upper one a woman is dancing before a harpist; in the middle a man offers a cup to a woman and a wine jar is visible between them; in the lower one a naked man offers a cup to a naked woman. This nude figure is similar to the goddesses depicted on the ringstones and on the gold leaves. Further interesting associations with other artefacts suggested by Allchin include a stone mould for cups from Kauṣāmbī showing a seated harpist with dancing women wearing bird masks, as well as a small spherical stone object with elaborate decorations. On the lower section of the latter there is a fantastic winged figure (a *yakṣa*?) playing a double flute, while on the middle band two scenes separated by vegetal elements show a harpist, a bird, a dancer and a standing couple on one side, and a man and woman worshipping a pile of rocks (an anthill?) apparently with a face depicted on it (Allchin 1995:265–8, fig 11.33; Agrawala 1983:fig 74; Lerner & Kossak 1991:52–3 figs 9.1–4).

Allchin, reflecting on the symbolism of dance, music, sex and intoxicating drink, suggests that the rituals connected with the ringstones' naked goddesses and other related objects might also be associated with the *devadāsīs* or deity's slaves. He remarks that the *devadāsīs* already existed in the 3rd–2nd centuries BCE, documented by an inscription in the Jogimara

Cave at Rāmgarh, where ritual dances might have been performed (Allchin 1995:269; Gupta 1980:169–9). Yet we wonder whether these scenes with harp players, dancers, masked and naked figures might allude to some sexual rituals or symbolism derived from the *Vrātya* tradition of the *Atharva Veda*. Apparently the *Vrātya* rituals underwent a complex process of transformation along with the development of the symbols connected to death and rebirth (Heesterman 1962). Attempting to demonstrate the archaic origin of the Śākta cults in Hinduism, Parpola has collected a variety of ethnographic, linguistic, archaeological and religious data ranging from the Bronze Age to medieval tantrism. He points to conspicuous similarities between some rituals of the Kafirs, the *Vrātyas* and the worship of *yakṣas* (Parpola 2002:303).[25]

It is possible that the cult of the ringstones might have embedded common elements into other contemporaneous rituals and traditions. Certain rituals appear to be distinctive in some segments of the urban population and we wonder whether this could be connected to the break-up of the old society of the *janapadas* that, in turn, caused a weakening of the tribal ties of kinship. In some instances the same social identity was challenged by the new centralised organisation. Consequently, a series of questions arise; is the cult of the ringstones' nude goddesses actually connected to Śāktism? It is difficult to confirm this because the material evidence is limited to the Mauryan and Shungan periods and we cannot prove any direct connection to later Śāktism. Perhaps we are facing an extinguished branch of the 'evolutionary tree' of that movement of spiritual practices and ideas that eventually converged into the Śākta movement. It is also possible that in some instances variants of the *yakṣa* cult or adaptations of the *Vrātya* tradition converged in these rituals. We can imagine that these 'transgressive' cults were assimilated into mainstream Brahmanism, like the *devadāsī*s that were later associated with the temples of Śiva. Was this ritual of the nude goddess distinctive of a specific group or rather of a transversal sect? We might further take into account the influences of socio-economics, trade, professional groups and the urban centres characteristic of the mid-first millennium BCE, as the organisation of professional groups eventually evolved into *jātis*, or sub-castes, offering defined social identities (Thapar 1984:90, 92, 100). From this perspective it is interesting to note that the *Mānava Dharma Śāstra* mentions various *Vrātya* clans of the *Vaiśya* order (Shastri 1982:68). We might also imagine that a *Vaiśya* group worshipped a goddess somehow analogous to Śrī Lakṣmī, the goddess of wealth (Chandra 1971). On the other hand, if we consider the Śākta connection, we might take into account that the later characteristics of the breakdown of caste barriers were more than likely preceded by an earlier transversal cult that was accepting of a variety of people without regard to their origin.

During the Mauryan period a new phase of syncretic imagery came about which lasted for several generations. Cultural and trading contacts with Greco-Bactrians and Parthians helped in the exchange of western symbols and ideas. With the formation of the Kushan Empire we can finally witness a fully-fledged reformulation of religious iconography in which important roles were played by female deities. A remarkable process of transformation of the Kushan mother goddesses (*mātṛkās*) began at this time.[26] This paved the way for the Gupta period identification of the *mātṛkās* with the *yoginīs* and *ḍākinīs* proper to the tantric cults. In fact, during the reign of Kumāragupta I, an inscription from Gangdhar dated 423 CE states that:

> For the sake of religious merit, the counsellor of the king caused to be built this very terrible abode and filled [it] with female ghouls (*ḍākinīs*) of the divine mothers (*mātṛ*) who utter loud and tremendous shouts in joy, who stir up the oceans with mighty wind rising from the magic rites of their religion (*tantra*) (Dehejia 1986:67; see also Banerjea 1956:494).

Conclusion

The material selected here from the Palaeolithic to the Early Historic period, though fragmentary and equivocal, is enough to suggest the geographical and temporal discontinuity and cultural disunity of the goddess cult in ancient India. Essentialist interpretations, on the other hand, assume an uninterrupted continuity of the cult of the goddess from prehistory to the present, and generally disregard historical change. Essentialisation of the goddess cult and the attempt to affirm continuities with the past and religious unity with fringe tribal/rural realities can also be seen in a culturally hegemonic perspective.

When a mythic past is believed to have been (historically) actual, it can act as a filter, blocking the perception of what does not fit the ideal image and favouring, beyond what real evidence shows, the features desired, such as freedom from sexist discrimination and aspirations for an egalitarian society. The re-imagined matriarchal feminist tradition is leading to a millenarian vision. The problem is that a goddess cult does not necessarily imply any evidence of matriarchy or better conditions for women in ancient societies. This ahistorical matriarchal past does not seem to be an active social model for current women's liberation movements.[27]

In studying the archaeology of Indian religions, in order to understand the actual meaning of the symbols in question, we might refer to historical and social contexts such as that of the Mauryan ringstones, or we may reveal the way old symbols are assimilated into new and wider contexts, as in the process of the assimilation of the *yakṣa* cult symbolism into Buddhism. The stratigraphic contexts of the Inamgaon bull and female figurines, like the conglomerate stone of the Māyādevī's temple, can easily be related to the 'ritual framing' as defined by Verhoeven. The same funerary associations of the Gandhāra Graves and the gold figurines from Lauriyā Nandangarh can be referred to through the syntax of ritual, as can all of the figurations on the ringstones. Rather than trying to demonstrate a continuous spiritual tradition of the Indian goddess, we must look at the change and discontinuity in the alleged religious transmission and iconography that have occurred throughout many centuries. We need to resist the flat timeless perception of patterns of culture, as if they can only represent unchanging wholes, for, in fact, as Hodder has emphasised:

> Objects or styles derived from other groups are given meaning in their new context, but these meanings may be based on, and may bring with them, meanings from the old. The new traits are selected and are placed within the existing system, changing it. The aim should be…to see…stimulus diffusion as an active social process working on and within systems of meanings which develop over the long term…(Hodder 1986:89).

In the long term we need to look for ideas and concepts that lie deep within the symbols, which, in turn, might have been transmitted and transformed, and not focus on a specific ritual, divinity, ideology or preconceived general rules. The use of analogy can 'broaden the mind and expand the horizon of interpretive possibility' (Insoll 2004:115). Nonetheless this can be misleading if 'sameness' between present and past phenomena is assumed, for instance using a monistic notion of an all-inclusive great goddess to establish the presence of 'the' Great Goddess in prehistoric India, 'where none might in fact have existed' (Insoll 2004:92–93, 141).[28]

With analogy we might look at some Hindu practices in order to compare and interpret the archaeological data, by applying a process close to ethnoarchaeology (like Marshall's attempt in interpreting the Indus religion). However, historically speaking, we cannot understand Vedic rituals simply by looking at the medieval tantras, even though the persistence of ritual elements, symbols or ideas evidenced in the *Atharva Veda* can be sought in later tantric traditions. This would certainly confer a sense of historic depth on certain ideas and would permit a clarification of our understanding of concepts and symbols, transmitted over time, that have been transformed in different contexts. Continuity in iconography and symbolic imagery does not imply continuity in mythology, because beliefs and meanings are likely to change over time and the study of myths can indeed reveal notions of change and adaptation (Trigger 1989:354; Insoll 2004:126).

The widespread distribution of clay female figurines (by itself a discontinuous evidence) has been commonly regarded as an indication of the 'pre-Aryan' origin of the goddess cult; hence it is taken as a possible evidence of a belief in a mother goddess already current in the Indus Valley (Chakrabarti 2004:20). In this way an essentialist notion of an 'Indian mother goddess' is taken to resolve the paradox of a discontinuity with a possible non-Sanskrit pre-Vedic past.[29]

As has been amply documented here, many scholars are still influenced by the notion of an uninterrupted cultic tradition of a presumed great goddess, a tradition held to have survived intact from the Palaeolithic populations to the Indus towns and to the Neolithic-Chalcolithic cultures of the Deccan up to the Early Historic period. The point here, though, is not just that the belief is mistaken; it is that the belief is just one manifestation of a tendency to read the concerns, interests and relationships of the present directly into the past. Such a tendency can interfere with our recognition of the complexity and dynamism of historical change. In the present case, for example, it would be possible in principle to see how the belief in an uninterrupted great goddess tradition could work for the modern concerns of certain Brahmanic groups in an effort to reaffirm over time an ideological hegemony:

> *The historical Brahmanic tradition appears to be indistinct because of its interest in canceling the traces of the historical discontinuities which reveal weakness and crises of the Brahmanic model and instead reaffirm the principle of an uninterrupted hegemony* [italic in the original] (Verardi 1996:226).

Where links with the ancient past are created to implement an alleged tradition at the service of a nationalistic agenda, implying ethnicity, cultural identity and historical unity, paradoxically it seems that the concern in advocating a continuous religious tradition betrays an actual break with the historical continuity (Hobsbawm 1983:7–8, 13).

Notes

1 See also Hodder (1986) and Shanks and Tilley (1989), which is an outline of the theoretical framework adopted in their previous books (1987a and 1987b).

2 On essentialism in archaeology, see also Shanks and Tilley (1987a:119–22; 1987b:147–51; 1989:6).

3 For male figurines see Jarrige (1984:fig 17.4) and Banerji (1994:19–20, fig II.2). Kinsley recognised that the grotesque connotation of the Zhob faces was due to 'crude craftsmanship or artistic stylisation' (1986:213). Piggott's interpretation was endorsed by Agrawala (1984:27) and followed without criticisms by Tripathi and Srivastava (1994:178–79).

4 Schopen has rightly criticised an analogous attitude by archaeologists and scholars in the study of Buddhism, assigning disproportionate value to literary sources in the definition of true religion (1997:13). Similarly Renfrew's remarks warn us against the dangers of gearing into our research 'our own culturally-encapsulated' view of what religion is' (1994:47).

5 On Vedic chronology see Witzel (1995:95–8).

6 On the pre-Indo-Aryan elements, see Bryant (2001:105–7, 298–300), also Witzel (1995:110–5) and Thapar (2002:14, 31). On the Indo-Aryan question, see also Erdosy (1995) and Bryant and Patton (2005).

7 Mode envisaged survivals of matriarchal traditions among the Indus people (1960:48–9). Kenoyer reconstructed a matrilocal pattern of burials by looking at the genetic analytic data of the Harappan's cemetery, concluding that some women held powerful positions in Indus society (2000:133–4).

8 Similar assumptions are still in vogue (see for instance, Sinha 2006:90,98).

9 See also Roscoe (1996), Atre (1998) and Clark (2003).

10 For an overview of these ideas, see Wood (1996).

11 For a distinction between matriarchal feminism and feminist archaeologists, see Eller (2000:89).

12 Srivastava (1979:8) sees the Indian deification of motherhood as a sort of compensation for the degraded status of women.

13 No conclusive information has been obtained so far for the rituals of the Indus people. Religious elements of the goddess can be inferred only from figurations on seals and from the mere occurrence of terracotta figurines, which are considered to be 'kept in almost every house in the ancient Indus cities' (Mackay 1948:146); see Chakrabarti (2001:42) and the important remarks in Ardeleanu-Jansen (1992).

14 These iconographic analogies can be ascertained within the phenomenon of Western Asian cultural interactions; see Amiet (1986:chapters 7–8) and Possehl (2002:215–36).

15 Mode (1960:98–100) reads some narratives with tiger motifs through the ancient folk tradition recorded in the Buddhist *jātakas*.

16 These were considered votive offerings to a fertility goddess (Marshall 1951:503–4).

17 Maula (1984) has attempted to explain the large rings and phallic stones as elements of astral calendars.

18 The headless goddess was identified with Viśirā, who in the *Mahābhārata* is worshipped for the welfare of children (Dhavalikar 1977:15–6, 49, pl. 10; 1985:77; Agrawal 1982:240–1, fig 150; Allchin & Allchin 1982:277–8, fig10.18; Chakrabarti 2001:48).

19 For Śītalā see Freed & Freed (1998:122–36).

20 Kosambi (1962:100–8) refers to the Jātakas as an earlier source preserving elements of the popular tradition.

21 To date only UNESCO reports have been circulated in a limited way.

22 'The Beloved of the Gods, the king Piyadassi, when he had been consecrated twenty years, came in person and reverenced the place where Buddha Śākymuni was born. He caused a stone enclosure to be made and a stone pillar to be erected. As the lord was born here in the village of Lumbinī, he has exempted it from tax, and fixed its contribution [ie of grain] at one-eighth' (Thapar 1963:261).

23 For Ṣaṣṭhī, personification of the 'sixth day', see also Crooke (1907:197–9), Joshi (1986:89–91), Jayakar (1989:161–2) and Freed & Freed (1998:122–3).

24 For detailed descriptions, see Gupta (1980:53–77) and Agrawala (1993).

25 On the *Vrātya*, see *Atharva Veda* Book XV, Choudhary (1964), Rolland (1973) and Shastri (1982).

26 On *mātṛkās* see Joshi (1986) and Kinsley (1986:151–60).

27 In stark contrast with this matriarchal model, a new type of nationalist Hindu woman is emerging inspired by the warrior goddess Durgā (see for instance Kovacs (2004)).

28 Assumptions that the past can be extrapolated from the present and analysed as it happened originally denote reductionist visions of the past and are similarly misleading in interpreting ancient phenomena (as in Bhattacharyya 1999:26).

29 In this regard see the interesting arguments by Sen (2005:65–6).

chapter three

Pārvatī as creator of *māyā* or victim of *māyā*: the role of Gaṇeśa's mother in the *Gaṇeśapurāṇa*

Greg Bailey

Though the Indian goddess, habitually known as Devī, or in a more abstract form as *śakti*, has been studied assiduously by anthropologists and textualists over the past 30 years, there is still room for more investigation. This is demanded by the centrality of this figure in South Asian religious life since even before Vedic literature, the multitudes of forms she takes when transferred into textual or iconographic form, and by the existence of complete theologies surrounding the goddess, a feature not present in other religions. Not only is the study of the mother goddess as a generic figure, operating on several different theological levels, a still valid enterprise, it is also important for what it tells us about the conceptualisation of both the feminine and of the roles women should normatively play in society. Of course, this conceptualisation often had to be read through images, which are often pathological, even to the culture which has produced them. Goddesses such as Kālī/Durgā, plus multitudes of tribal goddesses, and even the more benign Pārvatī, are frequently represented in extreme situations involving strong expressions of violence and emotion. Such oft-repeated imagery conveys a clear message. How it might translate into, or just translate, lived models of women is a secondary consideration. Nonetheless, it is a fundamental one because so much of didactic literature in Sanskrit and Pālī dealing with women is strongly misogynistic in its thrust and never gives us a picture of the ordinariness of everyday life which would have been the main context for women and men. What Purāṇic myth—the subject of this essay—has bequeathed to us is a masculine view of the role of women as mothers, or as ferocious warrior goddesses, with little in between.

One text that has been rarely studied at all, let alone for what it tells us about the mother goddess, is the *Gaṇeśapurāṇa* (*GP*), a Sanskrit text probably composed between the 14th and 16th centuries, perhaps on the basis of pre-existing material and from a geographical base located in Maharashtra. Yet, because of the centrality of the triad Śiva/Pārvatī/Gaṇeśa in the mythology of Gaṇeśa and of the tendency of Gaṇeśa's mythic activities to be centred around his role as son of Pārvatī, this text necessarily offers a good deal of material about Pārvatī and how, on the one hand, she relates to Gaṇeśa, and, on the other hand, how she functions as a mother. Thirdly, her ever-shifting relationship to Śiva is present, though it is heavily underplayed in the second book, a relationship that need not be explicitly developed as this had already been done in earlier Purāṇas and other folktales about Gaṇeśa (Dimmit & van Buitenen 1978:151–171; O'Flaherty 1981:129–143). Her status as a goddess is always present, but universally it is overshadowed by her role as a mother.

The *Gaṇeśapurāṇa* is a ritualistic and mythological text centred on the worship of Gaṇeśa, possibly composed for the use of various Gāṇapatya sects which had existed since at least the late 12th century. It contains a number of myths not attested in earlier sources, and a substantial reworking of many others well known from the Mahāpurāṇas (Bailey 1995:121–154). Divided into two books, the first is called *Upāsanākhaṇḍa* (*Ukh*) and deals primarily with the methods of worshipping Gaṇeśa and illustrates these methods with many myths and *stotras* which explain why the god should be worshipped, demonstrating equally his capacity as creator and/or remover of obstacles. The second book is named *Krīḍākhaṇḍa* (*Krkh*) and, true to its title, it focuses on Gaṇeśa's divine play, which also encompasses his role as an *avatāra*, explored over two very lengthy mythic cycles where he encounters and kills many different kinds of demonic figures. As the *avatāra*, Gaṇeśa is obviously a martial figure, but for most of these two cycles he is depicted as a child, living in two separate family units, the first consisting of Kaśyapa and Aditi (*Krkh* ch 4–74), the second of Śiva and Pārvatī (*Krkh* ch 75–155). In both cases motherhood defines the pre-eminent role of Aditi and Pārvatī respectively.

There is an intertextual complication here, of course. Because the *GP* so explicitly draws upon and reinterprets the classical mythology of the Śaivite Purāṇas, it was inevitable that Gaṇeśa's special birth and childhood would loom large in the *GP* itself. It had to if the *GP* was to remain true to the god's earlier mythological portrayal, where the original narrative parameters had already been set. In this portrayal the god stands psychologically and physically very close to his mother and at a considerable distance from his father. The tension between mother and son as a group, on the one hand, and the father, on the other hand, is strongly emphasised, and surely exaggerates true-life situations. The author(s) of the *GP* took great pains to explore Gaṇeśa's early life and family relationships and drew heavily from the classical narratives and the themes which shape them. In the *Ukh*, continuity with the earlier narratives is achieved by constantly portraying the interactions between a triad of father, mother and son, where the son is never Gaṇeśa, but some other child, and the father and mother are never Śiva and Pārvatī. The innovation in the *Krkh* is that Gaṇeśa is portrayed as a child in two different sets of families, the one where Kaśyapa and Aditi are father and mother respectively (in the *Kṛtayuga*), and the other where Śiva and Pārvatī play this role (in the *Tretāyuga*). There is a need for two families because Gaṇeśa appears as an *avatāra* in each of the four *yugas*, though only the first three *yugas* are dealt with in considerable detail. In the *avatāra* myth (*Krkh* ch 127–37) set within the Dvāparayuga, Gaṇeśa is again born into the family of Śiva and Pārvatī, but the narrative of childhood is not as rich as it is in the telling of the other two *yugas*. Typically, Śiva and Pārvatī are Gaṇeśa's parents and, apart from the *GP*, I do not know other instances where this situation is contradicted. I stress that the *GP* uses the Gaṇeśa birth myths as one of the sources of its several narratives, but it interprets them in its own idiosyncratic manner, bringing out a tone of originality in its portrayal of the interaction between Gaṇeśa and Pārvatī. Usually in the Mahāpurāṇas originality is found in the way traditional narratives are combined and recombined in new ways, not so much in the introduction of new content.

Pārvatī is, of course, a goddess[1] who derives her identity in part from her image as one aspect of the generic goddess in ancient and medieval Sanskrit literature, but more substantially from her role as wife of Śiva, by whom she is always seeking to be treated as the wife of a *gṛhastha*, and in part from her role as mother of Gaṇeśa and Skanda. The *Krkh* can be read on one of its levels as an exploration of her several attitudes towards Gaṇeśa and, through him, of her role as mother. As mother she is required to protect her son, a point stressed in the breach when in almost all cases it is he who protects her from destructive influences, even when she is not aware of this. In many passages she focuses only on her boy as a child, even though most other people in the hermitage where they live do know that the boy alternates between several different appearances and that on the highest level of reality he is the supreme god, *paramabrahma*. His appearance as a boy is necessitated by his role as *avatāra*, one he simultaneously plays with his role as Śiva's son. The disjunction between his position as *paramabrahma* and son is mediated through his role as *avatāra*, and throughout the *Krkh* there is virtually no individual who realises the simultaneity of all these roles and why they are essential for Gaṇeśa's identity, this despite the constant recognition in the text that he is not a normal child. Equally, the role of *avatāra*—especially since the *avatāra* is *paramabrahma*—brings with it the theme of *māyā* as the basic strategy of explaining the validity of the multiple identities of this figure. In turn, *māyā* understood as a constraining factor on the correct perception of a god/person's identity is directly connected with the inherent nature of women as mother.

It should be noted that the audience of this Purāṇa, whether it be of the Sanskrit text or its Marathi and Tamil summaries, knows all of the images of Gaṇeśa and the theology associated with them. This, at least, is what the many *stotras* and descriptions of iconic images of the god teach them. Even if there was only a partial knowledge, the particular themes of motherhood and *māyā* come up enough for them not to be missed and, more importantly, to be directly connected. Accordingly, we can assume the indigenous audience would be able to recognise which of the characters in the individual myths, and the more lengthy narrative units enframing them, noticed the limitations of Pārvatī's understanding of her son. Given the very large number of chapters (61–155, minus the 11 chapters of the *Gaṇeśagītā*) where she plays a central role, there is substantial opportunity to examine critically her epistemological confusion about the ontology of the god.

Epistemology and ontology

The basic dilemma faced by Pārvatī is concisely put by Viśvakarman after he has expressly come to the hermitage where Gaṇeśa is living in order to see the boy whom he knows to be 'marvellous' (*adbhuta* or *āścarya*), a term occurring almost in every chapter of the *Krkh*. Viśvakarman said,

> What is this extraordinary thing, Mother of the world? A boy will come to a mother, a great devotee will come to a god, a person seeking knowledge will come to a teacher, Śiva. Mother, what I have heard of your son is magnificent and utterly extraordinary. I have come to see him and I am eager to see both of you.[2]

In describing Gaṇeśa as *āścarya* and *paramādbhuta* Viśvakarman declares immediately his understanding of the complexity of the boy's identity. Gaṇeśa the boy may be 'magnificent' but the attribution of these two technical terms gives specification to this magnificence by indicating a particular ontological status. That which is 'marvellous' is *atimānuṣa*, beyond the range of normal human perception. Whilst in the *GP* Gaṇeśa is depicted in both *saguṇa* and *nirguṇa* forms, both can be regarded as *āścarya* in the sense that they either require special insight to see them or that they be offered as a *darśana* from the deity. For the rest of the time the god might conceal himself in one form or another through the application of his *māyā* and even confuse those sages or other gods who have been given a vision of his iconic form at a certain moment, not to recognise him at another moment. The comparison with Kṛṣṇa invites itself easily, though more in generalities than specifics, few signs of direct borrowings being apparent.[3]

In the passage just cited Viśvakarman is conflating (or just comparing) three forms of activity, similar because they represent an approach of a lesser person to another figure of higher status within the system whereby the relationship is given meaning in relation to other possibilities within that system. Of the three, the latter two are straightforward, whereas the first probably implies the image of a boy going to his mother in order to suckle at her breast. In all of the myths in the *Krkh* there is deliberate confusion created between the first and the third role as these are applied to the boy Gaṇeśa. He could also easily be the object of the second set of relationships, as there is no doubt that, when he is the object of devotion, he is capable of dispensing religious knowledge. In fact, the latter is usually provided automatically to his devotees, just as it is occasionally to his mother.

Viśvakarman himself becomes a devotee of the god, and throughout the chapters where he appears he is acknowledged as a figure who is 'jñānic' in knowing the god as he truly is. Much more interesting is Pārvatī, whose knowledge of her son can be understood at two, almost contradictory, levels. Her appreciation of the boy as supreme deity and son occur on two different registers and when the one prevails the other is entirely absent. Both registers cannot be held simultaneously in her mind and it seems as though this is not just a case of forgetfulness but a problem of the irreconcilability of two different forms of knowledge, a problem which can very easily be accommodated within most schools of Indian philosophy.

Emotion and role models

Pārvatī's problems with her son are explored across 20 odd chapters of the *Krkh* (80–100). These portray fairly similar plots involving Gaṇeśa at play with the boys in a spatial setting of a hermitage, one where life is supposed to proceed at a steady if predictable pace and where only auspiciousness prevails. Evil should be absent here, because being an *āśrama* the *puṇya* of the resident sages confers a sense of goodness on the environment. I note that we are dealing here with forest-dwellers of the third stage of the *āśrama* scheme as they are all married and many sons (but rarely young women) are wandering around. Outside of this hermitage the world exists in a state of *adharma*, since a malevolent demon named Sindhu is ruling, having overturned the 'dharmic' structures holding together the three worlds. But just as the world is not immune from the influence of inauspicious forces, so too can the hermitage be invaded by demonic forces. Always in the form of a male or female *asura/daitya*, this particular figure comes in disguise specifically to attack Gaṇeśa who plays the *avatāra* role even when he is resident in the hermitage. It is a microcosm of the world with the difference that it is a site of auspiciousness, a site compromised only by the arrival of the demon.

An illustration of the demon's intrusion and of the other themes I intend to discuss is provided in the passage I have included below, a complete translation of Chapter 84 of the *Krkh*. I have added Sanskrit words in many places, as they are illustrative of the themes and the shifts in epistemological registers with which I am concerned.

1 Brahmā said, 'In the second month, Gaurī, having dressed up the boy for
the evening, placed him in a cradle and sang very joyfully. Meanwhile two
2 daityas came to the boy as rats, taking this appearance by magic (*māyā
rūpadharau*). Named Kṣema and Kuśala, they wanted to kill him.
Wanting to fight and using nails and teeth as their weapons, these two
3 ferocious (*ghorau*) rogues went into the house near the watching woman
(*pālanābhyāśe*) and climbed onto his splendid body (*sphuradaṅga…*).
4 Ears were deafened by the sound of their cries and the blows of their feet
turned the entire Earth into a field ready for ploughing.

5 Picking up a stick she terrorised (*bhīṣayāmāsa*) both of them. Both
just fled and they jumped upwards. Still fighting, these two fierce
6 creatures fell onto the boy. That superb boy (*bālakottamaḥ*) woke up
when they struck him on his chest.

7 Śivā made a sharp cry and then became frightened (*bibhāya*).
But, in fear (*bhītitaḥ*), he moved his hands in a childish manner
(*bālabhāvena*) and when he struck them, their lives wasted, both fell
down. When she saw them vomiting blood from their mouth, Śivā
8 became quite confused (*bhrāntā*).

9 Barely alive these two were then taken outside by the hosts and
achieved liberation (*mokṣaṃ jagmatur*) because they were struck by
10 Gaṇeśa's hands. Their ferocious (*ghorau*) bodies fell, strewn over an area
of ten *yojanas*. When Pārvatī saw the two bodies as such there was a
11 huge uproar (*kolāhalo mahān*) amongst the hosts and friends.
Hermitages, trees, mountains and large houses were ruined by their
12 falling, lifeless, heads. After cutting (*chittvā chittvā*) up their bodies the
hosts took them outside (*ninyur bahis*).

13 Terrified with fear (*bhayavitrastā*), Pārvatī, who loved her son
(*bālakavatsalā*), quickly took the boy, and had him affectionately
14 (*snehena*) drink from her breast. The faultless wives of the sage
assembled and said to Pārvatī. 'You have great merit (*puṇyaṃ mahat*),
15 Gaurī, as a result of which this obstacle has been removed. The two huge
malevolent demons were killed by a two-month-old boy. In the future
there will be nobody like him in the three worlds (*anena sadṛśo na*
16 *bhaviṣyati*). Mother! This is a world of rākṣasas. It is necessary to be
diligent (*yatnaḥ kāryaḥ*) in regard to your child here. The rākṣasas will
stay in secret (*guptā*) and other asuras in a state of disguise (*asurā*
māyinaḥ).'

17 Brahmā said, 'After saying this the ladies left, but the hosts addressed
18 her. "Śivā this child of yours will kill every day. It will take us some time to
take these demons outside".'

Then the sages went and looked after (*rakṣāṃ cakrur*) the boy.
19 After bowing to them she gave them presents and dismissed them.

Then, in the third month, when people were preoccupied with their
20 own tasks, at midday, Pārvatī took the boy and slept on the bed. Some of
21 her servants slept, others were enjoying themselves and others gossiped
in the door. At that interval an asura named Krūra, huge and malevolent
22 (*duṣṭo*), entered Pārvatī's house in the guise (*veṣeṇa*) of a huge male cat,
deceiving (*vañcayitvā*) people's eyes like a dog. Having spotted Pārvatī
asleep, he then rejoiced, thinking, 'Whilst Girijā is sleeping, I will take the
23 boy away.' He deftly got onto the bed, took the boy by the head and got
24 under the bed. Right then the boy shrieked.

25 Girijā then awoke and spotting the child in the cat's mouth,
agitated with fear (*bhayavihvalā*), she screamed out 'Run! Run!' With
26 her eyes open, she fainted from distress (*duḥkhena*) and fear (*bhītitaḥ*).
27 But for as long as the cat was biting his neck, the boy, because of his
nature (*svabhāvāt*), held him on both his ears with his forearms. With a
blow of his foot to the area of the head, he felled the huge asura under
28 the bed. His heart pierced, he fled, went outside and fell like some ripe
fruit from a tree in a huge wind. His foul smelling blood fell onto the
ground, making people cover their nose.

29 Agitated with grief (*śokavihvalā*), the daughter of the mountain took
30 the boy and gave him a drink from her breast. At the sound of the child all
31 the servants came. Filled with curiosity (*kautukānvitāḥ*) they individually
touched his limbs, having decided in their minds that he was undecaying
and eternal.

32 The cat then became twelve yojanas in length and her friends and
servants were crushed. And the hosts gathered after they had seen this
33 special cat. They experienced extraordinary astonishment (*āścaryaṃ*
paramam) at the strength of the boy, thinking, 'On the one hand this
malevolent daitya creates an illusion (*māyino*), on the other hand there is
the blow from the boy's foot. He has killed in play (*līlayā*) those whom
Indra and the others could not kill.'

34 After receiving his permission the hosts went to their own abodes,
but some strong ones dragged the daitya away and left it outside (*tatyajur*
35 *bahiḥ*). Pārvatī placed him on her hip and entered her own house.

Then in the fourth month the sages' wives assembled. After taking
36 concoctions conducive to success when the sun was in the north, women
with and without children went with Pārvatī to her auspicious house.
37 Then Dākṣāyaṇī gave seats of honour to these women and made
obeisance to them after putting the boy on her hip. They were decorating
38 each other with turmeric and *kuṅkum* etc, after placing their children, who
were moving and standing still, on the ground. Then Pārvatī's boy also
39 played (*krīḍate sma*) amongst them and because of him all of them shone
40 like the host of stars and the moon.

When they saw him the wives of the sages spoke about him to the
daughter of the mountain. 'You are fortunate, Gaurī, having such a
41 splendid (*bhāsvatā*) son given by Śiva. Our boys too are shining
(*bhāsante*) because they are close to your son, in the same way that iron
gains a golden glow through association with treasure.'

42 They decorated each other eagerly with turmeric, *kuṅkum*, pieces
43 of sugar cane, sandalwood and garlic, sesamum, sugar balls, palm leaves
and many kinds of perfumes. Some smeared sesamum on their bodies
and others on their mouth.

44 At that moment a huge daitya named Bālāsura, who had a boy's
appearance (*bālarūpī*) and was of similar age, went to play (*krīḍitum*) in
45 their midst. He played (*cikrīḍa*) with Pārvatī's son, fighting as though
amusing himself (*vinodataḥ*), just as a jackal with a lion or a buffalo with
46 an elephant. After rubbing neck against neck they both fell roughly to the
ground. The malevolent (*duṣṭo*) demon then struck Gajānana on the head
with his feet. Taking his hair in his hands he violently dragged him. And
47 the malevolent (*duṣṭo*) demon himself roared, just like an old jackal in
the night.

48 When she saw these two like this, the daughter of the mountain said
to the women, 'Who does this rock-solid boy belong to? He has struck my son.
This rogue brays "Eaw!Eaw!" like a donkey. An observant woman says
49 this is the true nature of boys (*svabhāvo*). However, these two boys are
50 affectionately roughing each other up on the ground. They are grabbing each
other and dragging their hair about everywhere, whilst laughing and making
the other boys laugh, wives of the sages.'

51 Although knowing this was a huge daitya, Vināyaka continued
playing (*khelati*). Then the malevolent (*duṣṭo*) Bālāsura held the very
52 strong Gaṇanāyaka on the throat with his hands, drawing out his life. He
too seized him in a similar way and the asura's breathing stopped.

53 When they saw this boy—who was really a daitya—so agitated, the
54 women became depressed (*duścittām*) and shrieked out, 'He has
definitely killed this boy!' Some ran up but could not free the two. All the
men and women then said to the lovely Ambikā, 'You release him! The
sage's son will die!'

55 Then Pārvatī said to the boy, 'Release him! Release him! When
56 he is dead, the sages, filled with the heat of austerity, will curse us. In this
ball of creation there is no higher merit than the gift of life. Your great
power will depart because of their curse.'

57 Brahmā said, 'Whilst the daughter of the mountain was making entreaties
58 in this manner, his breath had immediately departed through his eyes like
bubbles. Then all of them saw that he was ten *yojanas* in extent, that his mouth
59 gaped and that he had fallen, crushing huge trees. The frightened women
60 (*bhītā*) quickly left from there, taking their sons, as if they were cows or goats
61 who flee in fear (*bhayāt*) when they see a troop of wolves.

But the daughter of the mountain, seeing her own tender son and whirling
62 him around, gave him the breast and had the propitiatory rituals performed
by the powerful Brāhmins. She gave gifts to them and she received many
63 blessings, thinking, 'I do not understand this asura magic (*āsurīṃ māyīm*). So
many come to destroy, then they are destroyed because of my son, the great
64 rogues. Who can oppress a person who is in the Lord's favour? '

65 Brahmā said, 'After giving ear to her speech, the sages' wives departed, and
the hosts, threw him far away, bathed and then went to their own homes. '

Whilst typical of this kind of narrative, the present chapter contains three demon-killing episodes (2–16, 19–35, 37–63), which, collectively, exemplify the themes defining the kinds of roles I am concerned about. Domesticity and localisation reign and mirror a view of a village under threat from marauding forces. Focusing initially on the text as story, clear emphasis is placed on the fear (derivatives of *bhī* occurring six times), especially of the women, when they are aware a demonic figure is in their midst. The demons are ferocious; the women are frightened. But of what are they frightened? Always the demons come in disguise and as animals (rats and a cat) in two cases, of a kind one would expect in a village environment, which is akin to how the hermitage is described. The third disguise is the boy/demon playing with the other boys, seemingly without any cares.

Each should seem to be harmless as they appear, but the reader/hearer of the myth knows they are far more than this. And this is where the different epistemological levels become clear within the context of the tales themselves. If the reader/hearer knows these three apparently harmless creatures are really demonic figures, this is not so for those who are required to deal with them or react against them. In the first episode, verse 4 suggests these demonic rats are no ordinary rats, as the sound of their feet is so great, a similar judgment if the giant size of the cat in verse 22 is taken into consideration and the violence of the boy fighting with Gaṇeśa in verse 46. Pārvatī is the woman who offers these reactions in each case and they are wholly typical of her as a mother who fears her son is about to be the victim of violence. But in each case, apart from the first, where the initial form of apprehension is effected through hearing, the mode of knowledge is sight (24 *nirīkṣya* and 48 *dṛṣṭvā*), an epistemology enabling her only to perceive her son as being under threat. Why someone would want to attack her son is not clear to Pārvatī, but that she is aware of the possibility is conveyed by the term 'watching woman' which utilises in part the verb *pālana*—from *pāl*, to protect.[4]

A sense of confusion, fear and even depression comprises the psychological reactions of Pārvatī and the other mothers who witness the attack on Gaṇeśa.[5] Fear is wholly understandable as it is an emotion spontaneously arising from an unprovoked attack where no cause seems to be apparent. The demons may be ferocious (*ghora* 3, 10), but this is not known to the watching women, yet still they are frightened. At a more problematic level is the sense of confusion Pārvatī experiences. Technical terms such as *bhrāntā* (8) or *duścittā* (54), used of the women in general, indicate a failure to go beyond the surface of the situation. The first is particularly striking as it describes Pārvatī's response at seeing the blood flowing from the rats' noses after Gaṇeśa has struck them. This means that, whilst her apprehension about the demons' true power is scarcely developed, her understanding of her son's true capacity is beyond her comprehension because it does not fit what she would normally expect from a small boy.

The different epistemological registers and levels of understanding shift into still higher profile when the reaction to the boy's killing of the demon is taken into consideration. It is commonplace in many of the other myths of similar plot for the boys to cheer Gaṇeśa's success and to announce that they have witnessed a miraculous event (*āścarya, adbhuta*). Miraculous, I assume, because Gaṇeśa is always depicted as being so small, the demon so large. Pārvatī's reaction, mimicked by many of the other women, is at variance with this. In the first of the three episodes in Chapter 84 she witnesses the death of the two rats (though, unbeknown to her, they really achieve *mokṣa*) which are immediately transformed into huge demonic figures whose size dwarfs the area surrounding the hermitage. Their heads are cut off, the people respond with uproar and Pārvatī is terror-stricken (13), even though she must know her son is alive. Or she is agitated with grief (29), or, finally, just relieved. In each case, except for the third, it must be the suddenness of the transformation that has produced her strong emotional reaction, not so much the transformation of her son, but of the demonic figure. Each of what seemed to be an animal or a boy appropriate for the hermitage has become something utterly different, even if her boy has not changed.

Only in the third episode is the story slightly more convoluted. Here the daitya, who has the appearance of a boy, is recognised by Gaṇeśa for what he truly is, leading the boy/Gaṇeśa to begin strangling him (52). Appalled by this scenario all of the watching women rush up and try to free the boy who is being strangled. Finally, Pārvatī intervenes with the words 'Release him! Release him!' (*muñca muñceti,* 55), a very simple but effective form of punning, because the same words can be taken as requesting he be given spiritual liberation of the kind given to the first two demons. The pun brilliantly glosses the two levels of reality operative here. Seen from the level of the naked eye she is simply asking him to be released so that he does not suffer physical death. Yet when viewed from the perspective of Gaṇeśa's real identity as the supreme object of devotion, the words highlight his capacity to confer liberation upon anybody. Yet Pārvatī does not understand the pun in the way the audience of the tale must.

In all three episodes (14, 30, 61) Pārvatī finishes by picking up her child—he is still only two months old—and giving him a drink from her breast. In all the other episodes she continues to offer the breast at the end of his demon-killing exploits.[6] This gives comfort to her and to him, though he makes nothing of it. It re-establishes the mother–son bond as some inextinguishable thing that appeared under threat when Gaṇeśa was actually fighting with the demons. Each occasion is a moment where emotion, fear mixed with affection, is released and the mother–son bond is reinforced by an act of physical nourishment. Note the mixed emotions associated with the brief act. In 13 she is 'terrified with fear' and then 'affectionately' feeds him and is accordingly 'loved by her son', the final compound occurring at the end of the verse in the Sanskrit, perhaps glossing his response after receiving her breast. In 30 she is 'agitated with grief' and then feeds him, whereas in a state of joy she whirls him around and then feeds him in verse 61. Given their widespread occurrence in these and other chapters, such verses may well be formulaic, but this merely serves to highlight their importance in the plot of the myth. I conclude that not only are they designed to reconfirm the mother–son bond, they also offer a reflex of her fear that she has not been watching the boy closely enough.

If these three verses (14, 30, 61) demonstrate yet again her strong commitment to motherhood, the immediately following verses reveal her incapacity to glimpse beyond the literal level of the action in order to understand the other conflict found here. In the first case it is the mothers of the other boys who reveal an awareness of another level, even if they cannot articulate it with absolute precision.

> The faultless wives of the sage assembled and said to Pārvatī. 'You have great merit, Gaurī, as a result of which this obstacle has been removed. The two huge malevolent demons were killed by a two-month-old boy. In the future there will be nobody like him in the three worlds. Mother! This is a world of rākṣasas. It is necessary to be diligent in regard to your child here. The rākṣasas will stay in secret and other asuras in a state of disguise' (14–16).

Everything is brought out in these lines: the paradox of a two-month-old boy killing huge demons, whose true size has now been revealed; the boy's uniqueness; the necessity for him to be protected; and the capacity of demons to engage in disguise. The contradiction between his killing of the demons and his need for protection is passed over here; I will return to it later. What is being suggested is that the boy appears as he really is, that a multitude of appearances are appropriate for him. The demonic figures are in disguise and will be revealed as they truly are only when they are killed. They can have only two appearances: the monstrous and the disguised (normal to the villagers). Gaṇeśa can have many appearances and his theological status is, in theory, the same in each, at least from the perspective of his worshippers. And this translates into his uniqueness. Uniqueness of a devotional god is an integral part of the theology surrounding such figures and glosses both their singularity and their supremacy in the hierarchy of gods.[7] Here though, the women seem not to be aware of the implications such a statement has for the other tenets they have advanced about the boy, nor do they develop the idea into a view of divinity associated with him.

Of more importance for my argument is the assumption about the world being filled with *rākṣasas*, meaning that there are dangers everywhere, though it may be referring to the condition of the world when it is overrun by demons, necessitating the intervention of the *avatāra*. More significant on the epistemological plane is the alleged secrecy of the *asura/rākṣasas* and their capacity to manipulate their appearance. This capacity is engineered by their status as *māyāvin* or 'possessors of *māyā*', the principal manifestation of which is a capacity to change their appearance easily and in a manner that convinces others that this is their true appearance, that they are not truly demons. All demons in the *GP* are shown to possess this capacity, and equally the women never seem to understand it, perhaps because their role as mothers causes them to be fixated on their sons simply as young boys, rendering them incapable of easily recognising the kinds of transformations *māyā* implies. Pārvatī admits this openly at the very end of this chapter when she reflects: 'I do not understand this asura magic (*āsurīṃ māyīm*). So many come to destroy, then they are destroyed because of my son, the great rogues. Who can oppress a person who is in the Lord's favour?' (62–64).[8] Two impressions emerge from this. Firstly, she cannot understand how the demonic figures are able to place themselves in disguise, nor can she see through this disguise. In this she is joined both by the other women and the boys. Note too that when the second demon appears as a cat, he is said to be in disguise and this deceives (*vañcayitvā* (22)) everybody's eyes. Secondly, each of these categories of observers only realises that *māyā* has been applied when the demon is killed and suddenly transformed, the principal expression of this being the magnification of the demon's size to gigantic dimensions. This incites reactions such as a huge uproar (*kolāhalo mahān*) amongst the hosts and friends (11), extraordinary astonishment (*āścaryaṃ paramam*) at the strength of the boy (33) and fear (60). Each of these is based on sight, on seeing the transformation that has occurred and/or the strength of the boy. The transformation is uniformly a dramatic one and the realisation of the strength of the boy comes as a shock. This is why it is so frequently described with the words *āścarya* or *adbhuta*, often with the adjective *parama*, both of which can also indicate a miraculous event, something very much out of the ordinary. Both are terms used very frequently within the devotional lexicon of the *GP*.

When Pārvatī declares her lack of understanding of the demonic *māyā*,[9] she is making a more extensive admission than she may realise. If the astonishment she experiences on seeing the demon is a reaction to the sudden doses of reality (unmediated by *māyā*) she is given, her knowledge of the process—as opposed to the result—of *māyā* seems straightforward. Yet she still does not understand that her own son, who to her is only a son, has also concealed his true appearance (*svarūpa*) under a veil of *māyā*. The astonishment of the boys at Gaṇeśa's extraordinary strength is not just an assessment of his strength; it also indicates a suspicion that he is much more than he appears to be. For Pārvatī, however, all this is quite irrelevant. She is fixated on his identity as her son.

Gaṇeśa's use of *māyā* is recorded everywhere in the *Krkh*, both in narratives where its actual application is presented and in *stotras* where it is listed as one of his attributes.[10] Its very frequent referencing in the text, in both ways, indicates how significant an aspect of his identity it is in the way this identity has been developed across the entire *GP*. But equally all the demonic figures are credited with the possession of illusion-making capacities,[11] which they use only as a means of creating a disguised appearance, one revealed to be unreal when they die. However, Gaṇeśa cannot die and if the demons' manifestation of their own giant forms is involuntary, caused by their deaths, Gaṇeśa's use of *māyā* is always voluntary as is his withdrawal of it. This is given immediate clarification in the case of those occasions when he shows to Pārvatī another appearance than that of a child. An example is Chapter 92 where Gaṇeśa lies on the ground yawning, Pārvatī peers into his mouth and is given a theophany.

42 In his mouth she saw the universe, the forms of the universe, the seven
continents and the Earth with its cities, villages, forests and mines,
43 Brahmā, Bhāskara, Śeṣa, Viṣṇu, the oceans and mountains, the
gandharvas, yakṣas, rākṣasas and the masses of sages and birds, the
44 moon, the sun, fire and the stars, things with consciousness and without
consciousness, the seven hells and the twenty-one heavens.

45 On seeing the three worlds in this way Girijā immediately fainted.
She opened her eyes, but remained confused for two hours. In her mind
46 she recollected Śiva and then became focused. She saw the boy standing
47 just as he was before and he was just as he was before. Her mind then
became clear due to his favour and she eulogised him.'

Pārvatī said, 'You are the highest self...all that is moving and unmoving
50 I have seen, but I cannot describe it. I was confused and fell to the ground,
but I became focused by recollection on Śiva, and so I saw the child in his
51 natural form in the state of a child.'

Brahmā said, 'When she had eulogised him in this way, he manifested
52 himself in an illusion and after she had fondled him, Śivā put him on her hip
and gave him a drink from her breast. Girijā entered the house and became
occupied with her household work. The sages and their wives went to their
own homes.'

Other such examples could be cited. All add to the realisation that Gaṇeśa does show himself to Pārvatī (also called Śivā and Girijā) in forms other than that of a child and that she is able to see him in these forms, forms entirely atypical of the kind of interests—domestic, more than devotional—with which she is constantly associated. Yet if he does show himself like this, she very quickly loses this special knowledge—it is always acquired in a vision—because it is in no way consistent with her image of Gaṇeśa as her son. If we interpreted this loss as a lapse of memory, we would be mistaken. Within the conceptual framework of the *GP* it should rather be seen as the god intentionally showing himself in a form she, his unwitting devotee, would desire. This is summarised beautifully in verses 50–51, lines redolent with the ambience of domesticity.

Besides this particular passage, where she does receive such a vision, there are only two places[12] where he appears in an iconic form. A further passage is the one just cited (92, 41–44) where she sees the world inside his mouth and on three occasions[13] she utters *stotras* or descriptions of him that could be made only by someone who has a knowledge of his iconic form. On eight other occasions[14] different figures, such as Śiva or prominent sages, give oral descriptions of the god in a form both iconic and reflective of his universal appearance. In none of these is any indication given of her being shown or seeing him in his elephantine form. It is usually the case that in *darśanas* that the god gives, or in *stotras* describing all his attributes, the god's elephant head is a point of focus, obviously because this is a sure sign of his divine form. When he appears like this it is an expression of his devotional favour to particular individuals whom he considers to be qualified to receive his devotion. There can be no doubt this aspect of the god's activity is being heavily understated in the case of Pārvatī, even if it can never be entirely absent.

But in its partial absence it reinforces the impression of Pārvatī's domesticity as the driving force behind her perception of Gaṇeśa. All her concerns are focused in this domain, a point brilliantly made in a later chapter (96) of the *Krkh*, where a conflict between Aditi and Pārvatī over who is truly the god's son, is narrated. I cite only the most relevant portions of the resulting argument:

48 Aditi said, 'Now you, Gaurī, must look, straight away, at my son, standing
here again!' She looked right at him and Gaṇeśa became her own son.
49 Aditi said to her, 'He is mine,' and Pārvatī said to her, 'He is mine.'

Whilst they were arguing in this way, the astonished gods said, 'This
50 god has neither beginning nor end, he causes the creation, the
preservation and the destruction, his forms are endless, his splendour is
51 endless and his energy has many female forms. Of which woman will he be
the son? Both women are confused by his illusion-making power.'

They said, 'He must be given into the hand of her whose son he might be'.

52 Brahmā said, 'Then after the gods had spotted the Lord in his different
forms, one said he was Vidhātṛ, and one that he was four-armed Viṣṇu.
53 One said he was three-eyed Śiva, one Varuṇa. The gods were
54 astonished. They said, 'We cannot make a decision. Both of you can
comprehend this supreme man by discrimination.'

55 Then Gaurī, taking that Lord as her own son, affectionately gave him
a drink from her breast. Aditi dried up, thinking, 'This is my son. Why does
he go to another? By a mistake I have become wrongly attached to
another's son.'

But the two women do not have the discriminating capacity (*viveka*)—the quality of distinguishing what is metaphysically real from what is not—to comprehend the true identity of the god. Yet even in saying this the gods themselves are mistaken because for them Gaṇeśa's true form is not known within a range of known alternatives. This scarcely matters, as the two women have no interest in subtleties of identity. To them the only real Gaṇeśa is the child they can nurse and suckle. In that sense the gods are missing the point completely and the two women know exactly where their interests lie. No proof is given in the final analysis, yet Aditi seems instinctively to know Gaṇeśa is not her son when he is feeding from Pārvatī's breast (cf Courtright 2001:53, 59).

Gaṇeśa's *māyā* and Pārvatī's ignorance

In all myths dealing with the *avatāra* at any period of Sanskrit literature where this figure appears, the *avatāra* uses *māyā* to conceal one of his appearances in order to lay stress on another. Moreover, the various types of individuals with whom he comes into contact know (usually fleetingly) this to be so. Where this knowledge of *māyā* becomes important is not so much in the indecision it might engender in a person uncertain of the god's true identity. Rather it is in the process of forgetting the role *māyā* plays that other identities of the god can be emphasised. In the case of Gaṇeśa three basic appearances (and their associated roles) are present in the *Krkh*: the god in his iconic form with an elephant head; the god as defined in theological terms especially in *stotras*; and, finally, the god as a boy. As the latter he grows into a youth[15] in the *Krkh* and is sometimes treated as a warrior by his demon antagonists, even if his boyhood, expressed physically and in attitude, is never in doubt. Pārvatī, despite the several occasions where she is visibly and intellectually reminded that Gaṇeśa is more than a mere boy, constantly forgets he has any other identity than this and is really disdainful of going beyond *māyā*.

All of these speculations raise the question whether Pārvatī would choose a different role if she were not so fixated onto her role as mother and whether the whole devotional movement allows any other possibility. That is, if a woman wishes to be a devotee, and there are examples of this in the *GP*, she cannot relinquish her role as mother, though men are able to renounce the fatherhood role as many ascetics who populate the *GP* have done. She must be a mother whilst still being a devotee, neither position being incompatible with the other.

A recent article by Robert Goldman provides a broad framework for understanding the role of the *avatāra* as one of conflicting identities. Working primarily from the *Mahābhārata* he argues:

> Crucial to the vital notion of *līlā* or play that provides the raison d'être for the avatāra in the Sanskrit epics is the idea that God on the Earth should not be universal or consistently recognised as such.
>
> ...the supporters, friends, and kinsmen of these gods on Earth [Kṛṣṇa and Rāma] are at best only occasionally aware of their true divinity, frequently forgetting about it immediately after a revelation or demonstration (Goldman 1999:105–6).

As Goldman (1999:114–5) argues this also includes the *avatāra* himself, who is sometimes portrayed adopting an entirely human attitude.[16] This forgetfulness can be understood in several modalities, some of which are explored in the *GP*. Where this text takes us further than either of the epics is in the underlying assumption that most women do not want to penetrate the god's *māyā*. Pārvatī's forgetfulness is almost total as is Aditi's, Gaṇeśa's mother, in an earlier section[17] of the *Krkh*.

This suggests that the *Krkh* is not just providing an easily understood lesson in the functioning of *māyā* as an impediment to the acquisition of metaphysical knowledge, but that it is deliberately counterpointing this with the capacity or incapacity of women to gain and hold this knowledge. It is the capacity that is significant here. Women clearly possess this capacity, as exemplified by the figure of Kīrti,[18] but do they want the knowledge? Does it have any significance for them? The *Krkh* is quite adamant that most do not. Motherhood and fostering of a son define their role as a woman. Anything else is incidental. However, incidental things do arise because devotional practices do not respect social boundaries. Historically women have been no more excluded from the devotional relationship than men and many have become exemplary figures.

If so, how can we explain this emphasis in the *Krkh*? Devotional practices can be performed knowingly or inadvertently. Examples[19] of the latter take the form of individuals having a meal before a Gaṇeśa image, not knowing that he is a god, and uttering his name for some reason or other. The god himself accepts this as a form of devotion. Another form this takes is for a person to focus intently on a particular figure, who may be a deity in disguise, where the focus itself is considered a devotional practice, irrespective of whether the focusing agent is aware that what is taking place should be considered in a devotional sense. Pārvatī's attention to her son's welfare is almost total and falls into this category of behaviour. Accordingly, devotional behaviour and maternal attitude could be seen to coalesce.

This does not, of course, resolve the problem. What is to be done about the women's—Pārvatī and Aditi—apparent addiction to *māyā*? An obsessive concern with the physical aspects of their son's upbringing[20] reflects a priority on the physical and perhaps psychological, but not on those aspects of existence associated with *ātman* and *paramabrahma*. Gaṇeśa overlaps with both of these. Yet whilst this might be regarded as wholly negative from a Vedantic perspective, their almost complete subjection to *māyā* means that whenever he reveals himself to them in his *svarūpa* as the elephant-headed god, this revelation is all the more powerful. So too is their forgetting of it, and their reversion to a wholly maternal attitude, all the more powerful. Such revelations are always a deep, if not the deepest, expression of the god's devotion to his devotee. However, for Pārvatī they are uncommon, occurring only three times (92, 42–50[21]) in the *Krkh*, though to this could be added three other occasions[22] where she utters a *stotra* in which she indicates the god's *paramabrahma* status.

In the final analysis I believe it would be trite to take Pārvatī's attention to Gaṇeśa as a homily addressed to mothers that they should treat their sons in the same way as they treat a male *bhakti* god to whom they exercise devotion. Gaṇeśa's earlier mythology in the *Mahāpurāṇas* places a very clear restraint on his depiction as anything other than a child or a youth. And if we take into consideration the strong devotional ambience of the *Kṛṣṇacarita* in its depiction in the tenth book of the *Bhāgavatapurāṇa*, a likely broad influence on the *Krkh*, then it is fully comprehensible that maternal affection should overtake devotional obsession. For the audience/listeners of the text, however, this will be construed as an act of devotion in its own right—one that may be all the more heightened because it does not follow the more formal applications of devotion.

Notes

1 Most clearly elaborated in *Krkh* 95, 5–14 where Viśvakarman offers a eulogy to her utilising all of the usual theological concepts associated with supremacy and devotion. Such *stotras* to her are rare in the *GP*.

2 *kim āścaryaṃ jaganmātar bālo mātaram āvrajet //*

draṣṭuṃ devaṃ mahābhakto vidyākamo guruṃ śive /

putrasya te śruto mātar mahimā paramādbhutaḥ //

tam ahaṃ draṣṭum āyāto yuvayor darśanotsukaḥ / (95, 19cd–21ab)

3 More precisely, the tenth book of the *Bhāgavata Purāṇa*, famous for dealing with the childhood of Kṛṣṇa, along with its precursor texts in the *Bālacarita* and the *Viṣṇu Purāṇa*, has had a direct intertextual influence on the *Krkh*. It does not call itself *bālacarita*, but it does contain perhaps a dozen *upākhyānas* where Kṛṣṇa is beset by and defeats demons, all of whom are working under the orders of Kaṃsa, and thus offers a parallel with the demons killed by Gaṇeśa who are acting at the behest of Narāntaka and Devāntaka, Sindhu or Sindūra, depending upon which cycle of the myths is being considered. Other parallels are the association of the respective gods with the boys, who are distinguished only on the basis of the larger mythological context: Gaṇeśa has to be associated with the *Gaṇas*, as he is their lord, and Kṛṣṇa is a suitable cowherd given his association with Viṣṇu the protector. At the level of imagery, the descriptions of rambunctious demons remind us of the demons who try to kill Gaṇeśa, but lacking somewhat (without being entirely absent) is the emphasis placed on these events as being miraculous and marvellous. For more details, see Bailey (2008).

4 Elsewhere, in other contexts, the boy's parents are consistently warned to maintain a watch over him.

5 Note that in other similar myths the boys as a group are attacked, not just Gaṇeśa, implying that it is the collectivity that is important, just as when a demonic figure overturns the established order of the triple-world, it is the 'dharmic' order affecting everybody that is of prime concern, not the individual.

6 See 96, 41, 54 and 99, 64.

7 See *Kūrma Purāṇa* 2, 29, 41; *Vāmana Purāṇa* 32, 10; *Sarohamāhātmya* 17, 17.

8 Cf 2, 87, 53. (Because of formatting conventions exact line numbers may vary slightly between translations here and the original text).

9 Cf 86, 51–53;

> Then she saw the Daitya extended for ten *yojanas*, his mouth agape, a tortoise vomiting copious blood. (52) He had violently crushed hermitages and trees of many kinds. Taking the boy, she happily gave him a drink from her breast, thinking, (53) 'I was not aware of those demons practising different kinds of illusion. Once more, through the favour of the three-eyed Śiva, I have found my son.'

10 See, 2, 5, 16–17; 6, 12, 35; 13, 27; 19, 47; 55, 13; 59, 5, 17; 71, 27; 81, 21; 83, 17; 91, 34; 92, 51; 100, 3, 33; etc.

11 See 4, 11; 19, 18; 20, 51; 39, 11; 60, 32; 86, 14; 90, 14; 91, 3; 92, 20; 93, 37.

12 Chapters 80, 4–7; 81, 16–18.

13 Chapters 80, 9–10; 91, 34–35; 92, 47–50.

14 Chapters 79, 27–33; 82, 4–6; 83, 10–15; 85, 9–16, 18–33; 95, 24cd–29; 103, 20–28cd; 116, 6–9

15 In this sense, I cannot agree with Courtright when he writes,

> For the moment it is important to notice the ways in which Gaṇeśa "submits" to his mother, attempting to remain close to her by keeping his youthful—indeed, childlike—form, and never grows up. Gaṇeśa's eternal youth matches Pārvatī's eternal adulthood. Because neither is subject to the ravages of time, they both remain temporally enshrined in a mother/son relationship (2001:109).

Probably accurate for the *Mahāpurāṇas*, where Gaṇeśa's mythology is initially developed, his image in the GP is considerably more complex than this because of the need to integrate several different forms of identity into one figure. Even so, though he does have two children (Kṣema and Lābha), nothing is known of them apart from their names.

16 Examples of this phenomenon in the *Krkh* can be found at 61, 19; 69, 28–35; 116, 21–3; 121, 51.

17 See 2, 5, 1–73, 45.

18 See, 48, 24–57.

19 A quite humorous example is *Ukh* 63.

20 See 116, 2–5, where Pārvatī expresses her fears about Gaṇeśa confronting Sindhu:

> 'Son, you have become exhausted in the battle with the cruel daitya. How did your tender limbs withstand the swords? That mighty strong daitya is like death and has powers of illusion. How did you defeat him in battle with your tender body?' The goddess wept compassionately, after taking her son on her lap. Then the group of sages and Śambhu pressed around Śivā.

Alternatively, this might be read as a sign of both her incapacity to know the boy as he truly is and her horror at a young boy confronting a hardened demon in battle.

21 Cf 80, 4–7; 81, 16–18

22 Chapters 80, 9–10; 91, 34–35; 92, 47–50.

chapter four

When Reṇukā was not a goddess

Rashmi Desai

Introduction

In oral traditions, in shrines established for her and in the *Sthalapurāṇas* (localised histories), Reṇukā as a goddess is well-established. The oral traditions are well documented by researchers on the ground, the numerous shrines also witness Reṇukā as a goddess, and localised texts such as the *Saṃhyādrīkhaṇḍa* and the *Kāñchīpuram Purāṇa* give detailed accounts of the deification of Reṇukā. Yet, there is ambiguity about Reṇukā's goddesshood. Most important among the worries is that the high literary tradition embodied in the epics and the major Purāṇas provide no instance of a human, let alone a female and a Kṣatriya, apotheosis. Further, it seems that her temples can be divided into two kinds; those of one kind house Reṇukā, her husband and her son Paraśurāma, whereas those of the other have Reṇukā alongside a companion goddess, usually of a low caste. The oral tradition can be separated from the high literary tradition.

This paper is based on the presumption that there are two sets of identifiable myths about Reṇukā, one of which explains how it is that Reṇukā came to be a goddess, while the other makes no mention of her as a goddess. To an extent the two myths share basic facts which give rise to the story as well as the characters involved. The facts are that a Brāhman *ṛṣi* decides that his wife Reṇukā has veered away from fidelity and so asks their son Paraśurāma to behead her. The son obeys the father. After this the facts diverge: oral traditions, which are sometimes picked up and recorded by anthropologists, include versions making Reṇukā a goddess, while the literary traditions portray her purely as a human being.

It seems that myths can be moulded to suit the social environments in which particular versions are told. Making suitable changes in a given myth to suit class and caste interests is nothing new. Guha shows how the myth about the eclipse, when suitably altered, enables the subaltern classes to justify their own pursuits (Guha 1985:17). In oral traditions, myths endure over long periods and are generally thought to survive as long as they are socially useful. However, in literate societies where they are written down, they become fixed and serve to provide glimpses of the society when they were relevant. The aim of this paper is to investigate the myth found in the *Mahābhārata* and to uncover its rationale in the society of the time (van Buitenen 1975:444–7). The contemporary usages and the mythic stories about Reṇukā as a goddess constitute a valid and interesting area of research. This paper, though, is concerned not with Reṇukā the goddess as such, but with her absence from the 'high' literary tradition (ie the epics and the Mahāpurāṇas). This absence is as eloquent as many a goddess narrative. Recognising it clearly, we can learn from the literary version of the Reṇukā story about such matters as the concept of matricide and class conflict in its cultural context.

The *Mahābhārata* story

Reṇukā is the wife of Jamadagni and the mother of Paraśurāma. A myth, perhaps the earliest written version of which appears in the *Mahābhārata*, tells the story of the beheading of Reṇukā by her son, Paraśurāma. JAB van Buitenen (1975:445)gives the following synopsis.[1]

> Reṇukā sees King Citraratha at play and is moist with desire. Jamadagni reviles her; he orders his first four sons to kill their mother. When they refuse, he curses them (5–10). Jamadagni then tells Rāma to kill her; he cuts off her head. Jamadagni grants him a boon; he asks for his mother's life, obliviousness and guiltlessness for himself, and normality for his brothers (10–15).

Reṇukā the goddess

This tale of matricide is unique in India and as such it has drawn the attention of Indologists, as well as scholars investigating contemporary Hinduism in south India. Thus, for example, HH Wilson (1961:321)[2] has recounted the tale in his translation of the *Viṣṇu Purāṇa*, although he was fully aware that it does not actually appear in that work. Scholars of contemporary religion working in south India have come across and documented varying versions of the myth. These accounts take Reṇukā to be the central character of the tale. They revolve around the fact of the separation of the head from the body. These versions are collected through fieldwork, so, while the accounts are given by the informants in their own language, they are documented by the researcher in the languages of scholarly discourse. Consequently, while the versions available in scholarly literature are not necessarily at variance with the truth, they are at the least mediated by issues that mould the discourse.

Characteristically, the fieldwork accounts add more facts to the *Mahābhārata* story. Thus one account adds to the basic account a low-caste woman whose body and head are separated so that she may fuse with the high-caste Reṇukā to produce two goddesses. In other accounts a simple separation of Reṇukā's head is enough to create two goddesses. In one account the very existence of headless icons is enough to identify them as Reṇukā.

Such elaborated versions are temple-related and seek to explain the existence of two goddesses, a high-caste Brahmanic goddess occupying the inner sanctum and a low-caste one represented by the body staying outside. The explanation stretches to different functions the goddesses perform for the worshippers and different modes of worship of each of the goddesses. As there are many temples of such kinds, the variations on this story and the elaborations are endless.[3]

As against this, there are other temples and religious sites that contain idols of Reṇukā, Jamadagni and Paraśurāma that commemorate the *Mahābhārata* myth by representing Reṇukā with only the head. Such temples and sites are associated with high castes and the Brahmanic *āgama* rituals. The following accounts from the documented scholarly literature illustrate the goddess myth.

Heidrun Bruckner's account (1994:437–48) is long and differs in some significant respects from the *Mahābhārata* myth. In contrast to the *Mahābhārata* version, here it is Reṇukā who insists on marrying Jamadagni. While this fact has little bearing on the issues that interest the author, Jamadagni's wooing of Reṇukā in the *Mahābhārata* has relevance in terms of an ongoing wife-taking, wife-giving relationship, as is discussed later. Bruckner also records a magical element; Reṇukā can carry a ball of water on her head with the help of a coiled snake because she is a *pativratā*. When she falls from this ideal, the snake escapes and she becomes wet. There is thus a physical cause for her wetness. The Sanskrit myth has no magic. Reṇukā's fall is caused by illicit desire.

Bruckner's account also introduces new factual evidence. While decapitating the mother, Paraśurāma also beheads a low-caste woman. The two heads get swapped in the process of revivification. Jamadagni now, even though there is no further misdemeanour on her part, refuses to take Reṇukā back and curses her with a skin disease and exiles her. There she meets Śiva, or Gorakhnath, who cures her and establishes a temple for her. She becomes Ellammā.

Wendy Doniger (1995:15–9)[4] provides two accounts of the origin of Ellammā, Allāmmā or Mariammā. In the first account the woman is already Mariammā, not Reṇukā. She is sentenced to death. At the moment of beheading she embraces a low-caste woman, Ellammā, so they both lose their heads. Later the husband grants them pardon and, in the process of revivification, the heads are transposed by mistake. Mariammā, with the Brāhman head, receives goats and cock as sacrifice, while Ellammā, with the low-caste head and Brāhman body, receives offerings of buffalo. Both forms are thus non-Brahmanic.

In her second account, Wendy Doniger reproduces an 18th-century French account by Pierre Sonnerat. The initial part of this account is substantially the same as in the *Mahābhārata*. When Jamadagni takes pity on the grieving son and asks him to bring two parts of his mother's body so that she may be brought back to life, he also teaches Paraśurāma a magical formula for the task. In haste, the son joins the head of his mother to the body of an outcaste woman who has been executed for her crimes. A monster is created with the virtues of a goddess and the vices of a wretch. She commits all kinds of cruelties. The gods appease her by giving her the power to cure smallpox. While her body is now worshipped outside the temple her head resides within it. In this account, the woman is Mariatale, but the husband and the son are Jamadagni and Paraśurāma.

Later on Mariatale gives birth to another son Kārtavīrya who is worshipped with offerings of meat, fish, tobacco and so on. In the *Mahābhārata*, Kārtavīrya is an enemy of Paraśurāma and is killed by him.

Michael Moffat (1979:248–9) gives what may be termed a subalternist account.[5] In his version, Jamadagni is identified with Śiva and Reṇukā with Pārvatī. On her trip to fetch water Reṇukā sees a reflection of a Gandharva couple in the water. After returning home, she tells her husband about this; incensed, he asks each of his four sons to cut off her head. Only Paraśurāma does so. In the moment of death Reṇukā/Pārvatī embraces a *chakkiliyan* woman and so, in the process of revival, the head of Pārvatī is joined with the body of a low-caste woman. Śiva, her husband, assigns her the task of removing pearls (pustules caused by smallpox). There are now two goddesses, one a vegetarian high-caste head, and another, a meat-accepting low-caste body. This composite goddess is known by many names, Mūlā, Mariammā, Peri, etc. In contrast to other accounts, this one makes a clear attempt to connect this goddess with Pārvatī of the classical pantheon. This goddess is now a consort goddess—a fact that is reinforced in that it is the male god who invests her with the curative powers.

When Reṇukā was not a goddess

From this point, though, we shall be concerned with the isolation of the classical version of the story which is resolutely of this world. As the deification of Reṇukā is brought about basically by the addition of 'facts' to the *Mahābhārata* story, it is not unreasonable to assume that the *Mahābhārata* account has a different meaning and purpose.[6] This chapter seeks to discover them by contextualising the myth from further material available from the *Mahābhārata* and another Sanskrit text, namely the *Brahmāṇḍa Purāṇa*, without adding 'the facts'.[7]

This exercise is based on specific characteristics of these two texts. They are in Sanskrit, written and hence largely fixed over time and carry a Brahmanic perspective. Insofar as the *Mahābhārata* has a Bhṛgu imprint, it may even have a Bhṛgu perspective. Both the texts have an all-India spread. It may be noted that these characteristics are in sharp contrast to the myths documented through fieldwork which are localised, in modern languages, diverse and of variable perspective.

To anticipate somewhat, the main contention is that, unlike the extended versions, the Sanskrit account of the myth has Paraśurāma and not Reṇukā as the central character. It follows from this that rationale for the myth is to be found in Paraśurāma's action both within the myth and in other myths that surround it in the text. It also follows that Paraśurāma's actions need to be explained in terms of some wider perspective. I argue that they can be explained by reference to two enduring aspects of social organisation in ancient India, namely, lineality and lineage solidarity on the one hand and the rivalry for primacy between the Brāhmans and the Kṣatriyas on the other.

The *Mahābhārata* account is succinct and highly structured. It is therefore instructive to look at it in a formal manner using the concepts of normative roles and their performance by the characters involved. Reṇukā is on a routine visit to fetch water but on this day she espies the Gandharva Citraratha sporting with his wives. She covets him,[8] wets herself (*klinnāmbhasi*) and returns (home) trembling (*vicetanā*, which can also mean total or momentary loss of consciousness). Jamadagni, her husband, who sees that she has 'lapsed from constancy and lost her Brahmanic beauty [*vivarjitan*, implying desertion rather than loss], reviles her'. He asks his four sons one after the other to kill her (*vyartham*, implying idle speculation). When they do not reply he curses them and so they lose their mind and become like animals, birds or inanimate things.[9] Now as Paraśurāma comes in, the father orders him to 'kill that wicked mother without compunction'.[10] He beheads her with an axe. Jamadagni now says, 'At my word you have done a difficult deed. Choose boons'. Paraśurāma asks that he forget the murder, his mother lives again and his brothers return to normalcy.

The myth as told has the following parts and characteristics. Although the story begins with Reṇukā's initial action, she remains passive and silent throughout the episode. Even her chance coming upon Citraratha and his wives is a passive and silent act. Upon being accused she does not remonstrate with her husband. Nor does she approve or disapprove of the actions of her sons. Even at death and resurrection she remains non-vocal. We may surmise that she accepts her guilt, but we have no proof of this. It is also possible that her silence indicates defiance. The issue is this—does she behave as an obedient and faithful wife?

Jamadagni, unlike Reṇukā, is both vocal and active and is present throughout the episode. He acts powerfully with all the others, but his authority has been violated. initially by his wife. and then by his four sons. Even Paraśurāma, by asking for a return to the *status quo ante*, may be taken to detract from his authority. We may then say that the role of the husband–father, while normatively fixed as superordinate to the others in the family, depends very much upon its performance.

The sons are divided into two groups for a purpose, which is to elucidate the correct father–son relationship. The bifurcation of the son's role represents two views, one of which is that matricide is unthinkable. However, this view is muted in its expression. The other view is that a lineage elder's commandments must be obeyed. This latter view can be interpreted to mean that patrilineal solidarity is stronger than the primary, but essentially emotive, relationship with the mother, which is secondary. The two views are advanced in a form not unlike that used in a debate. Thus there is a *pūrvapakṣa*, the initial view or argument, and an *uttarapakṣa* which is the correct answer or response. The story establishes a definite dominance-subordination relationship between the father and the son, which is based on the premise of lineality.

One more narrative device that is used can be seen in the telling of Reṇukā's death and resurrection as well as in the fall from and the restoration to normalcy of Paraśurāma's brother. In both cases there is a tripartite structure that is reminiscent of its employment during the rites of passage. Thus, initially, Reṇukā is pronounced guilty. She is polluted. Secondly, in that state she enters liminality through death. In the third stage she re-emerges sinless. In this drama Paraśurāma acts as the ritual specialist. First he kills and then he rejuvenates. Paraśurāma's brothers who violate father–son norms are sinful. They too enter liminality through losing their human status. They enter a new human status later through the agency of Paraśurāma.

We may now draw conclusions concerning the purpose (or rather the meaning) of the myth. It is undoubtedly didactic. Since two kinship dyads are involved, namely, the husband–wife and the father–son, one should consider both relationships for the message that the myth has for each of them. Thus we may well surmise initially that the myth, as told in the *Mahābhārata*, asserts male dominance. Reṇukā is the only female, both wife and mother to the two active males. She is passive and silent, whereas they are active and vocal. It matters little that both the men, the judge and the executioner, bring back normality, which is male dominance, once the principle is established.

However, I suggest that the myth is about much more than a slighted husband asserting and re-establishing male dominance. If one were to wonder why Jamadagni himself does not mete out justice/punishment but involves his sons, the answer would be that he interprets the slight as besmirching the family (ie Bhṛgu) honour. Therefore, the act of murder has to be carried out collectively with Jamadagni as the judge and Paraśurāma as executioner. We may wonder why it is that this is not expressed overtly. For an answer we need to recall the Sanskrit/Brahmanic predilection for brevity and for presenting didactic messages obliquely, often as puzzles that contain their own resolution. The message here is that of lineage solidarity. In other words, the betrayal affects the sons as much as it does the husband. To reinforce this interpretation we should place this myth among the other myths that surround it.

The myth among myths

In the *Mahābhārata*, the myth of matricide is the second of the five myths that constitute the hagiographic account of Paraśurāma. As we shall see, both Reṇukā and Jamadagni appear in these other myths, but they do so only in minor roles. The first myth concerns Paraśurāma's birth.[11] It explains why being born of a Brāhman father he should possess the propensity and ability to fight with weapons.

Simply told, the story is that the eponymous ancestor of the Bhṛgu clan to which Paraśurāma belongs gives two boons, upon being asked by Paraśurāma's paternal grandmother Satyavatī. She wishes that a son with Brahmanic characteristics be born to her, while another son be born to her mother with Kṣatriya virtues. The boons are granted but Satyavatī makes a mistake in carrying out the instructions and so the innate characteristics of the children to be born are switched. When she discovers her mistake she asks that her grandson and not her own son be born with warrior character. Thus it is not Jamadagni but Paraśurāma who is born a warrior. Amongst other things, this myth reduces the salience of the father.

This myth is preceded by yet another myth[12] from which Paraśurāma is absent. It is about the marriage of Ṛcīka, Paraśurāma's paternal grandfather, a *ṛṣi* and a Brāhman, to Satyavatī. Here Ṛcīka woos but also demands the Kṣatriya princess from her royal father. This myth establishes two themes, one of which is that the Bhṛgus are wife-takers to Kṣatriya kings. The second theme establishes, along with the myth of Paraśurāma's birth, that lineality is transmitted through the males. Thus Paraśurāma remains a Brāhman despite his Kṣatriya character and action. Further, this myth together with the birth myth, by focusing on the birth of Paraśurāma, accords subordinate status to the father, Jamadagni. It also explains why Jamadagni, who has Brahmanic characteristics, does not use weapons against his wife or even, later on, against his enemies. It is well known that *ṛṣis* curse rather than take up arms.

The third myth[13] concerns the slaying of the Kṣatriya king by Paraśurāma. In his absence the king Kārtavīrya visits Jamadagni's abode and is welcomed by Reṇukā. Ignoring this, the king sees and seeks to take away the celestial cow from the *ṛṣi*. When refused he inflicts physical harm on Jamadagni who simply shouts for help from Paraśurāma but does not himself fight back. Finally, Paraśurāma comes, sees the injured father and gives battle to the king and kills him. Compared to the earlier killing of the mother with a single blow from an axe, here the battle is described at great length. The description is one-sided in that it focuses on Paraśurāma's actions. Thus, Paraśurāma is established here, not only as the one with Kṣatriya characteristics, but also as a user of weapons and a great warrior. In the battle, Paraśurāma uses a bow and arrows (*astra*) rather than the emblematic axe (*śastra*) used to kill his mother. Reṇukā decides to die with her mortally wounded husband but is saved as he is magically revived by Bhṛgu, the founder of the lineage.

The fourth myth[14] is an extension of the previous battle. In it, the sons of Kārtavīrya visit Jamadagni's abode for revenge and to kill him. Paraśurāma is absent once again. When he returns however he laments copiously and performs funerary rites. He then vows to kill all the Kṣatriyas. He does so single-handedly 21 times and fills five lakes with Kṣatriya blood to offer it to his ancestors by way of propitiation. The vendetta against the king has now turned into a feud. Reṇukā dies upon the death of her husband.

In the last myth[15] Paraśurāma gives the Kṣatriya land that he had conquered to the Brāhman Kaśyapa and retires to the mountain Mahendra to pursue his Brahmanic duty of acquiring heat (*tapas*).

The myths are serially recounted and constitute a single chapter describing the actions of Paraśurāma. Despite this fact, van Buitenen titles the chapter (1975:443) after the king Kārtavīrya. The fact that it is about Paraśurāma is reinforced by the way the narrative is framed.

The myths are recounted by Akrūravraṇa, a disciple of Paraśurāma. Akrūravraṇa, as a Brāhman child, was saved by Paraśurāma from a tiger attack. The myths are narrated by him to Yudhiṣthira, the eldest of the Pāṇḍava heroes of the *Mahābhārata*, in response to his desire to know more about Paraśurāma. The locale is the forest (ie not a city). Yudhiṣthira and others await the arrival of Paraśurāma. When he arrives, they pay homage to him.

That Paraśurāma is the central character is also evident through the epithets used for him throughout the narrative. For example, in the second myth, his importance is declared: 'though born the last, he was the first of them all'.[16] In the same myth, his father granted him 'matchlessness in battle' and 'longevity'.[17] In his battle with Kārtavīrya he is described as 'slayer of enemy heroes'. In the battle with Kārtavīrya's sons he is called 'the conqueror of enemy cities', an epithet normally reserved for Indra. Finally, in several places he is referred to by his patronymic, Jāmadagneya, as well as his clan name, Bhārgava. In view of the brevity and restraint with which these myths are recounted, this is high praise. It emphasises his Kṣatriya character, especially as none of the usual descriptors of Brahmanness, such as learning, austerities, self-restraint, splendour, and brilliance, is used for him. They are used to describe only his father.

Paraśurāma in the *Brahmāṇḍa Purāṇa*

Volumes 22 and 23 of the *Brahmāṇḍa Purāṇa*[18] are a compendium of ancestral lists of Brāhman groups (among them are the Bhṛgus), rituals concerning ancestor worship and propitiation of dead ancestors. They also devote a substantial part of the text to recounting the deeds of the Bhṛgu hero Paraśurāma. In particular, it describes at great length his battles with Kārtavīrya and his sons. What is relevant to this chapter, however, is the evidence of lineality, affinal relationships with Kṣatriyas and lineage solidarity.

According to the *Brahmāṇḍa Purāṇa*, the Bhṛgu lineage is five generations deep until Paraśurāma. His ancestors are Jamadagni, Ṛcīka, Aurva, Cyavana, and the founder Bhṛgu. The lineage is one of the five derived from Brahmā's mind. All the ancestors occupy the same time period as Paraśurāma. This group's solidarity is reinforced by the fact that all of them appear on the scene to help each other at critical junctures.

All of them take Kṣatriya princesses as wives. Thus Bhṛgu is married to Khyāti, daughter of Dakṣa, the first king. Cyavana is given Sukanyā in marriage as a recompense for the offence given to him by her princely brothers. Ṛcīka demands Satyavatī in marriage from her father upon payment of bride price, which he collects from other princes and from his divine ancestor Varuṇa. Jamadagni woos Reṇukā, king Prasenajit's daughter, marries her and brings her to his forest dwelling to lead a harsh and austere life. The Bhṛgu marriage pattern is unidirectional and thus provides them with patrilineality, Brahmanic identity and a claim to superiority. Finally, there is no suggestion in the *Brahmāṇḍa Purāṇa* that Bhṛgus are priests to the kings—an omission that emphasises their independence.

Lineality and Paraśurāma

In the *Brahmāṇḍa Purāṇa* the identification and solidarity of the lineage are depicted systematically and deliberately in the identification of Paraśurāma as the young hero. In a relevant episode he embarks on a journey to visit his ancestors. At the outset he asks for permission to do this from his father and his wife. Next he visits Ṛcīka and his wife (ie Paraśurāma's paternal grandfather and his wife), by whom he is well received. He then proceeds to his great-grandfather Aurva and his wife. Having stayed for a time with them, he decides to visit Cyavana and his wife. Finally, he visits Bhṛgu and his wife. The description of each visit is elaborately marked by rituals of respect for the elders, both male and female. It is also formulaic. Paraśurāma addresses his father thus:

> For a long time I have been eager to see my grandfather. Hence with your permission I shall go to him.

Jamadagni replies:

> Dear son, go to your grandfather's house with pleasure for meeting your grandfather and grandmother.

At Ṛcīka's hermitage Paraśurāma pays homage. The description reads:

> The intelligent sage Rāma reported his name and lineage. With great joy, he touched the feet of his grandfather and grandmother with his head, as well as his hands.

The grandparents then embraced him and made him sit on their laps.

The pattern is repeated at each visit. However, at the Bhṛgu's hermitage, the description of the locale and the ritualistic meeting between Paraśurāma and his ancestor is most elaborate. It runs to 14 verses. The journey is not merely social. It leads Paraśurāma to the god Śaṅkara to obtain weapons which he will use ultimately against the Kṣatriyas.

Such elaborate rituals expressing respect and love establish levels of hierarchical relationships between the ancestors and Paraśurāma. The lineality, solidarity and hierarchy that are displayed here are not without meaning. They show that Paraśurāma's actions go well beyond family ties when he is asked to behead his mother. Later, these ties impose a duty of vendetta, when his father is killed, and of feuding, when his mother dies of distress. The *Brahmāṇḍa Purāṇa*, unlike the *Mahābhārata*, connects Paraśurāma with his mother by mentioning that he denudes the world of Kṣatriyas 21 times because his mother has beaten her breasts that many times. The point is that it is only with the mother's death that Paraśurāma sees his enemies not only as a single patriline opposed to the Bhṛgus, but also as a class. Having completed feuding successfully, he offers the land to an arch-Brāhman. What we may surmise from this is that not only Paraśurāma, the protagonist in the myth, but also the scribe of the *Mahābhārata* sees the society in terms of patrilines and group solidarities.

Reṇukā in the *Mahābhārata*

Reṇukā in the *Mahābhārata* is the daughter of an important king. She is a Kṣatriya princess brought up in the city and presumably in luxury. Although she is wooed, she is demanded by a Brāhman and a ṛṣi who, as his very name suggests, is hot-tempered and belongs to probably the most strident, anti-Kṣatriya clan. But Reṇukā in the myth is both a minor character serving the purpose of illustrating Brāhman-Kṣatriya uneasy relations and an instrument through which the relationship explodes into violence. She is neither a central character nor a *devī*.

The myth in the *Mahābhārata*

The Paraśurāma myth is not connected to the central theme of the main story of the *Mahābhārata*, which is about legitimate lines of succession to kingship. It adds little to the epic in terms of values. While the Reṇukā story is primarily about singular devotion to the husband and marital fidelity, the *Mahābhārata* abounds in tales of polyandry, rivalry between co-wives, bearing children outside marriage, fathering children to the wives of others and so on. The basic hostility between the Kṣatriyas and the Brāhmans that Paraśurāma embodies is conspicuously absent in the main story. The *Mahābhārata* is in fact, an epic strife amongst the Kṣatriyas themselves. Even the Lord Krishna who stands above all is not a Brāhman but a king, if not quite a Kṣatriya. (He is a *vṛṣṇī*.) The sole, but tenuous, connection that one can see is in the fact that the Paraśurāma myths are recounted by a Brāhman disciple of Paraśurāma to the Kṣatriya king Yudhiṣthira in the normal habitat of the Brāhmans—the forest. This is done in the presence of other Brāhman *ṛṣis*. It seems, therefore, that its inclusion is part of the 'bhṛguisation' of the epic. It is so because Paraśurāma is the greatest of the Bhṛgu heroes.

Notes

1 I have used the translation in English for convenience of referencing. The key Sanskrit words below are from Sukhthankar's edited version of the *Mahābhārata* in Sanskrit 1927–66. For a full version of this story see van Buitenen (1975:446–7).

2 In Wilson's account Paraśurāma is an *avatāra* of Viṣṇu, specifically born to kill Kārtavīrya, an oppressor of the humans and the gods.

3 It is neither possible nor necessary to list all the variations, let alone elaborate on them. Instead, I provide three examples. This is because as the title of this chapter and subsequent text affirms, my chapter is concerned with the issue of Reṇukā not being the goddess. Hence, I find it unnecessary to elaborate on the issues of Reṇukā's goddesshood. Further, none of the accounts provide details of the original narratives or the circumstances in which they are narrated. Also it is important to note that in the documentation produced by the researcher, an inevitable bias is generated by the academic interests of the reporter/ documenter.

4 In this essay, Doniger essentialises Reṇukā as the female. I prefer to see her as the mother in order to highlight the fact that matricide is unique and must therefore be explained.

5 This account is identical in part with Kāñcipurāṇam; see Shulman (1984:104–148).

6 The aim of this chapter is limited to pointing out the structural cohesion and secular purpose of the myth of matricide in the *Mahābhārata*. I am, however, aware of the existential hostility between the Brāhmans and Kṣatriya, particularly between the Bhṛgus and Kārtavīrya.

7 These two texts may have been composed at different times from each other. The contention here however, for the purposes of this chapter, is that they deal with the enduring issues of lineage, lineal solidarity and the varṇa rivalry between the Brāhmans and the Kṣatriyas.

8 Sanskrit *spṛhā* (desire) is preceded by *vyabhicāra* (adultery). This Sanskrit text is thus much more categorical in defining Reṇukā's guilt (The edition referred to in this summary of the myth is that edited by Sukhthankar (1942:888).

9 The curse is threefold and imposes muteness, chattering, and total inertness.

10 This reinforces the command.

11 Although the narrative may be read serially, there are in fact five myths, each of which can stand independently.

12 This establishes affinal relationship between the Bhṛgus and the kings.

13 This is a separate action which does not follow from Reṇukā's murder.

14 This myth arises from the killing of Kārtavīrya. However, the purpose here is to extend the interpersonal hostility into a generic feud.

15 The myth signifies the end of life purpose of Paraśurāma.

16 Through this description Paraśurāma is established as a hero.

17 This describes his capacity in the battle. Paraśurāma becomes an immortal, so longevity may indicate a portent.

18 *Brahmānda Purāṇa*, 1993:582–587. I have used the *Brahmāṇḍa Purāṇa* material to support the analysis of the *Mahābhārata* text. The latter text is the main subject of my scrutiny.

chapter five

The Lajjāgaurī: mother, wife or *yoginī*[1]

Jayant Bhalchandra Bapat

Although her true historical name remains unknown, the term Lajjāgaurī has been used to describe a nude deity with a striking image (figure 1),[2] who appears in a variety of forms in terracotta and in stone, varying in size and iconography and found in several parts of India. Available specimens range in date from approximately the 1st to the 8th century CE.

Scholars initially believed that the cult of the goddess Lajjāgaurī was confined mainly to the south of the Vindhya Mountains. Recent discoveries, however, indicate that it is far more widespread. Thus, although a large number of images are from Maharashtra, Karnataka and Andhra Pradesh,[3] images and seals have also been located in Uttar Pradesh and, recently, in Orissa to the east and in Pakistan in the northern Gandhāra[4] region (figure 2). Sisodia (as quoted by Tiwari 1985:202) has suggested that the goddess may have been known in Indian religions long before the 1st century CE and that the later Hindu and Jain iconographers may have borrowed from this source. He also thinks that such images have a tribal origin.

In this chapter I wish first to examine the iconographic elements of the image in relation to the myths that exist about Lajjāgaurī. Without entering into a debate about the precedence of iconography or mythology, I believe it is important to connect the mythologies with the Lajjāgaurī image, something that has not been attempted seriously by anyone other than the folk researcher Dr RC Dhere, who writes only in Marathi. Secondly, I also look at the ways this goddess is located in the Hindu pantheon.

Lajjāgaurī images

A very large number of the small images, which were probably mass-produced, have been found near Ter[5] and Paunar (Maharashtra), Kuduvelli (Andhra Pradesh), Naganathakolla (Karnataka) and Bhita (Uttar Pradesh).

Larger images, enshrined either inside Śiva temples or in separate temples dedicated to the goddess and sited next to the Śaivite temples, are present at Nāganathakoḷḷā and Siddhanakoḷḷā (Karnataka), and Kudavelli, Darasuram, Yellaḷḷa, Panchalingala, Bhavanasi, Belligamve, and Pratakota (Andhra Pradesh). A specific characteristic of the large images is the provision of spouts on one or the other side of the image (figure 3). This allows for the libations poured on the image to flow out during the *pūjā* to be collected as *prasāda* for the devotees.

Until now only one figure with a dedicatory inscription has been found at Nagarjunakonda (Dhere 1988:23). The one-line inscription written in Prākṛt (ca 3rd century CE) informs us that Mahādevī Khāṁaṇduvulā, the wife of Mahārājā Siri Ehavala Caṁtamūla, a king of Ikṣvāku dynasty, commissioned the image. The queen describes herself as *avidhavā* (one whose husband is living) and *jīvaputrā* (one whose sons are alive). These two adjectives hint at a connection between Lajjāgaurī and fertility. Further, it shows that, in addition to being a popular goddess, Lajjāgaurī was worshipped by royal families (Narasimhaswami 1952:137–9). Another figure of importance is from Vadagaon, near Satara in Maharashtra. It shows a naked, headless goddess with a standing bull to her right fashioned in terracotta (Radcliffe-Bolon 1997:16; Tiwari 1985:188). The presence of the bull has been interpreted by scholars (Radcliffe Bolon 1997:16; Dhere 1988:29) to mean that she is a part of Śiva's pantheon, most probably a form of Durgā or Pārvatī, the benign forms of the goddess, the mother[6].

Aesthetically, one of the most pleasing Lajjāgaurī images is in the form of a *pūrṇakumbha*, a pot brimming with life-giving water, from Karlapalem in Andhra Pradesh, currently housed at Vijayawada (Radcliffe-Bolon 1997:plate 12). This icon is yet another explicit statement of fecundity.[7]

In size, Lajjāgaurī images range from small figurines measuring just a few centimetres, to idols sculpted with great finesse, measuring over half a metre in height.[8] Because of her nudity and the prominent display of the breasts and the sexual organs, the image has been descriptively named 'the nude squatting goddess' or the 'naked torso-ed goddess' (*nagnakabandhā*).[9] As she is a woman in birthing posture, she has been interpreted as 'the mother goddess' (Kramrisch 1956:259–70).[10] The Lajjāgaurī image has also been identified with the Vedic goddess Aditi as well as the popular modern-day folk and Brahmanic goddess Reṇukā, a Paraśurāmakṣetra goddess in the regions of Konkan and Kerala (Dhere 1988:52).

Apart from an impressive art folio by Radcliffe-Bolon on the art-historical study of the Lajjāgaurī image (Radcliffe-Bolon 1997), another art-historical study by Janssen (1991:457–72) and the few articles discussed later in this chapter, not much material in the English language has appeared on this fascinating image.[11] However, an important book in the Marathi language, which incorporates a lively debate, is *Lajjāgaurī* by Dr RC Dhere (1988). Information about new finds of Lajjāgaurī images appear routinely in Indian newspapers from all over India.[12]

Etymology of Lajjāgaurī

The composite word Lajjāgaurī is made up of two separate words, *lajjā* and *gaurī*. Gaurī is identified as Śivā's consort, known also as Pārvatī (literally the daughter of the mountain) and Umā. The Sanskrit noun *lajjā* is translated as 'shame, modesty, and bashfulness or embarrassment'. It is derived from the root *lajja* carrying the same meaning (Monier-Williams 1986:895; Apte 1979:476). The compound word Lajjāgaurī would thus mean 'the bashful Gaurī' (*lajjitā gaurī iti*), or according to some researchers, 'the *shameless* Gaurī (Pārvatī)'. Philologically the latter meaning is awkward and even incorrect, because, if shamelessness were the intended meaning, we would expect the term to be Nirlajjāgaurī, or Alajjāgaurī (Gaurī without shame).

A priori, for a nude female figure that prominently displays the vagina and full breasts, bashful is not an appropriate description. Shameless Gaurī (Nirlajjāgaurī) would be the appropriate appellation for this image. Sankalia (1960:121) thought that the term Lajjāgaurī was a deliberate euphemism for a 'shameless woman'. The Marathi scholar Dhere (1988:29) suggests an alternative etymology for the word Lajjāgaurī. He argues that the word *lajjā* is a deliberate and artificial conversion (*Kṛtrīma parivartana*) of the word *lañjā*. The Sanskrit word *lañjā* is rendered 'an adulteress'. The closely related word *lañjikā* is rendered a 'harlot, a prostitute' (Monier Williams 1986:895; Apte 1979:476). Thus, according to Dhere, 'naked' would simply be an appropriate adjective for the goddess Gaurī who is without clothes.[13]

One could however argue that the prefix *lajjā* could still be valid for a goddess who, for some reason or the other, has lost her clothes and is embarrassed or bashful as a result. In my view, both the words *lajjā*[14] and *lañjā* are appropriate as they convey the intended meaning, that is, the bashful and/or the naked goddess.

Naming the image

Lajjāgaurī is an unusual name in that it is not found in the main body of literature that deals with iconography of goddesses.[15] It is also not found in tantric texts.[16] Although Lajjāgaurī images have been known since the 2nd century CE, the name Lajjāgaurī appears to have been used much later. Fleet (1881:103) was one of the first to report the name. In the environs of the well-known Śiva temple, Mahākūṭeśvara at Mahākūṭa near Badami in the state of Karnataka, Fleet came across a number of small shrines and a row of three cells on the western end. He noted,

> Scattered about the courtyard, there are a number of small linga temples, including two in the Northern style. And in one of a row of three cells towards the west end, there is a somewhat *notorious* and *very indecent* headless stone figure of the goddess *Parvati* under the name of *Lajja- Gauri*. It is probably not a very ancient figure [italics added] (Fleet 1881).

Independently of Fleet, but also in the late 19th century, the Marathi Pandit Ganeshashastri Lele-Trymbakkar (Leleshastri) accompanied Sardar Raghunathrao Vinchurkar, a chieftain of the Peshwas in Maharashtra, on a pilgrimage to Mahākūṭa. He describes this pilgrimage in his work in Marathi, *Tīrthayātrāprabandha* (An essay on pilgrimage), which includes a description of the image of Lajjāgaurī. He wrote,

> The Lajjāgaurī shrine is close to the shrine of Mahākūṭeśvara. The image of this goddess is very *peculiar and strange*. It is totally naked and is shown lying on her back in a position that a woman assumes during sexual intercourse. All her limbs are exquisitely sculpted and show meticulous detail. The image however has no head; only the torso below the head is shown. I have not heard of such an image elsewhere (Lele-Trymbakkar 1964:166).[17]

It may be noted that the learned Brāhman does not call her the mother, Pārvatī or Gaurī and explicitly emphasises the sexual aspect of the image. Being religious, unlike Fleet, he is not condemnatory.

Yet another mention of the name is by a layperson called Chapgar[18] who, in his diary, reproduced an illustration of Lajjāgaurī from a cave at Siddhankoḷḷā[19] in Northern Karnataka. In mentioning this, Sankalia comments,

> An explanation of the survival of such a goddess in India was provided by the late Shri Chapgar. He has noted that the figure is called 'Lajjāgaurī', that is, a shameless woman. Hence her head is never shown. Nowadays, women who do not get children worship 'Lajjāgaurī'. Butter and red lead are applied on the vagina and breasts and they pray for children (Sankalia 1960:111–23).

Dhere (1988:26) believes that the name Lajjāgaurī, or its alternative form Lañjāgaurī, must have been in use from the 6th century CE. He supports his conclusion by citing an inscription, once again, from Badami in Karnataka. The Cālukya king Maṅgaleśa caused a rock temple to be carved at Badami, which was dedicated to Lord Viṣṇu. The inscription of 578 CE, on one of the pillars of this temple, records the gift of the town Lañjīśvara to the Brāhmans at the temple for the dual purpose of performing the ritual of Nāgabalī and for feeding them. Dhere does not mention the language of the inscription. At this temple, another inscription in Kannada, also by Maṅgaleśa, records the donation of a part of the income from the town of Lañjigeśvara for the regular worship of the deity. Dhere explains that, 'according to the experts in the study of inscriptions in this area, both the names Lañjīśvara and Lañjigeśvara denote the present day town of Nandikeśvara'. He further notes that the *Śākambharī Māhātmya*, a Sanskrit treatise adoring the goddess Śākambharī which claims to be a part of the *Skandapurāṇa*, says that Lajjāgaurīśvara is one of the famous shrines at Mahākūṭa. Both Nandikeśvara and Mahākūṭa are part of the present-day town of Badami.

Dhere argues that Lajjāgaurīśvara, the name by which the Śiva shrine is now known locally, is a Sanskritisation of the names Lañjīśvara and Lañjigeśvara. Since the names of Śiva shrines often incorporate the name of his consort Pārvatī, Dhere believes that Pārvatī was known by the names Lajjā, Lañjā and Lañjīkā at least in the 6th century. To him, these names also suggest that Pārvatī was worshipped as the peculiar headless nude image ever since that time.

Iconography of Lajjāgaurī

As the images of Lajjāgaurī date from the second to the seventh centuries CE, a long time span, they include variations in features. Two art historians, Frans Janssen (1991) and Carol Radcliffe-Bolon (1997) have suggested a fourfold typology for Lajjāgaurī images.[20] Radcliffe-Bolon, in her extensive study of Lajjāgaurī, points out, 'The icon of goddess Lajjāgaurī, a most sophisticated symbolic image drawing on epochs of artistic and cultural layering of meaning, illustrates a process of ongoing generational, cultural, and artistic imagination' (Radcliffe-Bolon 1997).

Both Janssen and Radcliffe-Bolon have divided Lajjāgaurī images into four forms:

1. *Uttānapāda* Pot (*pūrṇakumbha* form) (figures 4 and 5).[21] The Sanskrit word *uttānapāda* literally is 'with lifted legs', and *pūrṇakumbha* is 'a completely filled pot'. This type of Lajjāgaurī image represents the personified pot full to the brim with life-giving energy signifying regenerative power. The legs render the pot partially anthropomorphic. A pot or a vase containing lotus flowers has held a special place in Indian art as signifying life, wellbeing and procreative power; the *pūrṇakumbha*

motif (figures 6 and 7) is often a part of the decoration of temple walls. The lotus flower is a well-known symbol and a metaphor for the vagina in Indian art and literature. The *pūrṇakumbha* sculptures depicting Lajjāgaurī show a vagina, but no breasts.

2. Lotus headed image without arms (figures 8 and 9).
3. Lotus headed image with arms (figures 10, 11, 12, 13, 14).
4. Fully anthropomorphic images, which have a human female head as well as all other body parts. Radcliffe-Bolon says that these fully anthropomorphic forms were popular in Gujarat and Rajasthan (figures 15 and 16).

From the rendered drawings and photographs, one notes that the most common features of these images with a headless torso are the naked female body or a part of it; and, in most cases, a lotus replacing the head. Often, the sculpture also has several lotus flowers surrounding the image. The breasts are large and prominent, not pendant, and are somewhat flattened, suggesting that the body is supine. The legs are folded sideways with feet pointing upwards so as to accentuate the vagina. On the more elaborate sculptures, found in especially dedicated shrines such as the one at Alampur, a raised fold is noticeable on the lower part of the stomach. This is gynaecologically accurate in that it is an evidence of the descended uterus of a woman who is about to deliver a child. The fold is quite different from the *trivalī* (three folds) on the lower abdomen above the navel of a woman, which, according to the treatises on Kāmaśāstra, is an attribute of the beautiful lotus woman, the Padminī.[22]

Myths of Lajjāgaurī

Like any other myths, those of gods and goddesses reflect the manner in which the populace of the time perceives real or imagined phenomena. At least five myths exist which explain the existence of this naked and headless image.

1. The ethnographer and historian, JF Fleet, visited Karnataka in the late 19th century. He recorded the following version.

> The story about it is that Parvati asked Siva what was the meaning of the term adultery. Siva replied that he would shortly shew her what it meant and then, locking Parvati, richly apparelled, in a room, went away. After a little while, Parvati found out that all her clothes had been torn by mice, and was at a loss to know what to do. Just then a tailor appeared, and offered to mend them all on the condition, to which Parvati rashly assented, that she

should grant him whatever reward he might ask for. On finishing his task, he demanded to have intercourse with her. Parvati, however, knew that the tailor was Siva himself, and though with reluctance and fear, consented to what he asked, and laid herself down in the posture for it. But Siva then assumed his original real form, and Parvati, overcome with terror and shame, and unable to hide her face, caused her head to sink down into the ground and so to disappear (Fleet 1881:102–5).

2. The writer of the Marathi *Devikoṣa* (lexicon on Devi) has recorded another myth about the image at Mahākūṭa

> Once, Śiva and Pārvatī were sporting together in a lake when a devotee happened to come there to pay homage to Śiva. Both Śiva and Pārvatī felt highly embarrassed. Śiva ran to the temple and coalesced with the *liṅga* whereas the abashed Pārvatī assumed an invisible form and disappeared into the lake itself. The highly embarrassed and naked Pārvatī, therefore, acquired the name Lajjāgaurī (Prabhudesai 1968:499).[23]

3. The Brāhman, Ganeshshastri Lele, mentioned earlier, was told the following story about the origin of Lajjāgaurī by the people at Mahākūṭa:

> Once Śiva felt like testing Pārvatī's devotion and gave her a woollen quilt to look after. He then assumed the form of a rat and made a hole in it. When Pārvatī saw the hole, she was petrified because she feared Śiva's anger. In the mean time, Śiva returned in the guise of a tailor and when Pārvatī asked him to repair the hole, he agreed to do it only if Pārvatī had intercourse with him in return. Fearing Śiva's anger, Pārvatī reluctantly agreed. While they were having intercourse, Śiva discarded the guise of the tailor and reappeared as himself. This embarrassed Pārvatī in the extreme. As a result, her head fell off and the rest of her torso remained in the position of a woman having intercourse (Dhere 1988:30).

4. The myth from the 'Sthala-Mahātmya' of Alampur in Andhra Pradesh, a town well known for several temples dedicated to Śiva. One of the temples in this complex includes a shrine, which is at present defunct but formerly housed a beautifully sculpted image of Lajjāgaurī, which is at present in the museum at Alampur. There exists a Sanskrit work called the *The Sthala-Mahātmya of Alampur* (The Greatness of Alampur as a Holy Site). It consists of five chapters and claims to be part of the *Skandapurāṇa*. The myth about the naked goddess, Lajjāgaurī, included in this work is revealing.

> Reṇukā was the devoted wife of the seer Jamadagni. Every day, she fetched water required for her husband's rituals from the Tungabhadra river, bringing it each time in a freshly made unfired clay pot. Her daily routine thus consisted of going to the river, making a fresh clay pot from mud, filling it with water and taking it back to the *āśrama*. Because of the heat of her devotion to her husband, the unfired clay pot would stay intact, not disintegrate. However,

one day, this heat proved to be inadequate. On that occasion, she saw a king dallying amorously with his young and beautiful queen in the waters of the Tungabhadra. Upon this, momentarily, Reṇukā was stirred by desire. Even this small transgression resulted in the loss of her ascetic heat so that she was unable to keep the clay pot in one piece. Despondent, she returned to the *āśrama* without water. Due to the power of his ascetic heat, her husband Jamadagni found out what had transpired. He was incensed, and being known for his short temper, ordered each one of his sons in turn to behead her instantly. The first three sons refused to perform this dreadful deed.

Paraśurāma the youngest, on the other hand, obeyed his father. Pleased with his obedience, Jamadagni asked Paraśurāma to seek a boon. Upon this, Paraśurāma asked his father to bring his mother back to life. Jamadagni however replied that it was impossible for Reṇukā to come back to life in her erstwhile form because her head had fallen into a pot of water in a shoesmith's shop and hence become impure. It was therefore improper to attach it to the torso. Hence, Jamadagni granted that Reṇukā's head would be worshipped as Ellammā and the torso would be known as the 'mother goddess earth'. Thus, the head of Reṇukā at Alampur became known as Ellammā and the torso came to be worshippd as 'Bhūdevī', the mother goddess earth. Ellammā is the *grāmadevatā* at Alampur (Dhere 1988:41).[24]

Scholars agree that the southern Indian goddess Ellammā has coalesced with Bhūdevī—Reṇukā. Along with the author of the *Sthalapurāṇa* described above, the locals at Alampur and Sañgameśvara have called the naked headless images Bhūdevī, the goddess earth. The populace also believe that the headless torso is that of Reṇukā. Dhere says of the myths,

When one sets aside the elements of mystique and wonder infused in the myth in its folk version, the real meaning of the myth becomes apparent. The goddess that was worshipped in the form of an unsculpted stone was the same one whose images were made in the form of the *yoni*, the female generative organ. Her *prākṛt* name was Ellammā whereas her Sanskrit name was Reṇukā.

However, irrespective of her name, people firmly believed that she was the 'goddess earth.' Women worshipped her in order to obtain children. Ellammā, Reṇukā and Bhūdevī were the three names for the same goddess. It is clear that the myth about Reṇukā losing her head was fashioned to explain the headlessness of the image (Dhere 1988:44).[25]

5. A playful version of the myth has appeared on the internet:[26]

Once Shiva and Parvati did not step out of their cave for a thousand years. Impatient to meet their lord, the seven cosmic sages, the *saptarishis*, walked in without announcing themselves. Parvati, who was caught unawares, was so embarrassed that she picked up a lotus and covered her face. The image of Parvati with a lotus over her face came to be known as Lajjagauri, the shy Parvati. Irritated by this intrusion, Shiva and Parvati decided to isolate themselves. They moved far into the inaccessible caves of the Himalayas.

Some say it was the cave at Amarnath, Kashmir. Here, away from all interruptions and distractions, they explored the limits of ecstasy. For the first time sensual pleasure, *bhukti*, became the tool of spiritual emancipation, *mukti*.

Lajjāgaurī myths: a comment

A detailed analysis of these myths is out of place in this chapter. Some remarks, albeit cursory, are, however, in order. To start with, the first and the fourth tales attempt to explain the headlessness of the image. The second and the third tales explain the nudity and etymology of the name Lajjāgaurī. The fifth tale tries to explain the presence of the lotus flower that replaces the face of the goddess and the etymology of her name.

Some salient elements can be identified after perusing the five myths. These are, the rat, the lotus, the sexual intercourse of Śiva and Pārvatī and the downfall of Reṇukā, also arising from thoughts about sexual intercourse. All these motifs have a common sexual element that moves the story ahead, and there is some virtue in identifying Lajjāgaurī as the wife/consort sporting with Śiva. It is noteworthy that only the term Ellammā, which is applied to Reṇukā, indicates the motherly aspect. The rest are about sexual intercourse. However, as seen earlier, from the devotee's point of view, divine sexuality is transformed into asking the image for children. Even a cursory examination of the five variations of basically the same myth shows that the main purpose of the myth is to explain and convey the nakedness and, more specifically, the headlessness of the image. While the image de-emphasises her personality and renders anonymity, the myths invariably identify her as Pārvatī. In a painting or sculpture, it is the face that completes the anthropomorphic character and enables recognition. As Howard Eilberg-Schwartz points out, 'removing the female head relieves woman of both identity and voice and reduces her to a mere sexual and reproductive body' (Eilberg-Schwartz & Doniger 1995:1).[27] In the case of Lajjāgaurī, the sculptor is trying to portray the universalisation of the female body as a mother. There is a deliberate attempt at blurring the identity of the image.

In sharp contrast to the myths, the gaze of the female devotee and even the intention of the sculptors interpret the images as those of the mother. The women in seeking a child for themselves see her as a fellow, archetypal mother, while the sculptor decidedly conveys the fact of giving birth.

We may argue that, as Lajjāgaurī's sole function is to reproduce and to sustain, she is fashioned minimally. She has, therefore, been endowed with a prominent *yoni*, the generative organ, and ample, full breasts, the means of sustenance. Hands and feet are often shown, if at all there, merely to provide human character, or maybe to hold a child later on, but the face is totally absent because it is superfluous. Face recognition is innate evidence of intelligence and, in iconography, face is an important marker. There seems to be a deliberate reluctance on the part of the iconographer to invest the image with consort-hood. The replacement of the face by the lotus flower has a twofold purpose: it signifies auspiciousness and once again the *yoni*. In the *pūrṇakumbha* depiction, which emphasises fullness and hints at perpetual pregnancy, even the feet are rendered superfluous. Apart from the organs of regeneration and sustenance, she has no need for any other limbs or characteristics. We may then speculate that, while the myths are androcentric, the images and their worshippers are gynocentric. We may also add that the sculptors and the worshippers have a better understanding.

The lotus

In studying the iconography of the Lajjāgaurī image, the presence of the lotus warrants elaboration. The question that comes to mind is—what aspect of the significance attached to this flower in Hindu mythology connects it to the peculiar iconography of Lajjāgaurī?

Hindu mythology and the Indian lore generally have associated the lotus flower with goddess Śrī, also called Lakṣmī. Śrī is the symbol of the idealised wife. The Ṛgvedic *Śrīsūkta*[28] equates her with Bhūdevī or Pṛthvī, the goddess earth, who is also described as the Mahāyoni (the great *yoni*)—the origin of the universe. The hymn describes the goddess Lakṣmī, or Śrī, as the spouse of Viṣṇu: 'the cherished one of Mādhava, and dear to Achyuta'. It also describes her as lotus-born, lotus-handed, seated on a lotus (*padmasthitā*), with a complexion like the lotus (*padmavarṇā*), wearing lotus garlands (*padmamālinī*), lotus-thighed, and looking like a lotus (*padminī*). Her other name Kamalā also means lotus-like.

The *Lakṣmīsūkta* takes the association between the lotus and Śrī even further when it says[29]

> Oh lotus-faced goddess! You, who are born out of the lotus, whose thighs are like lotus and who is lotus-eyed, grant me that which will bring me happiness. Oh lotus-faced Kamalā! Your seat is the lotus leaf, your eyes are like the petal of the lotus flower, you are dear to everyone in the universe, keep your lotus feet near me. Oh goddess who lives in the lotus, one who holds lotus in the hand, you are adorned with fine, white apparel and white garlands…

There is a close association between water, the goddess Śrī and the lotus. The *Śrīsūkta* says that water makes Śrī soft, moist and billowing (*ārdrā*), and clayey,[30] which makes her fertile[31].

In a different context, the *Matsyapurāṇa* (168:15–6; 169:1–18) describes the birth of Brahmā the creator from a golden lotus that emanated from the belly button of Lord Viṣṇu. It is this close association of the lotus in Purāṇic mythology with the generative aspect of mother earth that has led to the female vagina being termed a lotus. One should then have little difficulty in seeing the lotus replace the head of the Lajjāgaurī image. The lotus symbolism serves many a purpose: it gives the much-valued anonymity to the image; it is suggestive of procreation and recreation; and it shows the connection of Lajjāgaurī to Pṛthvī, the mother goddess who is identical with Śrī.

Epic and Purāṇic mythology also calls Pārvatī 'the mother of the world'[32] and myths about Lajjāgaurī equate her to Pārvatī. A question that naturally arises is—if the lotus is so closely associated with the consort of Viṣṇu, how is it that the lotus-headed Lajjāgaurī is recognised as Gaurī? I advance a suggestive/conjectural explanation. Firstly, Śiva as a god, let alone Mahādeva (the great god), is rarely mentioned in the *Ṛgveda*. On the other hand, Viṣṇu, by various names, and his consort are, by comparison, quite common in myths and hymns. Only later, probably from southern India, Śiva came to acquire significant prominence alongside of Viṣṇu.[33] By a further association Gaurī, as Śiva's consort, came to be seen as mother, and the symbol of the lotus, the symbol of motherhood, was transposed from one goddess to another, so that Śridevī remained essentially, or was reduced to, the consort goddess and Gaurī became the archetypal mother. One may point out that while the Pṛhivī-Bhūdevī is the wife of Viṣṇu, she is the mother to the peasant.Thus in the context of Śrī and Pārvatī, the lotus seems to have been adopted as a transformational symbol.

Which images should be termed Lajjāgaurī?

It was Janssen who initially proposed that the Lajjāgaurī image evolved in four stages. According to him, the initial Pūrṇakumbha form led to the ones with a lotus head, which in turn produced ones with limbs. The final form in this transformation was the fully anthropomorphic form. Later investigators such as Radcliffe-Bolon, Nath (1990:42–7), Sonawane (1988:27–34) and Jamkhedkar (2004:23–39) seem to agree. However, I see a fundamental problem in accepting the suggested evolution of this image. My reasons for this belief follow.

In my opinion, it is reasonable to believe that any conjecture develops only after a certain amount of verbal corpus is generated; it cannot be the other way around. It is true that verbal myths may be added or subtracted during the process of iconisation. None the less, the priority itself must be given to the verbal myth.

Given this, the fact that none of the myths quoted above mention or emphasise the Kalaśa, suggests that the Kalaśa form cannot reasonably be assumed to be the progenitor of the other forms. If the Kalaśa was indeed the very first form, then there should have been myths about the Garbha/womb in describing the Lajjāgaurī. The myths do equate Lajjāgaurī with Pārvatī, the mother of the world and hence the primordial womb in Hindu thought. However, none of the myths make a mention of this fact.

Further, all the Lajjāgaurī myths are about the loss of the head and its replacement with the lotus. The anonymity provided by the headlessness is the most important characteristic of this image. Therefore, the fully anthropomorphic images in Group 4 (referred to on page 83–84) do not fall within the scope of the myths and hence cannot be included in discussing the Lajjāgaurī.

To me, many naked female sculptures in India have been too easily and erroneously identified as Lajjāgaurī. But nude female figures are not confined to India; they are universal. Even in India, they are profuse both in time and space. Right from the Kushan times, Indian art abounds with examples of sculptures of voluptuous women with abundant breasts and prominent vaginas (Czuma 1985:plates 90, 95, 97, 102; Mehta 1976:plates 7, 9–11, 13). However, they are contextually identifiable as *yakṣīs* or other celestial damsels and none of them have been called Lajjāgaurī.

The figures from Arna and Bhinmal (figures 15 and 16) that have been labelled as Lajjāgaurī by Radcliffe-Bolon and others do not fit the requirements discussed above. They both have loin garments and could well be dancers. Similarly, the naked image in cave number 21, the Rameshwar cave at Ellora, has been included in the definition of Lajjāgaurī by Radcliffe-Bolon, Janssen and Dhere. The same can be said about the figure found in Gujarat and discussed by Sonawane in the paper quoted above. I believe this to be a mistake. It may well be that some images with heads were erroneously called Lajjāgaurī by the locals in some areas and the name then stuck. However, to me, they do not have any connection with the lotus-headed Lajjāgaurī images found in excavations or with later sculptures installed in temples dedicated to Lajjāgaurī.

Eroticism, self-display, pornography and Lajjāgaurī

From the descriptions by Fleet and Ganeshashastri Lele-Trymbakkar, quoted above, one notes that, in 1881 at least, the image was considered to be that of goddess Pārvatī. Fleet called it 'notorious and very indecent'. Similarly, Lele-Trymbakkar called it 'peculiar and strange'. The image has also been called erotic, self-displaying (Radcliffe-Bolon 1997:5) or simply pornographic. It is, of course, possible that the shrine was known as such to Fleet's informers. In all likelihood they would have been Brahmans. While the descriptions by Fleet and Lele-Trymbakkar can be attributed to Fleet's Western eye and Christian and Brahmanic prudery of the time, one cannot deny that the image is unusual and out of character with mainstream Hindu religious iconography.

Is Lajjāgaurī self-displaying? One ought not to think so. An examination of figures 17 and 18, both of which have been described in literature as 'self-displaying' (White 2003:111) shows that they are not Lajjāgaurī. To start with, both of these figures attract the viewer's attention to their vaginas by the deliberate act of opening the labia with both hands. Secondly, in both of these self-displaying figures, the vagina has been shown to be larger than life in relation to the other body parts. This is not so with the Lajjāgaurī images, where the vagina is shown as a mere line. It may be that this was a deliberate attempt to hint at the perpetual virginal character of Lajjāgaurī as mother earth, the Bhūdevī, who is perpetually pregnant, yet a virgin.

Can one class Lajjāgaurī as obscene and indecent? The definitions of these concepts vary enormously from culture to culture, from society to society, from religion to religion and over time. While Brahmanic elite Hinduism, especially in the last few centuries, may have seen her as obscene, one must not forget that the Brāhmans did accept the worship of Śiva in the form of his phallus and have venerated it for thousands of years. They sought to subsume eroticism through sublimation of symbolism, but in literature and *nātya* they embraced erotica openly.

One must also remember that women who are unable to produce offspring and are the main devotees have venerated Lajjāgaurī images for centuries[34] and that several of the images were housed in shrines in close proximity to Śiva shrines. Given such a contextual background, one could hardly call the Lajjāgaurī image obscene and indecent.

Is Lajjāgaurī erotic? She may be so. Eroticism is something that encourages and legitimises sexual activity, leading to it being viewed as an essential aspect of *prakṛti*. Pornography, on the other hand, attempts to raise raw and unadorned lust, devoid of emotion.[35] In the words of Roger Uren, a contemporary erotologist,

> The concept of the 'erotic' is quite different to things pornographic or obscene and has no negative connotations. It relates to that which is designed to encourage, to normalise and to legitimise sexual activity, both by arousing or tantalising the senses and by creating an intellectual view of the society/ the world/ the cosmos, in which sexual activity is a natural transaction. Sexual art, in addition to the above, embraces not only the encouragement of sexual activity but also art designed to highlight the importance of fertility, reproduction and the reproductive organs. This concept includes unambiguously erotic items such as couples engaged in sexual congress, but also, in Chinese art, paintings of peaches, or rocks shaped like peaches, which symbolise the vulva. The basic facts of gender and the reproductive process determine much about what is erotic and symbolic of fertility etc. These are concepts that are heavily conditioned by culture.[36]

Lajjāgaurī image in the global context

In the universal context, it is possible to speculate about the reasons for the creation of the Lajjāgaurī image. Although she did not discuss Lajjāgaurī in particular, Murray (1934:93–100) reviewed female fertility figures and other researchers have subsequently used her work in attempting to classify Lajjāgaurī type images. Murray divides fertility figures into three categories: the universal mother, or the Isis type; the divine woman, or Ishtar type; and the personified *yoni*, or Baubo type (figure 19).

She described the groups as follows: the true or universal mother is a type of figure with full breasts, which are often exaggerated in size or number. Such a figure is often shown with a child in her arms, either being suckled or held up to her face. The child is an essential part of the iconography, either actually held or implied. Many images are also shown as pregnant women. The divine woman is always shown as a young woman, hardly more than a girl. Her rounded limbs are made as beautiful as the skill of the sculptor would permit. She is portrayed sometimes nude, sometimes lightly clad and sometimes completely clothed. She has not yet borne a child. She is a woman whom a man desires: beautiful, exquisite, alluring, potential mother but still a virgin.

For the last category, the personified *yoni*, or Baubo type, Murray cites examples from Neolithic Egypt, England and Ireland. The idea here is to emphasise the genitalia, that is, the vulva and the pudenda. The figure is commonly represented with the legs spread out so as to display the pudenda. These are strongly marked and are often exaggerated in size and somewhat distorted in their position. In some cases, the figure is shown squatting with the knees raised and turned outward. Murray calls this the Baubo-Phryne or frog-like attitude. In every case, the outward spread of the thighs is essential for this posture. The pose of the arms is varied: sometimes they are raised in a prayer-like attitude; sometimes they are held forward as in invitation; sometimes they are laid on the thighs to stretch the legs apart in order to emphasise the pudenda. Murray argues that in ancient world, the most realistic of such figures was the goddess Baubo from Egypt, also common in the late Roman times.

Even a cursory look at the images of Baubo (figure 19) is enough to convince anyone that Lajjāgaurī is not Baubo. Murray herself has classified Baubo as the 'Vulva Personified'. Lajjāgaurī is much more than just the vulva. In addition to the organ of generation, all Lajjāgaurī images pay equal attention to the breasts, the organ of sustenance. Also, Baubo cannot properly be described as being in the birth-giving position.

Codrington examined a toad-like image in the Mathura museum, and identified it as Baubo type (figure 20).[37] The underside of the toad figure shows a female who appears to be squatting and has flattened breasts. It reminded Codrington of the British Sheila-na-gigs. This figure has also been incorrectly identified as Lajjāgaurī.

In an insightful article, Stella Kramrisch (1956:259–70) reported a detailed study of the Lajjāgaurī image from Alampur (figure 14) in Andhra Pradesh. This image, to which I have referred earlier, is at present in the Alampur museum. It used to be housed in a special shrine dedicated to her amongst the Śiva temples known as the Navabrahma temple complex. Kramrisch reports that the rather large (91.44 x 101.6 centimetres) image is carved in dark stone with a high degree of polish. By comparing the descriptions of the goddess Aditi in the *Ṛgveda*, the *Vājasaneyī Samhitā* of the *Śukla Yajurveda* and the *Atharvaveda*, Kramrisch hypothesises that Lajjāgaurī is the mother earth Pṛthvī, who is the same as Aditi. Kramrisch says that,

> As Aditi, she is the all-sustaining mother from whom the universe is born. The Vedas describe her as the wide one, the widely spread bounteous earth who, with her legs spread open (*uttānapāda*), gives birth to all that is (Kramrisch 1956).

Kramrisch's detailed and poetic description of the image is convincing and supports her hypothesis that the figure is about to give birth (see figures 3, 14, 21, 22 and 23).

> It lies facing upward on a nearly square plane. The rim frames the figure and allows water poured on it during worship to flow off through the spout to the left of the figure…Legs are drawn up laterally and bent at the knees.

> The soles of the feet are turned upward. Their modelling and contraction of the toes show the tension and struggle, which attend the process of giving birth…The arms are bent upwards and the hands, each holding a lotus bud, are laid on the shoulders while the forefingers, in a sensitive and relaxed movement, touch upon the petal of the large and open lotus blossom that crowns the image, as its neck and head. A small and delicate bead necklace links chest and flower by the curve of its outline. It reposes on the surging modelling of the body, which gains powerful volume in the large, flattened globes of the breasts with their lotus nipples…Thin anklets, quickened with serpentine energy, cling to the feet. But for these serpent ornaments, the figure is naked. The lower half of the body is modelled in the throes of muscular convulsion, from the palpitating flesh of hips and abdomen to their bud-like opening in the middle…
>
> Embedded and floating on the surging model mass, the lotus crowns the woman who is all body, gravid mass akin to that of the paleolithic Venus from Willendorf, who, though she has a head of hair, is without face… For the mother goddess is altogether body, incarnate purposive potentiality whose fulfilment, the womb, is between the symmetry, right and left, of the two breasts, hands and legs.
>
> Spread within, and coerced by the square limit of the base, the mass rises with curves, which are as tense as they are elastic. Their arcs hold the tidal waves of the life giving body. Its boundless abundance is stemmed by the square field of relief. The overall conception of altar and life-giving body imparts monumental calm to the modelling. It is accentuated by a greater frequency of vibration in the modelling of the upturned soles, suggestive of muscular contractions in the agony of giving birth (Kramrisch 1956:259–269).[38]

From the style of the modelling, Kramrisch believes that the Alampur image belongs to approximately the 8th century CE, about the same in space and time as another image at Mahākūṭa, which dates from about the year 600 CE. She sees a deeper message and primal vision in the image and says that this 'All-mother' is born of the waters by which she is surrounded, floating on them on her altar during worship.

> She is 'our Lady of Abundance.' And she is earth, Pṛthvī, the broad one, spread on the water, the support of all living beings…As Earth, Womb and Altar, the image of Aditi is surrounded by the waters. The lotus flowers on them. Aditi is the Air, Aditi the mother, the same also Father and son (Kramrisch 1956:268).

With so powerful and poetic a portrayal, one is tempted to agree with Kramrisch that the image is indeed that of a mother about to deliver. Yet, one can only wonder whether giving birth is really so sublime an event or whether this is the sublimation of an essentially painful experience. Further, cannot this description also be of a woman waiting in anticipation of sexual love?

In an anti-poetic mode, Sankalia (1960) disagreed with Kramrisch that Lajjāgaurī was the Vedic goddess Aditi, on the grounds that there were no images from the Vedic period. He concurred with Mr Chapgar that Lajjāgaurī was a euphemistic term for a goddess whose real name should be a 'shameless woman'. To Sankalia and Chapgar, the shamelessness was the reason for the absence of a head. Sankalia compared nude females from many parts of the world with Lajjāgaurī and similar images found all over India and came to the conclusion that the goddess was originally Baubo who was brought from Egypt to India and became Indianised in the process.

Basing his observation of the myth of goddess Śakambharī in the *Markaṇḍeya Purāṇa*, MK Dhavalikar (1987:281–93; 2002:219–35) has argued that the Lajjāgaurī is none other than Śakambharī, the headless goddess of vegetative fertility. After examining some stone plaques found in Orissa, Mishra and Mohanty (2002:311–21) arrive at the same conclusion.

In a paper discussing eroticism in the temple art of Orissa, Donaldson (1975:75–100) reviewed a large number of Indian temple sculptures.[39] Included in the discussion was the ubiquitous Lajjāgaurī from Alampur. Amongst the several universal explanations he suggested for the presence of such figures on Indian temples, the ones directly relevant to Lajjāgaurī are: their use as touchstones for testing the man on the path of renunciation; for the sexual education of the young and ignorant; their use in initiation ceremonies for young brides; their use in the representation of ritualistic orgies; and the growing influence of tantrism, as in the Kaula and Kāpālika cults during the early medieval period.

To Donaldson, the most plausible explanation for the presence of such imagery was that it was auspicious and had the power of averting evil and was, therefore, employed for prosperity and/or protection. He further argues that the nude female had been looked upon as auspicious throughout the history of mankind and that this was especially so in Indian art. The emergence of Śāktism and tantrism signified the return to the indigenous spirituality, the belief in fertility worship, the magic of formulas and initiation rites, sacrifices, and, above all, a return to the worship of the female principle. For both the *tantrikas* and the *śāktas*, woman is the *brahman*. The goddess incarnates herself in every woman and the very act of being a woman thus becomes sanctified; to worship a woman is to worship the great goddess herself.

Jagdish Narain Tiwari (Tiwari 1985) wrote on the goddess cults existing in India in the first seven centuries of the Christian era. In his work, he devoted a chapter entitled 'The Nude Squatting Goddess of India' to the Lajjāgaurī image. Like Sankalia, Tiwari disagrees with Kramrisch's identification of Lajjāgaurī as Aditi Uttānapāda. He feels that the Brahmanical texts would have mentioned this fact if she were identical with Aditi. He agrees with Sankalia who proposes that Lajjāgaurī was originally the personified *yoni*-type goddess Baubo, who was imported from abroad.

Tiwari quotes a verse from the *Matsyapurāṇa*, which describes Pārvatī as one whose husband is not born (because Śiva is beyond birth) and who is *uttānahastā* (with hands raised) and *svacchāyayā vyabhicāribhīḥ caraṇaiḥ* (literally one whose feet are in an improper posture because of her own form). He interprets the verse as referring to Lajjāgaurī with her peculiar iconography. He feels that the words *vyabhicāribhīḥ caraṇaiḥ* and *svacchāyayā* have been deliberately chosen to reflect the goddess's offensive posture.[40] Tiwari further notes that, even by the time of the *Matsyapurāṇa*, her absorption was far from complete and the nude goddess existed on the fringes of Purāṇic Śaivism. The *Matsyapurāṇa* is the only *purāṇa* that alludes to the goddess, which Tiwari takes to mean that, although she must have had a popular cult of her own through most of her popular history in India, she remained a figure alien to the Brahmanical tradition. Attempts were made, nonetheless, to absorb her into the Brahmanical Śaivite pantheon by regarding her as Pārvatī and as the consort of Śiva.

Tiwari makes an important observation that the cult of Lajjāgaurī may have a connection with *cakra-pujā*—the worship of the female sexual organ in the tantric tradition—either as a diagram or as an actual nude woman.[41]

The possibility of this last connection has also been echoed recently by White (2003:115). He notes that, according to the Indian treatises on Kāmaśāstra, while men and women can both be called lotus-faced, lotus-eyed or lotus-mouthed, only woman is 'lotus-vulva-ed'. In other words, the lotus has been used as a symbol for the vulva, especially in tantric literature. After examining the Lajjāgaurī image from Saṅgameśvara in Andhra Pradesh, White points out that the image was laid horizontally allowing a channel and a spout to carry away the libations poured over the body. He hypothesises that, in this situation, the mouth (and also the nether mouth, that is, the vagina) of the female consort becomes the transfer mechanism for the germ plasm of the divine. The fluids that flowed over her lotus face and open *yoni* were later consumed as the figure's *prasāda*—her edible grace.

White's work deals with *yoginīs*, the semi-divine females who had the ability to fly and who were able to grant special boons (*siddhis*) to their devotees. The cult of *yoginīs* was prevalent in all parts of India before Muslim invasions. White is thus suggesting that the Lajjāgaurī image was used as a vehicle in the tantric worship of the *yoginīs*. It is also worth noting that places such as Mahākūṭa, which boasted large and beautifully sculpted images of Lajjāgaurī, were known to be great centres of tantric worship.

We thus come to the main reason for this chapter—why the Lajjāgaurī image? Was she worshipped as mother earth, as Pārvatī, or as Lakṣmī or Śakambharī, the mother of the universe who also provides the entire world with food? Was she a folk goddess such as Reṇukā, or Ellammā/ Yellammā who granted children to barren women? Was she a goddess in higher Brahmanic religion, who served the same purpose? Finally, was she used as a vehicle by the left-handed tantrics to propitiate the *yoginīs* who gave *siddhis* to their tantric devotees? In view of the available evidence, I believe that the answer to all of these questions has to be in the affirmative. In other words, the Lajjāgaurī image was probably worshipped to promote all of the above ends.

I believe that the problem can be examined further on two levels—of archaeology and of interpretation. On the level of archaeology, it may be possible to study the archaeological evidence by examining the sites where the images have been found and to ascertain their period, type, etc and then postulate the functions this goddess may have performed at various times in Indian history. On the level of interpretation, one can say that the sculpture itself is but a text and, as such, the gaze of the beholder is important. Most of the work cited above has dealt with the former and as yet, owing to the lack of concrete historical evidence, no satisfactory answers have been obtained. On the level of interpretation, one can think of three possible ways of looking (gazes) at the problem:

1. Socio-ideological elaboration. The general population, and especially village folk, look at an object usually with a view to fulfilling their personal needs. In the case of Lajjāgaurī, this was, and still is, practised by village women desirous of begetting children.

2. Elaboration involving the Brāhmans and the appropriate tradition they represent. This involves recognising only the male of the family who performs elaborate ritual worship with the help of a priest, once again to obtain personal gains. This is *sakāma-bhakti*.

3. Tantric elaboration. This is the process adopted by those who are tutored to think in this fashion; that is, it is a structured gaze. It parallels physiological steps such as, in left-handed tantrism, the union of male and female, the mixing of their body fluids and their consumption, the resultant bliss etc. Such a process goes step by step.

The basic dichotomy is between folk Hinduism and the Hinduism of the learned. One is, of course, aware of many other dichotomies within Hinduism, such as Vedic Brahmanism versus Purāṇic beliefs.

Conclusions

We have cited strong evidence from several sources that, as early as the 2nd century CE, small look-alike images of Lajjāgaurī were made in large numbers, probably in a mould, indicating that they must have been part of the regular worship regime for the common folk. In addition to a number of finds from southern and northern India, we have recent evidence of the Lajjāgaurī seals found in northern Pakistan, that is, Gandhāra. This area was a stronghold of Buddhism and finding these seals indicates that, even in areas where Hinduism was at a low ebb, the folk worship of Lajjāgaurī was still popular. The finding of an image from Nagarjunakonda, where the Lajjāgaurī is shown next to a Buddhist stupa, suggests that the goddess may have been shared by Hindus and Buddhists alike. The Gandhāra seals show a trident next to the Lajjāgaurī image. Another image from Vadagaon in Maharashtra state shows a Nandi bull next to the Lajjāgaurī image. These two finds suggest that the goddess belonged to the Śaivite pantheon. Tiwari (1985:195) quotes a verse from the *Matsyapurāṇa*,[42] which tends to support the view that the Lajjāgaurī and Pārvatī are identical. It would not be unreasonable to assume that the small images of Lajjāgaurī would have been housed in shrines in people's homes, amongst other images such as the Śivaliṅgam.

The majority of the large images appear to have been made in such a way that the goddess was designed to lie on her back. The well-preserved images in this group show a ridge just below the stomach, a fact that seems to have been ignored by most researchers, apart from Kramrisch who also comments on the somewhat flattened breasts. Legs are drawn up laterally and bent at the knees. The soles of the feet are turned upward. The supine position, the ridge below the stomach, the large flattened breasts and the position of the feet strongly suggest that the sculpture is meant to portray the goddess in the process of giving birth.

On balance, I agree with Kramrisch that Lajjāgaurī is the 'life giving and life sustaining all mother'. In Hindu mythology, she has appeared under many names. In her capacity as the mother of the world, she is Pārvatī, the wife of Śiva, the father of the world. To the village folk, she is also the Kṣhetrapālikā, the guardian of the fields. She is Śakambharī, the provider of food. She is the same as Ellammā or Yellammā, the goddess whom the village folk worship. She is Joguḷāmbā, the mother who puts her children to sleep by singing lullabies to them.[43] She is the patron goddess of the village folk and tribes such as the Dombaris and the Gols. And she is none other than Reṇukā, the personal deity (*kuladevatā*) of many of the Maharashtrian Brāhmans.

In her striking iconographic form, she has been with us for almost 2000 years. Brahmanic gods and goddesses must conform to human shape and form. On the other hand, to the unschooled mind, which can think in much more abstract terms, the organs of creation and sustenance are what matter in an image of the mother. Portraying them and them alone completes the wholesome picture of the mother. I end with a quotation (my translation) from Dhere (1988):

> Lanjikā-Mahākoṭeśvarī-Lajjāgaurī is the great *yoni* that creates the whole universe. She is the beginning of it all. She begets all the living and non-living things. It is the milk from her breasts that keeps all the living things going. The sole reasoning behind her creation by the primitive man has been to portray her as the organ of generation and of sustenance. First of all, she is the goddess of creation of the world. It follows therefore that she is also the goddess of its sustenance. Her *yoni* signifies creation and her breasts sustenance. It is no wonder then that only these two organs require prominence in her iconography.

Appendix

Figure 1: Stylised line drawing of Lajjāgaurī.

Figure 2: Line drawing of Lajjāgaurī from Gandhāra, Pakistan.

Figure 3: Alampur Lajjāgaurī. The spout to take away libations can be clearly seen (photograph by the author).

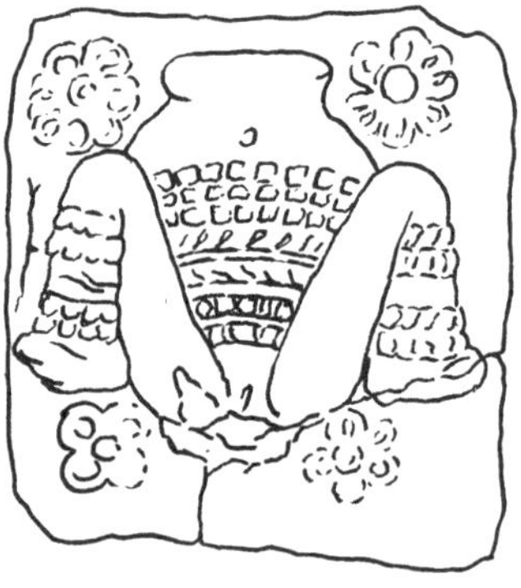

Figure 4: Line drawing of Lajjāgaurī in the *pūrṇakumbha* form from Ter, Osmanabad District, Maharashtra, 3rd–4th centuries (terracotta in Ter Museum).

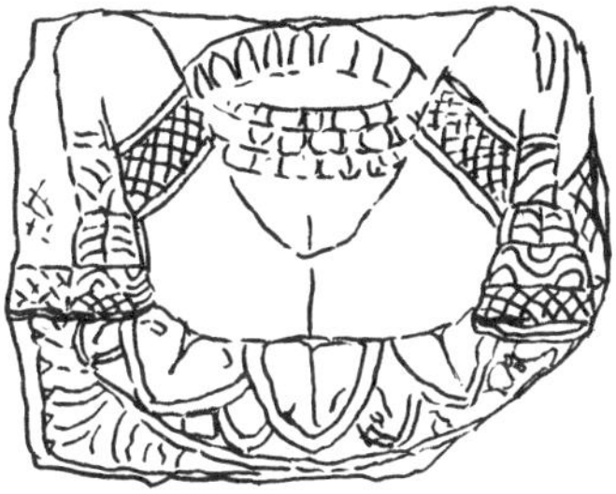

Figure 5: Line drawing of another Lajjāgaurī image in the *pūrṇakumbha* form, Ter, Maharashtra.

Figure 6: Line drawing of the *pūrṇakumbha.*

Figure 7: Line drawing of *pūrṇakumbha* and a Buddhist *stupa*, Nagarjunakonda, Guntur District, 3rd–4th centuries, terracotta (5 x 5 centimetres) in Andhra Pradesh Archeological Museum.

Figure 8: Line drawing of Lajjāgaurī without arms from Ramatola, Bhandara District, Maharashtra.

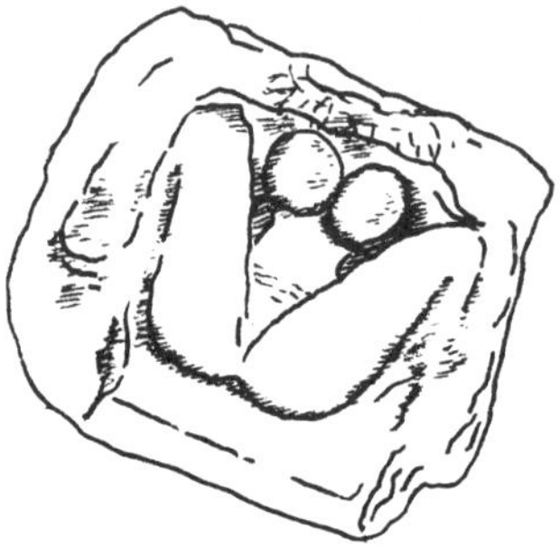

Figure 9: Line drawing of Lajjāgaurī from Vardha District, Maharashtra (11 x 7.6 centimetres).

Figure 10: Line drawing of Lajjāgaurī from Panchalingeśvara temple, Kurnool, Andhra Pradesh.

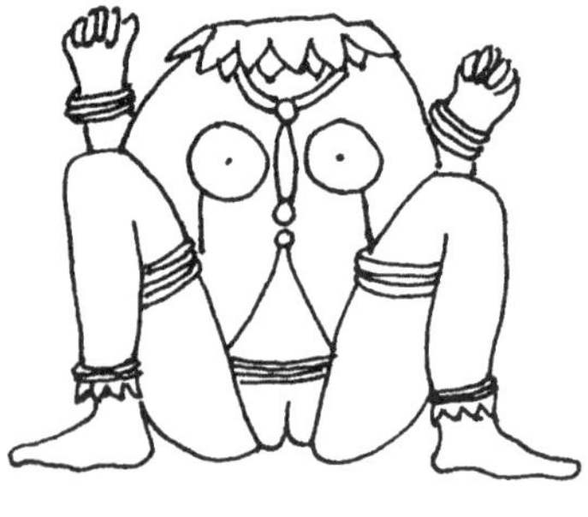

Figure 11: Line drawing of Lajjāgaurī image with arms, Siddhankoḷḷā cave.

Figure 12: Line drawing of Lajjāgaurī image with arms (6 x 5.5 centimetres), Alampur, Andhra Pradesh.

Figure 13: Line drawing of Lajjāgaurī from Paunar, Naganathkolla, Andhra Pradesh.

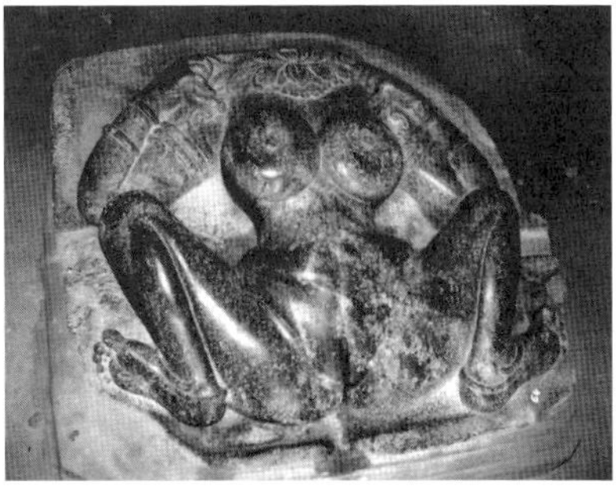

Figure 14: Lajjāgaurī from Alampur Museum (see Kramrisch 1956) (photograph by the author).

Figure 15: Line drawing of stone figure (height 41 centimetres) from Arna, Jodhpur District, Rajasthan, 7th century.

Figure 16: Line drawing of stone fiure from Bhinmal, Jalore District, Rajasthan, 7th century.

Figure 17: Line drawing of sexual display at Basantpuri temple, Kathmandu, 7th century.

Figure 18: Line drawing of exhibitionist woman, Malva Mahal, Chhapri, Madhya Pradesh.

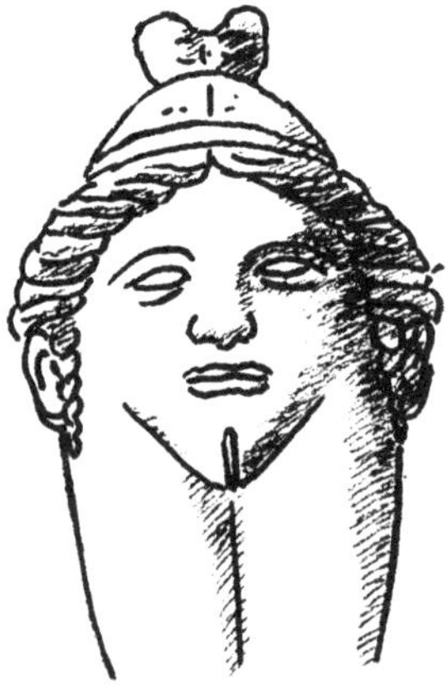

Figure 19: Line drawing of Baubo, personified vagina.

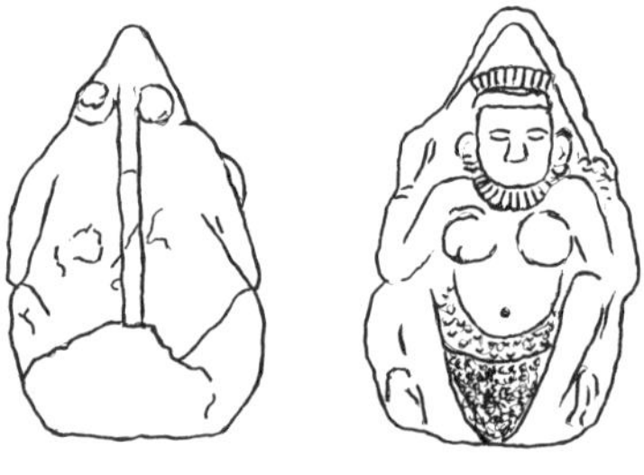

Figure 20: Line drawing of figure (height 7.62 centimetres) from Mathura, Uttar Pradesh (in Victoria and Albert Museum, London).

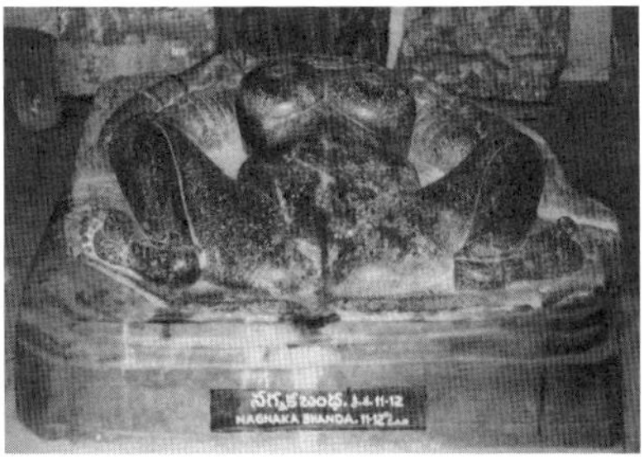

Figure 21: Alampur Lajjāgaurī. Note the flattened breasts and the ridge below the stomach; the hands hold lotus buds.

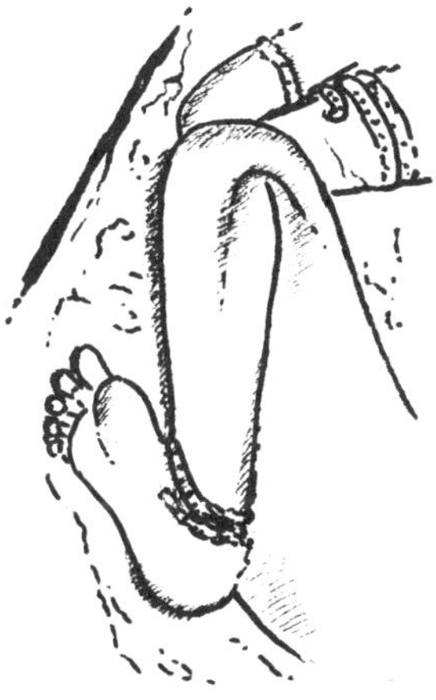

Figure 22: Line drawing of Alampur Lajjāgaurī. Note the modelling and contraction of the toes.

Figure 23: Line drawing of the other Lajjāgaurī image from Alampur. Note the evidence of the worship of the vagina of the image by application of butter and sindur (the red auspicious dye used to signify a married woman).

Figure 24: Line drawing of the Śivaliṅgam and Lajjāgaurī images from Siddhankoḷḷa.

Notes

1 I dedicate this article to Dr RC Dhere, an outstanding scholar and researcher in the folk culture of India, who put me on the trail of Lajjāgaurī.

2 I am indebted to my friend J who chooses to remain anonymous, for the superb line drawings produced in this chapter and Chapter 10.

3 The sites where Lajjāgaurī images have been found are: Maharashtra State (Ter, Mansar, Pauni, Nevase, Paunar, Mahurzari, Ellora, Vadagaon, Nanded); Andhra Pradesh (Kondapur, Kudavelli, Nagarjunakonda, Yellessvaram, Kesaragutta); Uttar Pradesh (Bhita, Zhusi, Kosambi); Karnataka (Mahakuta, Chikamahakuta, Nāganathakoḷḷā, Aihole, Siddhanakoḷḷā, Bilagi); Rajasthan (Arna); Gujrat (Bhuj, Amreli, Bhavka, Sathal, Valabhipur, Randella); Tamilnadu (Darasuram).

4 The Orissan discovery was reported by Dr Mohanty in newspapers in the 1980s. I am grateful to him for providing me with a photograph. For the discovery of the Lajjāgaurī seal in Gandhāra, see Nasim Khan (2002, 2003), also Gail and Mevissen (1993:247–52).

5 Ter, the ancient city of Tagarapura in the Osmanabad district of Maharashtra yielded a very large number of images during excavations. The original discovery was made by Mr Lamture, who has established a small museum in his house. The Government of Maharashtra has also established a museum at Ter, which houses some 30 images.

6 The term 'mother' has been used here simply to indicate that the icon is subject to worship. The wider question of whether the Lajjāgaurī is a goddess is one of the subjects of this chapter.

7 In Hindu mythology, the Kumbha, a pot brimming with water, represents the womb of the mother. In equating the womb with the Kumbha, the Vajasaneyī Samhitā of the Yajurveda says that the latter is the progenitor of the human race.

8 For instance, the Kuduvelli image measures 89 x 104 centimetres and the Darasuram image measures 114 x 84 centimetres.

9 It is not clear as to how this name came about. However, several scholars have referred to it (eg Radcliffe-Bolon 1997:1).

10 It was in fact James Campbell who, in 1884, confirmed that the Lajjāgaurī image at Mahākūṭa was lying on her back, ie in the birthing positon. See Campbell 1884:666.

11 The Lajjāgaurī image has often been mentioned in books on Indian art and sculpture, if not specifically by that name. Kelkar (2002) mentions two Lajjāgaurī images in Vidharbha. Das Gupta (1961:301) shows one such image and calls it only a nude headless figurine. Poster (1986:121) calls her a nude goddess with a flower head. The Arts Council of Great Britain, *Catalogue of an Exhibition on Tantra* (1971) shows the Alampur image and simply calls it 'the genetrix of all things'.

12 In the past 20 years, newspapers in Maharashtra have regularly reported new finds of Lajjāgaurī images. Some examples of this reporting are:,' Discovery

at Kandhar', *Kesari* 23 December 1984; 'Discovery in Goa', *Kesari* 10 March 1988; 'Discovery at Nira-Narsingpur', *Tarun Bharat*, 13 June 1990; 'Discovery near Nanded', *Maharashtra Times* 25 March 1992.

13 Dhere sees no contradiction in the descriptive terms prostitute and harlot applied to the Lajjāgaurī image. In his words,

> It is not unnatural to call a goddess responsible for procreation by the name harlot. She is ever ready for the male seed. The mother of the world is considered to be a virgin. The male has only a subordinate impregnating role in her life. In Hindu thought, a prostitute is considered to be auspicious because she is never going to be a widow. This explains the custom in many parts of India of tying the *maṅgalasūtra* (the traditional black bead necklace given to the bride at the time of the wedding as a mark of a long happy married life) around the bride's neck by a prostitute, a woman who will never be a widow (Dhere 1988).

14 Interestingly, one of the meanings of the word *lajjā* in the Kannada language is the vulva. One could, therefore, place the word Lajjāgaurī etymologically in the Kannada language. It would then mean, 'Gaurī displaying her private parts'.

15 One of the few places where this goddess has been mentioned by the name Lajjāgaurī is the comprehensive four-volume encyclopaedia of goddesses in Marathi (Prabhudesai 1968). In her study of erotic sculpture, Devangana Desai (1975) shows a photograph of the Alampur figure but calls her only 'the nude goddess'.

16 For instance, Lajjāgaurī is not listed in Bühnemann (2000–2001).

17 This is part of the present author's impending translation of Dhere's work (Dhere 1988); the translation and italics are mine.

18 Mr Chapgar seems to be an enigmatic figure. Although Sankalia, Dhere and Radcliffe-Bolon have mentioned him, there is no indication as to who he was and what made him research the Lajjāgaurī image.

19 Chapgar gives the name of the village incorrectly as Siddan-Kote. I visited this village, about 20 km from Badami, on a recent trip to India.

20 Janssen examined several Lajjāgaurī images dating from the second to the 7th century and came up with their classification in a fourfold typology (Janssen 1991:457–72). This typology has been further expanded by Radcliffe-Bolon (1997).

21 The line drawings have been made from original photographs included in the works of Dhere and Radcliffe-Bolon.

22 Kokā Pandit, the author of the Hindu treatise on love, *Ratirahasya*, divides women into four groups: Padminī, the lotus woman, Citriṇī, the whimsical woman, Śaṅkhinī, the fairy woman, and Hastinī. It is the Padminī who is described as follows:

> The Padminī has tender limbs like lotus stems, her sexual secretions smell of lotus. She has the eyes of a startled doe; the edges of her eyes are red. She hesitates, out of modesty, to expose her beautiful breasts.

> Her nose resembles a sesame flower. She is virtuous and respectful by nature. Her face is white like a jasmine flower. Her sanctuary of Eros seems like a full-blown lotus. Her body is thin and light and she walks delicately like a goose. Her words are mixed with sighs like a goose, her figure is slight, her belly divided into three parts (Daniélou 1994:92).

23 These translations from Marathi are mine.

24 The translation is mine.

25 The translation is mine.

26 At www.crystallotus.com/shiva/11.html, viewed 3 March 2005.

27 See also Wendy Doniger's chapter, 'Put a bag over her head,' in Eilberg-Schwartz & Doniger (1995).

28 Although it may have been interpolated later on, the *Śrīsūkta* appears at the end of the fifth *maṇḍala* of the Ṛgveda. It is however quite old, since it has been mentioned by Yāsk and Śaunaka. This *sūkta* contains 25 hymns addressed to goddess Śrī or Lakṣmī. The *Agnipurāṇa*, *Viṣṇupurāṇa* and *Brahmāṇḍapurāṇa* recommend that goddess Lakṣmī should be worshipped by recitation of the *Śrīsūkta*. See Hall 1859:121–135.

29 It is thought that the *Śrīsūkta* must have been placed there later in the Ṛgveda Samhitā. The *Lakṣmīsūkta* often appears at the end of the *Śrīsūkta* and is therefore a later addition. The verses I have translated here are:

padmānane padmaūrū padmākṣī padmasambhave I

tanme bhajasi padmākṣī yena saukhyam labhāmyaham II

padmānane padminī padmapatre padmapriye padmadalāyatākṣī I

viṣvapriye viṣvamanonukule tvatpādapadmam mayi sannidhatsva II

sarasijanilaye sarojahaste dhavalataranśukragandhamālyaśhobhe I

bhagavati harivallabhe manodnye tribhuvanabhūtikarī prasīda mām II

30 The words Ciklīta and Kardama have alternative meanings in that they represent two seers by the same name. The verses containing these words would then mean: 'Oh Ciklīta/Kardama, please stay in my home so that the divine mother will also stay in here'. (See Hall 1859:121–35). However, in view of the mythological equation of Lakṣmī with earth, and the association of water and mud with germination of seed and later springing up of crops, I prefer my earlier interpretation.

31 In the context of the lotus, the words Ciklīta and *ārdrā* are used to emphasise moisture. However, in the context where a woman is also indicated, they refer to the moisture in the vagina due to erotic desire.

32 The Jnānasamhitā (Adhyāya 1, Śloka 1) of the *Śivapurāṇa* starts with the following invocations to Śiva, Pārvatī and Gaṇeśa:

jagataḥ pitaraṃ śambhuṃ jagataḥ mātaraṃ śivām I

tatputraṃ ca gaṇādhīśaṃ natvaitadvarṇyāmyahaṃ II

(Having bowed to Śiva, the father of the world, Pārvatī, the mother of the world and their son Gaṇeśa, I now describe the following). Mahākavī Kālidāsa, in his epic *Raghuvaṁśa*, pays homage to Śiva and Pārvatī in a similar fashion:

> *Jagataḥ pitarau vande pāravatīparameśvarau* I (I bow to the Gods Pārvatī and Śiva, the mother and father of the world.)

33 Almost 90% of the Brāhmans from Maharashtra, for example, consider themselves as Śaivites.

34 During recent fieldwork in Maharashtra and Karnataka, I visited the village of Siddhankoḷḷā near Badami. On the banks of a small stream is a shrine dedicated to a *siddha* (*yogi*). Next to this shrine is a huge rock with a large hollow at the bottom. Chapgar, quoted above, describes this hollow as a cave. In this hollow are two large images: one of Lajjāgaurī, and the other, of Śivaliṅga (see figure 25). When I visited the shrine around 11 am, someone had just performed a *pūjā* of both the images. They were both adorned with fresh flowers and turmeric and vermillion. Oil and vermillion had also been applied to the vagina of the Lajjāgaurī image. The locals told me that women wanting children visit the shrine regularly and worship the goddess. In Melbourne, a friend from Andhra Pradesh recently told me that her sister, who lives in Kurnool, was unable to conceive for a long time. She performed a ritual worship at a local Lajjāgaurī shrine and has since been able to have two children.

35 For a discussion on pornography and eroticism, see Faust 1982.

36 From personal communication with Roger Uren (who writes under the name John Byron), an expert in erotica, particularly Chinese erotica. I am indebted to him for his insight and help. He gives some fascinating examples of the culturally bound nature of eroticism. As he points out, no one outside the Chinese world would associate a peach with the sexual organs of a woman. Another example is the role of bound feet in traditional China where they were regarded as extremely arousing. There are well documented accounts from pre-modern China of men going to a brothel and paying to view a pair of bound feet, dressed in delicate shoes, displayed beneath the fringe of a curtain. At the sight of the bound feet and bound feet alone, the men would masturbate—a practice that was entirely a consequence of cultural conditioning (Byron 1987). I am well aware that Uren's distinction between pornography and eroticism may be too categorical in the general evaluation of Indian religious art. However, in the case of Lajjāgaurī, I think it is sound.

37 Codrington (1935:70–87) argued that, although naked goddesses displaying their charms with hands touching the pudenda were known in India, they needed to be differentiated from the highly specialised, highly worked figurines such as the Mathura figurine. To him, this figurine must have been cast from a mould and, therefore, in demand in quantity. He thought that the figurine was of the Baubo descent, rather than of indigenous description.

38 In order to ascertain whether the position of the Lajjāgaurī image was one of self-display or that of a woman during childbirth, I consulted a gynaecologist and obtained from him the exact description of a woman during childbirth:

> At the time of delivery, a woman is always made to lie on her back. The legs are spread apart and kept in that position with the help of stirrups. The hands are usually folded and made to lie sideways. As a result of the release of the lactating hormones, breasts are considerably enlarged and because she is made to lie on her back, they appear flattened in the centre. The vagina is larger but not necessarily dilated, except of course during delivery. The uterus, at the onset of the pregnancy, almost touches the bottom of the rib cage. However, as the pregnancy progresses, it moves downwards towards the vagina, causing a ridge to appear across the stomach.

Even a cursory examination of the larger sculpted Lajjāgaurī images would show that they depict the position of the goddess at the time of delivery and that she is shown lying on her back. One can clearly see the ridge that Kramrisch mentions. It would be wrong to describe such a position as 'squatting'. A squatting position would not normally be one assumed by a pregnant woman at the time of childbirth. Also, since the hands are not touching the vagina and since the vagina appears only as a vertical line or slit, this position of the image cannot be described as 'exhibitionist' either.

39 Donaldson listed several universal explanations for the presence of such figures on Indian temples. As well as the ones discussed above, these include enticing people in the war-torn countries to indulge in free sexual activity so that soldiers could be available for the king, representing the symbolic union of the individual and the world soul, representation of the of the sacred syllable Aum, representation of heavenly rapture and bliss, use in the initiation ceremonies for the young bride, and attracting gross-minded people to the temple. He also suggested that they were the representation of the erotic activities of the Devadasis, the temple courtesans, or the result of the growing influence of tantrism during the early medieval period.

40 It is not certain why Tiwari used the word 'offensive' to describe the Lajjāgaurī image. Perhaps he meant, 'aggressively erotic' and hence offensive to him.

41 Tantric sex is discussed in more detail by John Dupuche in the chapter that follows this.

42 The exact text of the verse that Tiwari quotes is:

> *uttānahastā satataṁ caraṇair vyābhicāribhiḥ* I
>
> *svacchāyayā bhavīṣyeyam kimanyad bahu bhāṣyate* II (*Matsyapurāṇa,* 154, 156)

43 According to Dhere, the word *joguḷa* in south Indian languages means a lullaby; since *ambā* is the mother, Joguḷāmbā is the lullaby-singing mother. At Alampur, there is a small but well-known shrine of goddess Joguḷāmbā, which is part of the Bālabrahmeśvara temple. However, the image there at present is clearly not of Lajjāgaurī. It has a prominent head with a crab and a lizard on a very large forehead and has protruding fangs like those of a boar. In two of her four hands, she holds a human skull and a sword. I was unable to find out when this image was installed at Alampur. It must, however, have been later than 1830, because

King Sarfroji II of Tanjavur (1798–1832) visited Alampur and the shrine of Jogulāmbā. Sarfroji composed poetry on his pilgrimages and, in describing the greatness of Alampur, he mentions that 'the Jogulāmbā shrine is known for the headless image of the mother earth'. He then goes on to describe the Reṇukā myth to explain the headlessness of the image, saying that if barren women place butter on the vagina of this goddess and consume it as *prasāda*, they are guaranteed pregnancy (Mahadik 1952:53).

chapter six

Devī and tantric practice

John R Dupuche

Any consideration of the Devī must face the scandalous and repulsive aspects of extreme tantric practice. Can these be explained away as the fancy of an overheated imagination? Is the goddess to be interpreted into irrelevance? This question is all the more penetrating when we consider that Abhinavagupta, one of the major figures in Indian thought, gives full weight to an extreme tantric practice, the Kula ritual.

Abhinavagupta, the major author of the tradition we are considering and the leading figure in Kashmir Śaivism, proposes an interpretation of the goddess which aims at both preserving the horror of the practice and allowing it authentically to be accepted. He wishes to enable the practitioner to take up intelligently and wholeheartedly the ritual which the right-minded people of his day dismissed as an aberration and to arrive at supreme consciousness—union with the goddess.

This study acts as a counterweight to the many corruptions of tantra so well surveyed by Hugh Urban (2003). It also avoids the other extreme—the mitigation of the Kula ritual proposed by Lilian Silburn (1983). This chapter neither defends the indefensible nor condemns or justifies. It only attempts to clarify practices which must be considered in any full presentation of Devī.[1]

Sanderson, in his study of the history of the tantric traditions (Sanderson 1988), notes a progressive shift away from the worship of the god to the worship of the goddess and away from reputable Vedic practices to extreme 'unlawful' rituals. The Kula and the Kaula traditions are to be listed among these extreme rituals (Sanderson 1995:23, 79). According to White, they constitute the 'sole truly distinctive feature of South Asian Tantric traditions' (White 2003:13).

Sanderson holds that the Kula tradition belongs to ascetics who are linked to the Kāpālika (skull-bearers) and *yoginī* cults and to the cults of the cremation ground, whereas the Kaula tradition is an adaptation that allows for the householder (Sanderson 1985:214 n.110). If the ordinary person undergoes the same experience as the Kāpālika, but more simply and indeed more powerfully, his domestic ritual is to be deemed at least equivalent. The terminology of the Kāpālika or *yoginī* cult could then be transferred to the domestic context and the externals of those cults could be justifiably abandoned as superfluous.

The actual word *kula* has a plethora of meanings, which cross-refer. It first relates to the family or grouping of the *yoginī*s and of the 'Mothers'. It also refers to the human body, to the body of power, to the cosmic body, and even to the totality of things. The practitioner is already, in his own body, the embodiment of the 'Mothers' and of the cosmos, but, by being initiated into a particular 'Mother' and by entering into a 'family', he also enters into one or other level of his own body and becomes master of the powers identified with it. By piercing all the circles of his body he is master of all and attains the central deity that is the true self of the worshipper of whom the eight 'Mothers' are the projections.

Abhinava, in his presentation of the Kula ritual in Chapter 29 of his encyclopaedic *Tantrāloka* (Light on the tantras) in which he surveys all the tantras of his day and reinterprets them in the light of the Trika school to which he belongs, presents the goddess first of all at the supreme level of consciousness and then in the more limited form of lesser goddesses and female figures, at the subtle level of speech in its various forms, and at the gross level of the sexual fluids. He then outlines rituals that allow the practitioner to move up and down these various levels, which imply and flow from each other. Each aspect is to be seen in the context of every other aspect.[2]

Theoria and praxis involve each other. An adequate understanding of an extreme tantric practice, which is the purpose of the following pages, requires both a presentation of the basic concepts and a description of the ritual. Indeed, it is only in the practice of the ritual that the tantric attitude is actually experienced.

The following pages, therefore, cover several major aspects of the Kula tantric ritual:

1. What is the nature of the goddess (Devī) and her more frequent emanations according to the Kula tradition? After all, the goddess is the ultimate object of worship. Who is she? How is she manifested?

2. The goddess is supremely embodied in her mantra (*vidyā*). Which are the principal mantras of the Kula tradition and what do they mean? It is by reciting them, even more than by performing the ritual activities, that the goddess is enjoyed and her powers secured.
3. Particular emphasis is given to the substances, the three Ms, of the Kula tradition, in which the goddess is embodied.
4. A further section sets out the basic, daily (*nitya*) ritual and the central ritual with an external *śakti* (female sexual partner) as described in Chapter 29 of the *Tantrāloka*. These rituals show how, in fact, the Kula tradition was lived and how it achieved its purpose.

SECTION A: THEORIA

Part 1—Devī

Devī as consciousness

Abhinavagupta teaches that consciousness, 'I am', is the highest reality and since it cannot be ignorant of itself, consciousness is self-illuminating. If Śiva is considered to be consciousness, the goddess inseparably joined to Śiva is the 'consciousness of consciousness'. Indeed, it is this 'consciousness of consciousness' that is the particular focus of the rituals described in this chapter. In other words, it is the goddess who is above all worshipped and whose powers are sought.[3]

The union of Śiva and the goddess is not a monism since there is a distinction between consciousness and its self-knowledge. This distinction is not, however, a dualism, for they are not separate. The usual comparison is that of the fire and its capacity to burn. The philosophy is neither monistic nor dualist but non-dual (*advaita*)

The idea of Devī as consciousness takes the reader out of the usual presentations to be found in myth and imagery. She cannot ultimately be described or imagined; she is not to be associated with any particular place or associated with any ritual to the exclusion of others; she is all and contains all and is in all. She is not the subject of discourse so much as an experience that cannot be named.[4]

This self-revelation is the supreme word (*paravāc*)—which is the supreme goddess, the supreme mantra—of which all other words and revelations, powers and substances, realities and persons, are the lesser manifestations so that the goddess is surrounded (*āvaraṇa*) by lesser manifestations or lesser goddesses, which eddy in ever broadening circles to the point of inertia (*jaḍatā*). But since the goddess, even in her lesser manifestations, is never without her 'male' counterpart, there are circles upon circles of gods and goddesses paired in sexual union.

Many goddesses are named in Chapter 29 and its *viveka* (Dupuche 2003:Appendix 5) and can be understood as persons or personifications. They variously refer to the supreme goddess or to her attendants, but it is the following women who chiefly claim our attention.

Devī as a woman

1. patnī

The Kula tradition has been handed down from the divine realm to the perfected beings (*siddhas*) and from them to humans such as the guru who transmits it in turn to his disciple. The Kula ritual itself is defined (*Tantrāloka* 29.2) essentially as the worship of lineage of the *siddha*s and their wives (*patnī*). Thus the listing (*Tantrāloka* 29.29ff) of the perfected beings also names their wives. These are arranged in a *maṇḍala* which need not delay us here (cf Dupuche 2003:203ff).There is a certain ambiguity in the Kula tradition, which is handed down both by the guru and by the *śakti*.

2. dūtī

The term *dūtī*, referring to the female sexual partner in the Kula ritual, does occur in *Tantrāloka* Chapter 29, but Abhinava prefers the term *śakti*, for which reason the major emphasis in this section will be given to the description of the *śakti*.

3. yoginī[5]

De Mallmann (1963:169–82) has given a full description of the characteristics of the *yoginī*s. However, even though these fantastic creatures provide a basis for the role of the *yoginī* in *Tantrāloka* Chapter 29 and its investigation, the *yoginī*s of Chapter 29 and Jayaratha's commentary are vastly different. Although he uses the terminology of the Kāpālika and *yoginī* cults, Abhinava demythologises the *yoginīs* who cease to be the wild hordes of terrifying females needing to be placated with what is most precious—blood and semen. Instead, they become the sexual partner who, nevertheless, destroys the sense of the ego (*ahaṃkāra*), which constitutes the essential stain (*mala*). This is disconcerting, for the limited individual clings to division and its cravings. The loss of egoity is profoundly feared and resisted. The domestication of the Kula ritual by Abhinava means that the female sexual partner is invested with all the imagery of another era. She has the essential role of the mythical *yoginī* but not her outward appearance. To be associated in sexual rites with the female partner is effectively to enter the cremation ground and to join the company of the perfected beings (*siddhas*) and the *yoginīs*. Instead of acquiring the *yoginīs*' magical powers, the Kula practitioner attains the transcendent powers of consciousness and bliss from which the cosmos derives. To become Śiva is to possess *śakti* (*śaktimān*).

While Abhinava prefers the term *śakti* to describe the female sexual partner in the more private and domestic context, he also mentions the *yoginī* whom the Adept will visit on his tour of the sacred sites. She will recognise him as belonging to her own section within the broader range of Kula practitioners and will perform the ritual with him, granting all that can be obtained from her 'mouth'.

4. śakti

The Kula ritual focuses above all on the *śakti* who must therefore be described more fully. From the goddess who is the self-revelation of consciousness, all other revelations derive; and from the goddess who is *śakti* and the primordial manifestation of Śiva, the universe in all its aspects is emitted. Thus the cosmos is an array of innumerable *śaktis* streaming out from the one *śakti*, the one consciousness.

Abhinava gives long descriptions of the internal or imaginary *śaktis*, where they live, their names, how they are arranged around the central and presiding *śakti*, the goddess from whom they emanate. In this way the goddess has 'personality' but this description is not at the heart of the Kula ritual which concerns the 'external *śakti*', that is a real woman. *Śakti* can be internal, consisting of the whole range of emotions and interior experiences. Indeed, the practitioner is to consider his own self as nothing; he is only an expression and a conglomerate of *śaktis* (*Tantrāloka* 29.64).

Because a woman is able to give birth, she is the particular manifestation of the unlimited power that gives rise to the universe. She also provides the sexual fluid. Because the male (*śaktimān*) does not have this capacity, he is the particular manifestation of Śiva, who is inactive and by himself ineffective.

The female sexual partner in the Kula ritual, the 'external *śakti*', is not the practitioner's mother, sister, daughter, or wife etc (Dupuche 2003:129–34). She is a woman who takes on the position of a consecrated female in relationship to the practitioner and grants him every boon and gift, 'bestowing both enjoyment and liberation' (*Tantrāloka* 29.103b).

She is brought to the ritual and consecrated to that purpose. Abhinava quotes Kallaṭa: The guru 'should ritually prepare [the *śakti*] because by her very being she is superior to his own body' (*Tantrāloka* 29.123b). The *śakti* is female by her very nature (*sva-bhāva*) and is the source of the sexual fluid (*kuḍagolaka*). Her body is superior to that of the guru because she is female and is the means of *maithuna*. But she must also be ritually prepared (*bhāvitām*) by him.

She is chosen for the ritual without regard to caste or age. What is required is not that she possess every feminine quality, but that she identify completely with her male partner. This point is made at length by Jayaratha in his commentary. He first quotes a text describing a woman with every sexual quality and every aspect of beauty, the seductress *par excellence*. He quotes the description of another type of woman who is demure, dutiful, observant and attractive in another way. He notes that these contradictory qualities make it impossible to find a woman who has every quality. How then can any single woman portray the feminine in all its aspects? To this question Abhinava provides the answer—the sexual partner must have the essential quality of identity with her partner; she is to be *śakti* to his Śiva. 'The characteristic quality of a *śakti* is that she is in no way separated from him who possesses her. Let him, therefore, bring [a *śakti*] of this sort, but without regard to castes etc' (*Tantrāloka* 29.100b).

And since the primordial *śakti* is the source of every other *śakti* and every aspect of femininity, the female partner with the characteristic quality, whether she be old or young, beautiful or ugly, is 'everywoman'. 'The Kula ritual can also involve an adulterous union with the wives of an outcaste, a *kṛṣṇa*, a bowman, a butcher, a tanner, a eunuch, a bone-splitter, a fisherman, a potter' (*Tantrāloka* 29.66), who are ritually impure since they are involved in dealing with impure substances. Union with such women, which can in part be explained as a reaction to the respectability of Brahmanism, allows the practitioner to transcend the divisive concepts of pure and impure and to reach supreme consciousness.

Abhinava does not go into further detail on the attitude involved. It is Jayaratha, his faithful commentator, who explains that the focus of the practitioner is not to be on a passing orgasm but on eternal bliss. He quotes:

> He should enjoy a beautiful woman for the sake of achieving steadiness, never because of lust (*Tantrāloka* vol 7:3363 line 5).
>
> The aforementioned perfect expression of sexual desire, as it is called, is not to be performed for the sake of enjoyment. [It is to be performed] for the sake of considering one's own consciousness: is the mind steady or fluctuating? (*Tantrāloka* vol 7:3363 lines 4–5).

In this way the practitioner transcends the divisive concepts of aversion and desire, beauty and ugliness. He goes beyond orgasm and time to the abiding transcendent state of Śiva and *śakti* joined in eternal *maithuna*.

In the face of this most scandalous aspect of this extreme tantric practice, questions naturally arise. How can such abuse of women be a means to the highest spiritual state? What sort of goddess is she, if she allows her representative to be used in this way? That, of course, is precisely the point. The extreme tantric ritual intentionally contravenes all the Vedic views of *dharma*. The practitioner rejects the *dharma*. Indeed, the true *dharma* consists in not being troubled by *dharma*. The practitioner is completely free. He will drink of the forbidden alcohol and mate with women of forbidden castes and eat proscribed meat and fish. To him nothing is fundamentally repulsive or attractive. Being permeated by consciousness; indeed, being consciousness itself, he is at the source of everything and, therefore, does not distinguish between pure and impure, good and evil, righteous and unrighteous. These mental constructs have no meaning for him. Or again, he wishes to enter into the paradox of clean and unclean and arrive at its source. He does not depend on anything yet is involved in everything.

The supreme goddess, consciousness, is attained precisely by union with a woman of the lowest caste whose husband is involved with the slaughter of living beings and the production of alcohol—an adulterous woman. The goddess is not apart from such a woman but is expressed in her and is attained by means of her. Thus, the lowest of the low is in fact divine. This teaching is intended to be liberating, for it means that what others despise is, in fact, to be infinitely esteemed, for she is the expression of the goddess and grants every good. The goddess is to be found everywhere. Far from being repelled by such a woman, the goddess identifies with her. She is the *mūrtī* of the goddess. Far from being angry with the practitioner for 'abusing' the woman, the goddess draws close to him and grants him all her powers, the greatest of which is her bliss.

Such a woman is, in fact, the 'personality' of the goddess. Consciousness does not have any aspect since it is the source of every aspect. The goddess, therefore, is not to be imagined in the usual forms of iconography, beautiful, crowned, smiling, seated on the lotus, holding various instruments. There is no appeal to iconography in the Kula ritual for the simple reason that the *śakti*, even in her repulsiveness, is the image of the goddess.

The reconciliation of these contradictions—the use of the low-caste woman and the worship of the supreme goddess—means that all mental constructs must be abandoned in favour of what surpasses them all—consciousness itself.

How can one accept the demeaning of such a woman and, therefore, of all women? Is this ritual not an unendurable offence against the rights of women? Is not the practitioner profoundly abusive of such a creature, poor, despised, unprotected by a husband who has no rights just as she has no rights? Is the practitioner not using her as a vehicle for his own purposes, without regard for her own needs? How can such a practice be termed in any sense 'spiritual'? Does it not open the door to every abuse? Is not such teaching a distant echo of the sadism of *Justine* (de Sade 1969)? To which the answer must surely be 'yes'.

While ritual and morality are distinct, they do relate. Indeed, ritual is performed as the expression of insight; and, conversely, ritual introduces the practitioner into the essential revelation. One leads to the other. If morality and ritual do not imply each other, the ritual is emptied of meaning, while morality is relegated to the internal forum. Ritual, insight, the internal and the external forum all constitute a whole. The philosophical underpinning of the Kula and its practice cannot be divorced from each other. That is precisely the reason why the Kula is problematic.

At the same time also a note of caution must be added. The moral value of an act cannot fully be assessed if it is perceived simply and only in another moral context. Anachronism is an uncertain guide. For example, the tradition of slavery, which is now acknowledged to be intolerable, was accepted as normal right into the 19th century. Democracy and universal suffrage were unimaginable only a few generations ago. From another angle, Jayaratha, the faithful commentator, takes greater pains to justify the use of wine than to explain the use of women; he provides 25 quotations to explain it (*Tantrāloka* vol 7:3299–3304). He does not even attempt to justify the use of women. Nor was there any problem with the existence of the *devadasīs* of Puri, for example, who were disbanded only last century (Marglin 1985). It is more than likely that future generations will look back on our times and stand aghast at our lack of moral perception on some issues.

Part 2—Devī as mantra (*vidyā*)[6]

Since the highest goddess is the supreme word, she is also, non-dualistically, her phonic manifestation. She is her word and is found in her word. The *vidyā*, which expresses her, is also the means to invoke and claim her. For this reason, the *vidyā* is an all-powerful tool and its divulgation is surrounded by secrecy, indeed obfuscation, in order to ward off the unauthorised.

The worshipper receives his particular *vidyā* from the initiating guru who himself belongs to a tradition stretching back to the supreme goddess who is the supreme word from which all traditions and scriptures and mantras descend. The *vidyā* received in initiation introduces the disciple into his particular *kula* and, by worshipping the *vidyā*, he arrives at ultimate reality.[7]

While there are hierarchies of *vidyā*, just as there are hierarchies of goddesses, the Kula ritual emphasises the following:

1. Mālinī is an arrangement of the 50 Sanskrit phonemes where vowels and consonants are mixed as a garland (*mālā*) and, since the vowels are understood as seed and the consonants as womb, their mingling produces the emission (*visarga*) of the universe so that Mālinī is primarily emanating and is focused on the world of objectivity.
2. Parā, whose phonic form is SAUḤ, is called 'the seed of the heart' (*hṛdaya-bīja*) and 'the seed of the nectar' (*amṛta-bīja*). It is also called '*trika*' because it consists of three phonemes and because it encapsulates the system called Trika that dominates the outlook of Kashmir Śaivism. When Parā is recited in the direction of reabsorption, 'S' represents the objective world, 'AU' the three energies of will, knowledge and action, and 'Ḥ' the supreme *brahman* which emits the universe. When Parā is recited in the direction of emission, 'S' symbolises Śiva as the highest *brahman*, 'AU' retains its meaning as the three energies of will, knowledge and action, while 'Ḥ' represents the emission. Abhinava also interprets SAUḤ as referring to the liquids of the Kula ritual. In his commentary on verse 18 of *Parātrīṃśikā* he points out that, just as the knowledge of SAUḤ alone is sufficient to secure every supernatural power (*siddhi*), so too the mere consumption of the liquids is to attain the fullness of power (*Parātriṃśikāvivaraṇa* 1985:266 lines 4–9).

3. Mātṛsadbhāva is also called Saṇkarṣiṇī and Kālāntakī and Kālasañkarṣiṇī. 'Mātṛsadbhāva' originally meant 'The Essence of the Mother Goddesses' but Abhinava interprets it to mean 'The Essence of (All) Agents of Cognition'. Her phonic form is the one syllable KHPHREṂ. Thus the supreme deity, consciousness itself, is feminine. In Mātṛsadbhāva the reabsorptive aspect is more prominent, so that by reciting this *vidyā* the practitioner achieves the ultimate state of total absorption.

4. Mātṛkā. The term *mātṛkā* originally designated the mythological figures called the 'Seven (or Eight) Mothers'. However, in the phonematic speculation of Kashmir Śaivism it refers to the set of 50 phonemes in their normal order, from A to KṢA. Mātṛkā and Mālinī are associated. In Mātṛkā the subject predominates and therefore Mātṛkā is absorptive and 'fiery', whereas in Mālinī objectivity predominates so that Mālinī is emitting and 'cooling'.

5. Rudra-śakti, which consists of Mālinī enclosed (*saṃpuṭa*) by either Parā or Mātṛsadbhāva. It is a means of acquiring both liberation and enjoyment, since Mālinī is principally concerned with objectivity and enjoyment, while Parā and Mātṛsadbhāva are primarily concerned with subjectivity and liberation.

6. Śakti-bīja—ĪṂ or HRĪṂ—contains all the power of *śakti*. To know the *vidyā* is to have its power. Its communication confers juridisdiction. According to whether the practitioner wishes to achieve one or other effect, he will use one or other phonic form of the goddess. Śiva is powerless without *śakti*; the practitioner is all powerful if he has received the *vidyā* of her who is the supreme revelation.

Part 3—Devī as bodily substances

Preliminary considerations

While all objects are manifestations of the supreme goddess, women are the more perfect symbol since they give birth and thus symbolise in their very being the emanation of the universe, as we have seen. The sexual fluids, which are considered in this part, not only issue from the *yoni* as the symbol of emanating power, but also arise from the experience of sexual pleasure (*bhoga*) and so manifest the bliss of Śiva and *śakti*.

The following comparison is instructive since it provides the link between mantra and substance. Jayaratha quotes, 'As a result of savouring everlasting bliss, the [sound] '*HĀ-HĀ*' occurs in the throat [of the sexual partner]'

(*Tantrāloka* vol 7:3400 line 8). The cry of pleasure (*sīt*) and the fluids that arise from pleasure serve the same purpose. Just as the *yogī*, by attending to the sound that results from the experience of bliss, is himself drawn into that bliss, so too, by coming into contact with the sexual fluids, the *yogī* is taken into the pure consciousness that produced them.

One may ask, given that as the phonic expression of the goddess the *vidyā* contains all the powers of that deity, what need is there to consume the substances? Is this not especially the case if the Trika, the single *vidyā* SAUḤ, which is more exalted than the Kula ritual, makes ritual unnecessary? True, but some find the Trika too exalted and must use methods more suited to the level of grace (*anugraha*) given to them.

The three Ms

The Kula ritual uses not the five Ms (*pañca-makāra*) of other tantric rituals—*mudrā* (parched grain); *matsya* (fish); *māṃsa* (meat); *madya* (wine); *maithuna* (intercourse)—but the three Ms (*tri-ma*) of meat, wine and intercourse.

Abhinavagupta makes the point that the three Ms are for ritual use only; one must not fail to use them during the ritual nor abuse them outside the ritual, for to do so is to be a 'bonded animal' (*paśu*). Jayaratha gives a telling quotation:

> Without a guru, without a deity, like dullards, O Parameśvarī, forever consuming wine and meat, they are 'bonded animals'. There is no doubt about it (*Tantrāloka* vol 7:3357 lines 3–4).

In other words, the use of these substances is not for the purpose of acquiring a state of consciousness that does not exist but to express externally what is already present internally. Jayaratha makes this clear:

> Therefore the [set of three Ms] is to be utilised by the person who has entered upon the Kula path for the reason that he is in every way committed simply to manifesting his own bliss. [The set of three Ms] is not [to be utilised] out of greed. If that were the case, how would [the use of the three Ms] differ from worldly usages? (*Tantrāloka* vol 7:3357 lines 7–10)

Meat gets scant mention in the ritual. Wine (*madya*) is preferred over the 'manufactured' (*kṛtrima*) alcohols (*ali, āsava*), such as grain-alcohol, mead and rum, since it develops naturally from the grape itself, just as the sexual fluids arise naturally from the body. The significance of alcohol in the Kula ritual lies in its 'divinising' effect, but equally in its sinfulness, for even a small amount, even a whiff, is gravely wrong. Indeed the *Laws of*

Manu enjoin extremely severe penances for any contact with it (*Manusmṛti* 11.91–98, 147–151).

In the first instance, the term *maithuna* refers to the act of sexual intercourse, but is extended to include the substances that are produced during intercourse, the male (*retas*) and female (*rajas*) sexual fluids. These can be used either in their liquid form or, more practically, as a powder or granule.

A whole series of words is used to describe the substance. Abhinava identifies *amṛta*[8] with *kuṇḍa-golaka*.[9] The term *vāma* can mean 'on the left-hand side' (where the consort sits), or 'improper' (as in 'sinister'), or 'beautiful woman', or 'emitting'. The 'nectar-of-the-left' (*vāma-amṛta*) has all these meanings: it is the 'unclean' female sexual fluid. Menstrual blood (*rakta, puṣpa*) can also be used in ritual. The word *aruṇa* (menstrual blood) also refers to the female procreative sexual power. Since in the human life cycle intercourse is the first (*ādi*) act (*saṃskāra*), the ritual which produces the fluids is called *ādi-yāga*, the 'primordial sacrifice'.

The three Ms are also called 'oblation' (*caru*)[10] which ordinarily refers to boiled rice etc, but in the Kula ritual consists of the 'five jewels' (*pañca-ratna*) which are not the traditional five jewels of gold, silver, coral, diamond, pearl (Monier-Williams 1983:864.3) but 'male urine, semen, menstrual blood, phlegm, faeces' (*Tantrāloka* vol 7:3420 line 7). It is taken as the human equivalent of the *pañcagavya*, the five products of the cow, namely milk, curd, ghee, urine, and dung. If goddesses take the form of cows (*Tantrāloka* 29.16a) such that the *pañcagavya* are sacred, are not the bodily products of the deified human also sacred?[11]

But what is the point of using such a horrific concoction? The answer is given quite simply: Śiva transcends pure and impure, licit and illicit, pleasure and horror. He is not governed by such divisive concepts for he contains all in himself and, through his *śakti*, gives rise to all. Indeed, what some consider to be impure, such as wine or bodily fluids, are most pure 'because of [their] proximity to consciousness' (*Tantrāloka* 29.128a and cf. *Tantrāloka* 15.164cd–167ab). By producing them and even consuming them, the practitioner shows that he has the mind of Śiva, indeed is Śiva.

Again, the three Ms stand in relationship to each other: the meat and the wine are to intercourse as means to result. By consuming wine and meat, the practitioner experiences an exhilaration which leads to intercourse and its fluids. The Devī is expressed in these substances just as she is found in the woman of lowest caste.

Furthermore, by taking what has arisen from consciousness, the practitioner is taken back into consciousness. The vessel contains every value, from the most sublime source to the most material object and, to unenlightened eyes, the most repulsive. The rituals of the cremation ground, all the paraphernalia of skulls and ash, trident and corpses, are replaced by the natural symbols of meat and wine, intercourse and, above all, the fluids that arise from intercourse. They relate to art and theatre about which Abhinava has much to say in his *Dhvanyālocana* where he investigates the nature of resonance (*dhvani*), that is the power of suggestion in poetry. The three Ms, like theatre and poetry, can transport the practitioner to the highest state. Because they are natural, they are at once simpler and more powerful: they derive from and impinge on the very person of the practitioner. They have an immediacy and power which mere words and explanations do not have.

The 'oblation' is of particular significance in this process. Abhinava proposes four means (*upāya*), the most exalted of which is really a non-means (*an-upāya*) because in fact there is no path to follow; the goal is reached suddenly and totally, due to an intense descent of energy (*śakti-pāta*), an immense outpouring of grace (*anugraha*). There is no need for repeated practice or deeper understanding.

> The revelation [of this Light] is given once and for all, after which there is no means (*Tantrāloka* 2.2b).

> The reality of Consciousness shines forth by its own radiance. What is the value, therefore, of those [means to make it known]? (*Tantrāloka* 2.10a)

According to Jayaratha, the term 'non-means' (*an-upāya*) can also be understood as a 'very reduced means' (*alpa-upāya*) (*Tantrāloka* vol 2:312 line 13), or a 'subsidiary means' (*parikaratvam*) (*Tantrāloka* vol 7:3420 line 12). He lists a certain number of them.

> The sight of the perfected beings and *yoginīs*, the eating of the 'oblation' (*caru-bhojana*), a teaching, a transition (?) (*saṃkramaḥ*), spiritual practice, service of the Teacher (*Tantrāloka* vol 2:312 lines 13–4).

This approach is not 'aesthetic' if this word is taken to mean 'superficial'. It is 'aesthetic' if this term refers to the heightening of sensation and experience such that the ultimate reality is perceived and recognised. For the purpose and point of the Kula ritual is not to placate the *yoginīs* or to obtain their powers and the pleasure of intercourse with them but to attain the state of ultimate consciousness and the condition of Śiva and *śakti* united in supreme, eternal bliss (*ānanda*).

SECTION B: PRAXIS

Part 4—the ritual

It is one thing to contemplate the horrific ideas in theory and quite another to see them actually practised. Indeed, it is the actual practice which has provoked such scandal.

Chapter 29 of the *Tantrāloka* is carefully structured. The Introduction (*Tantrāloka* 29.1–17) and Concluding Rites (*Tantrāloka* 282–92a) enclose the two main sections: the Rituals for the Initiate (*Tantrāloka* 29.18–186a) and the Rituals of Initiation (*Tantrāloka* 29.186b–281) which interrelate to make the point that only the initiated can perform the rituals. In other words, the Kula is not just a point of view but a tradition; it cannot be learned from a book but must be communicated by gifted guru to worthy disciple. Indeed the ritual is the outward expression of what has already occurred within the disciple. The ritual and its elements are therefore understood only from within the tradition. Those who remain outside because the divine grace has not illumined them will be at best curious and at worst repelled. This indeed is the very purpose of the use of certain substances—to distinguish between those who, by Devī's grace, stand within and those who are excluded from her *kula*.

This being said, Abhinava is not slavish in his presentation. He reinterprets the Kula ritual, which he respects, on the basis of his philosophy of the Trika, as he had done with other traditions. He wishes to show how the Trika can accommodate and surpass every other system. He does not reject or devalue but incorporates.

In the Introduction Abhinava lists the six 'sacrifices' or 'supports' which provide a solid framework for the many rituals he describes. Only two will be described: the first, the daily ritual and the third, the ritual with the external *śakti*.

The daily (*nitya*) ritual is given in shorter (*Tantrāloka* 29.18–23) and longer (*Tantrāloka* 29.24–55) forms.[12] The shorter form gives the essence and basic pattern of all the subsequent rituals and consists of a few simple steps:

1. The practitioner enters the 'hall of sacrifice' and regenerates himself by placing (*nyāsa*) either Parā or Mālinī or Mātṛsadbhāva, the feminine mantras, on his body. By investing himself with the goddess by one of her mantras, he becomes Bhairava.[13]
2. Now that he is divinised, he fills the vessel with the substances.
3. He then performs an aspersion with the substances and consumes them. Just as the mantras, Parā etc, transform the practitioner who places them on himself, so too the contents of the vessel transform him when he uses them. Because he is the god he is invested with the goddess and acquires all her powers. By sprinkling the area around himself with the contents of the vessel and by drinking them the practitioner consecrates himself and all creation. The outer and the inner are one.

The same basic pattern is repeated in Sacrifice 2, performed with the 'internal *śakti*', where the practitioner imaginatively places on his body the various sacred sites (*pīṭha*) so that he becomes the abode of the goddesses. It is his divinisation. He then enters the heart of consciousness and performs the oblation into the fire. But it is in Sacrifice 3, Abhinava's preferred Kula ritual, performed with an 'external *śakti*', ie with a real woman, that the worship of the Devī and the use of the substances are most pronounced.

It is performed in terms of the Circle Sacrifices described in *Tantrāloka* 28.60b–111.[14] These involve the guru seated in the middle with the disciples arranged around him. In a ritual expression of the emanation and re-absorption of the universe, the substances are handed out from the guru, as from Śiva himself, and passed from row to row as far as the outermost circle and then back again. By re-enacting the vibration (*spanda*) of the universe in this way, the participants become the cosmos and acquire its powers.

The Circle Sacrifice can be done in five ways: i) with the guru and his disciples only; ii) with these and their wives; iii) with these and choice courtesans; iv) with these and the wives of outcastes; v) with all these types mixed in together. Sacrifice 3 is a case of the fourth Circle Sacrifice so that the practitioner's wife does not take part but the outcaste women do.

Having outlined these basic principles Abhinava goes on to describe a series of rituals organised according to the various triads of the Trika. Thus, Sacrifice 3 is structured in three parts or three 'emissions' (*visarga*)—'emanation' (*sṛṣṭi*), 're-absorption' (*saṃhāra*) and 'union' (*saṃghaṭṭa, melaka*), some of which are further divided into threes. Moreover, these texts can be read on three levels: gross (*sthūla*); subtle (*sūkṣma*); or supreme (*para*). This chapter cannot describe the many rituals but will focus only on part of the first 'emission' which focuses on emanation (*sṛṣṭi*), and involves three stages: action (*kalpa*); thought (*vikalpa*); and beyond thought (*nirvikalpa*).

Abhinava gives the basic principle for the activity (*kalpa*):

> And the sacrifice, viewed externally, is called 'satiation' (*tarpaṇa*); and as a result there is an expansion (*vikāsa*) (*Tantrāloka* 29.107b).

This is possible because of the interconnection between the many *cakra*s and sub-*cakra*s (*anucakra*); for the whole person is a network, a *maṇḍala* (wheels within wheels), of interconnected faculties which are arranged in such a way that the satiation of one *cakra* leads to the opening of another, as a lotus opens under the warming rays of the sun, until the principal *cakra* (*mukhya-cakra*) begins to function, namely the sexual organ which is called 'principal' precisely because it affords the greatest bliss (*Tantrāloka* 105b–106a) and because it is essentially related to supreme consciousness.

A whole morality is contained here, for the religious act is no longer a set of external rites whose observance will lead to blessing. Any act which leads to the attainment of Sivahood is religious. But, on the other hand, if a particular satisfaction does not lead to the expansion of consciousness, it is useless and its repeated application is proof of folly. Thus the emphasis is not on the act but on the experience.

Indeed, the emphasis is on the immediate, unreflective (*nirvikalpa*) experience of union with the *śakti* and the fluid she produces. Her very anatomy provides her with the 'fully opening and closing central path' (*Tantrāloka* 122a), her *yoni*, which makes her best able to lead the practitioner to consciousness. This central path (*madhya-pāda*) is also called: the *yoginī*-'mouth' (*mukha, vaktra, vadana*) or '*śakti-cakra*'; the 'Picu-mouth' (*picu-vaktra*), meaning the 'lower mouth' as distinct from the five other faces of Śiva which point north, south, east, west and upwards; the central-sacred place (*madhya-dhāma*); or womb (*janma, janma-ādhāra, -sthāna*). The male sexual organ (*liṅga, nala*) is also called 'mouth'. Both male and female sexual organs are called the 'primary identifying mark' (*ādy-ādhāra*).

All three—consciousness, the 'mouth of the *yoginī*' and the sexual fluid it emits—correlate with each other. Consciousness is the ultimate reality (*tattva*) and from the female sexual partner the fluid (*tattva*)[15] is emitted. This emitting is the 'saying' by the 'mouth' of the *yoginī*. Just as supreme consciousness cannot be described, so too the flow must be experienced and cannot be 'put into writing'. Just as the mouth of the guru utters the mantra that leads to consciousness, so too the 'mouth' of the *yoginī* communicates the unique experience of consciousness, immediately. This sexual fluid results from consciousness and leads to consciousness. Just as the guru considers the initiate to be his son, so too the *yoginī* by her 'mouth' begets him into the family (*kula*) of the 'Mothers' and into the Kula tradition.[16] Just as consciousness is the pre-eminent circle because it produces the highest bliss, so too the 'mouth' of the *yoginī* is the principal circle because it gives the highest pleasure. When the practitioner joins his 'mouth' to the 'mouth' of the *yoginī*, when the sexual organs are joined, he comes to consciousness, he is *tattva-jña*,[17] 'one who knows reality'. Even to taste the fluid is to engage in 'mouth to mouth' and, therefore, to arrive at the union of Śiva and *śakti*. The practitioner is the 'hero' (*vīra*) who eats the 'food of heroes' (*vīra-bhojya*).

Although Abhinava makes full use of the substances, he has shifted the emphasis from activity to awareness. In this way, perception and sensitivity predominate over the 'magical' powers of the substance or a crude 'rubricism'.

There are two outcomes: the male practitioner becomes supreme Bhairava so that he is universally present (*vyāpti*); if the *yoginī* conceives, her child will, since he is conceived while his parents are in that state, be 'of himself a repository of knowledge, a Rudra' (*Tantrāloka* 29.162a), and even in the womb he will be a *yoginī*-child (*yoginī-bhū*).

Conclusion

This chapter has tried to show that the extreme tantric practice called the Kula ritual, for all its weaknesses and limitations, especially in the eyes of the modern reader, cannot be simply dismissed as a perverse aberration. Abhinavagupta demythologises the fearsome *yoginīs* and replaces them with the sexual partner who nevertheless destroys the limited sense of the self. She eliminates the dualism of pure and impure, licit and illicit. The householder is the ascetic; the ordinary is extraordinary. Liberation and enjoyment coincide; the outer and the inner are one. All is valuable; all is a manifestation of the goddess and a means to attain the full expansion of consciousness. Even the repulsive is divinely revealing. What others consider unacceptable is, to the enlightened mind, the very means of spiritual advance. Far from being designed for persons of low character or undeveloped spiritual sensibility, the Kula ritual is designed for 'the most advanced gurus and disciples' (*Tantrāloka* 29.2a). The practitioner becomes Bhairava such that his every word is mantra and his every action is sacrifice. He achieves the goal of being 'liberated while living' (*jīvan-mukta*).

Notes

1 The history of the tantras and of the role of the goddess in this history is complex and uncertain. Chapter 2 of this volume, by AA Di Castro gives interesting insights into the way this history might be traced.

2 Greg Bailey's chapter on Ganeśa's mother, Parvatī, shows how the *Ganeśapurāṇa* ranges from presenting Parvatī as goddess to presenting Parvatī as simple mother, with neither emphasis excluding the other. Similarly, the various levels at which the Devī operates in the Kula ritual must be seen in relation to each other.

3 There is a certain ambiguity, nevertheless, as to whether the term 'consciousness' (*saṃvit, cit,* etc) applies primarily to Śiva or to Śakti, the goddess. Cf. the phrases: 'The nature of consciousness, ie of the goddess' (*Tantrāloka* 29.118a), and 'Supreme consciousness is called "the goddess"' (*Parātriṃśikāvivaraṇa* 1985:198 line 1).

4 Thus Devī in Kashmir Shaivism as in the Kula ritual differs markedly from the presentations of her given in other articles of this volume.

5 David Templeman's study on the *ḍākinī,* in Chapter 7, helps fills out the idea of the *yoginī* who is in some way related and similar.

6 In the case of female deities the mantra is referred to as *vidyā.*

7 In Chapter 9, Effy George gives a present-day example of how the Goddess is still worshipped as 'the supreme deity, the beginning and the end of the cosmos'.

8 The word *amṛta* occasionally also means 'wine'.

9 He defines it as that which '...comes from the union of the heroes and their counterpart, [their sexual partner]' (*Tantrāloka* 15.166cd). Jayaratha confirms the point: '...the nectar is the so-called sexual fluid (*kuṇḍa-golaka*) which arises during the perfect fusion of the [hero and the *yoginī*]' (*Tantrāloka* vol 6:2524 lines 14–5).

10 By metonymy they are also called 'vessel' (*argha-pātra*) and perhaps even 'lamp' (*dīpa*).

11 Jayaratha expands 'the five jewels' to 12: 'Male semen, male urine, and menstrual blood, faeces and phlegm; human flesh, beef, goat's flesh, fish, fowl; onion and indeed garlic: these are the beautiful set of twelve ingredients.' (*Tantrāloka* vol 7:3306 lines 4–6).

12 Perhaps the figure of the Lajjāgaurī, presented by JB Bapat in Chapter 5 of this volume, gives some idea of how the Kula ritual may in fact have been practised in the home, especially in the daily ritual

13 In this ritual the appellation 'Bhairava' is often preferred to 'Śiva'.

14 It is not entirely clear whether Sacrifice 3 takes place in a group or in private.

15 The whole of reality consists of 36 categories (*tattva*). However, the knowledge of Śiva, the 'category' *par excellence*, produces bliss and a sexual flow, which thus signifies all the categories and grants access to them and to their powers. The sexual fluid is, therefore, also called *tattva*, 'substance'.

16 The Kula tradition was first taught by Ardhatryambakā, the daughter of Tryambaka who is considered to be one of the perfected beings (*siddha*) and the founder of the non-dualist Śaiva tradition. She had a twin brother, hence her name 'Half of Tryambaka' (Ardhatryambakā).

17 The word *tattva-jña,* with its synonym *tattva-vid*, also refers to the person who has taken the 'oblation' (*caru*) and who has been absorbed into the highest category, consciousness itself.'

chapter seven

The *ḍākinī* in Tibetan hagiography

David Templeman

The study of the *ḍākinī* has reached new levels of maturity and insight. Several recent books dealing either fully or partially with the topic demonstrate a broad awareness of the *ḍākinī*'s role both in tantric and in psychological terms. Authors such as Janet Gyatso (1998), Adelheid Hermann-Pfandt (1990, 1992–3), Judith Simmer-Brown (2002) and June Campbell (2002) have widened the context in which the *ḍākinī* may be viewed and in so doing have brought a wealth of original interpretative material to our attention. In this mass of frequently detailed information, however, there appears to be an element not yet discussed and it is this I wish to discuss here. I take this opportunity to raise the question, 'How does the *ḍākinī* function within the ritual setting of a *maṇḍala*, and what are the processes by which they manage to become so intimately associated with the bestowal of gnosis?' Attached to this question is the corollary, 'How did these minor, sometimes nuisance-like Indian deities become such major figures in the enlightenment process, especially as recorded in the Tibetan tantric tradition?' This contribution will use the genre of Tibetan hagiographical writings as its main contextual basis.

*Ḍākinī*s: from India to Tibet

Those who have read even a few Tibetan hagiographies will have already come across the figure of the *ḍākinī*, most likely as a rather strange sort of character who combines menace and tenderness, ugliness and beauty, and apparent unconcern with ultimate engagement. Descriptions of the *ḍākinī* in the Tibetan literary tradition tend to expand and embroider upon the rather brief and attenuated Indian descriptions we may find in tantric texts and accounts in collections of stories such as the Indian work, the *Vetālapañcaviṃśati*—the so-called 'Twenty-five Corpse Stories' which date perhaps to the 10th century CE. Clearly the Tibetans found the Indic descriptions of *ḍākinīs* to have touched something within them. The detailed Tibetan writings concerning *ḍākinī* activity reflect their preoccupation with their already existing cults of female deities and an acute awareness of the dangers such spirits were believed to bring. Later on, however, the Tibetans' intimate awareness of the role of the *ḍākinī* in the tantric process, in what had, to a great extent, become a nation familiar with the imported arts of meditation even in that early period, enabled them to write with authority about the role of the *ḍākinī* in the personal meditation processes. In other words the *ḍākinī* had been ascribed a soteriological role which had been, to a great extent, absent in the Indian understanding of the *ḍākinī*. As an example of the Tibetan understanding of the outer form of the *ḍākinī* we may cite the description of the troupe of *ḍākinīs* who inhabited *Śītavana* or 'Cool Sandalwood Grove' cemetery, one of the eight great cemeteries (*śmaśāna*) of India and said to be located in a forest to the northwest of Nālandā University in modern day Bihar. What is described is horrific, to say the least, and shows something of the Indian antecedents of the *ḍākinī* cult in terms of raw energy and urgency of these beings, as well as the Tibetan tendency to embroider and add their own local genius. It is recorded in the 14th-century hagiography of the eighth century (possibly) Tokharian *yogin* Padmasambhava, who visited Tibet and laid the foundations for the flourishing of Buddhism.

> As for the *ḍākinīs* there, they were innumerable.
> From the eyes of some of them, sun rays emerged;
> Some of them had thunderous voices of dragons and rode upon buffalo;
> Others held knives and their eyes were wide and staring;
> Others held aloft piled up skulls and rode on tigers;
> Others, holding human corpses, rode on lions;
> Others rode on *garuḍas* while eating entrails;
> Others rode on jackals and had lances from the tips of which shot flames;
> Others had five faces and made offerings of lakes of blood;
> Others had hands beyond counting in which they held exemplars of all types of creatures;
> Others, having severed their own heads, held them in their own hands;
> Others, having plucked out their own hearts held them in their own hands;
> Others, having split asunder their own chest cavities, ate their own entrails and intestines;
> Others, having displayed their male or female sexual organs, then hid them from sight,
> While all the while riding stallions, bulls, and elephants (*U rgyan Ghuru* n.d. 166, line 6–167, line 5).

Not only were the *ḍākinīs* terrifying, but the location itself had its own peculiar terrors. For example, the Tibetan pilgrim Chag lo tsā ba, who visited the site in 1234 CE, said that the grove was filled with venomous snakes with spotted bodies, with heads the size of a man's thigh. He also noted that when they slithered through the trees the branches would shake and crack with their weight (Roerich 1959:85).

Certainly we can see from the description of the *ḍākinīs* that we are in an ancient world, one in which the norms of blood, death and a fascinating and yet repulsive sexuality prevail. We may also note the Tibetan accent on portraying the *ḍākinī* in great detail along with their more frightening and bizarre activities and note that these are rarely the focus in Indian literature. Indian *ḍākinī* descriptions tend to accent their unpredictability and their rather dangerous allure as well as their almost human nature, whereas Tibetans embroidered their gory and terrifying aspects.

Ḍākinīs and their role in the *maṇḍala*

It struck me when re-reading Martin Kalff's doctoral thesis on the *Abhidhānottara-Tantra* that he had made a very important point in his discussion on the nature of the *ḍākinī.* He noted in passing, that the *ḍākinīs* were frequently distinguishable from other (female) goddesses by their 'collective nature and a strong human component' (Kalff 1979:77). His point, drawn exclusively from a study of tantric texts themselves, was obvious in terms of both the text and iconography in which *ḍākinīs* frequently appear in cycles and in forms similar to human beings. However, over and above this, it also contained a strong resonance in terms of certain aspects of hagiographical writings in which my prime interest lies. Kalff's point here was to distinguish the *ḍākinī* from other *laukika devas* (worldly deities). In this observation he caused me to think about their role in Tibetan hagiographies, a genre I had previously worked on, to see whether his observation was entirely accurate. Certainly, in the context of his thesis (the union of female and male deities in the *Abhidhānottara-Tantra*), what he had especially noted was the type and role of the *ḍākinīs* in the three inner circles of a *maṇḍala*, which surround the central Great Bliss circle (*mahāsukha cakra*). These circles are those of Mind (*citta*), Speech (*vāc*) and Body (*kāya*), moving from the inner circle to the outer. The *ḍākinīs* actually *become* the very structure of the *maṇḍala* itself, inasmuch as they help to 'act out' the role of the central deity, in Kalff's case the deity *Saṃvara*, located in the circle of Great Bliss. By 'act out' I mean here that they vivify and exemplify the transcendent nature of the central deity located in the central Great Bliss circle.

On viewing a *maṇḍala* in its painted form, the neophyte might be tempted to regard the *ḍākinīs* as static, merely painted and possibly decorative figures.

However, the written texts see them rather as alive, moving figures who are engaged in an endless cycle of song, dance, debate and other activities which serve to exemplify the teachings of that particular tantra in whose *maṇḍala* they are found. Certainly iconographically speaking, they give the appearance of being filled with energy, their poses wild and sometimes provocative, but, within the context of initiation and the *gaṇa* ceremony attendant on it, we must ask ourselves what it is that they actually *do*. We find little to answer this question in the tantric texts themselves, apart from some rich and marvellously detailed accounts of the *ḍākinīs'* clothes, bodily poses and physical peculiarities. Nevertheless, in their painted form for example, they still remain, to a certain extent, static figures, without an apparent function. We may know of their significance from the tantras but we have yet to know exactly how such esoteric detail is imparted to the *sādhaka*.

I believe that it is in the hagiographical genre that we find the most detailed descriptions of their actual role in imparting gnosis, and it is to these works we should now turn.

Kunga Drolchog's hagiography of Kṛṣṇācārya.

Perhaps one of the most detailed sources for the role of the *ḍākinī* in the imparting of tantric initiation is in the account of the life of the Indian *mahāsiddha* (great tantric adept) Kṛṣṇācārya, who lived in the 11th century. One of the most interesting versions of his life was written by the Tibetan scholar Kunga Drolchog, somewhere between 1525 and 1560 CE (Kun dga' grol mchog 1982). Kunga Drolchog was a lineal descendent of Kṛṣṇācārya, so his account of his own predecessor is of great interest to us here. To what extent it is an authentic memory of his past life has been discussed elsewhere (Templeman 1994).

Encouraged by his master Jālandharipa to seek out a *ḍākinī* who, he warns, may appear somewhat disagreeable looking, Kṛṣṇācārya sought to gain the *ḍākinī*'s blessing on a set of bone ornaments and to bring them back to his master. These ornaments are both real and symbolic. They represent the complete transformation of the Five Ignorances into the Five Transcendent Wisdoms. They are to be worn as ornaments in the performance of tantric ritual as a sign that the performer has attained that level of realisation. The ornaments in themselves represent the deeds, the *caryās*, performed with a complete understanding of Perfection of Wisdom (*prajñāpāramitā*) in action.

In the hagiography we see the role of the *ḍākinīs* in possibly its most expanded and detailed form, and through it we may observe the actual role of those enigmatic females—that is, what they actually do within the circles of the *maṇḍala* itself.

When Kṛṣṇācārya approached the sacred land of Urgyen, said to be present-day Swāt in Pakistan, he was immediately approached by *ḍākinīs*, who gently guided him into the land itself, and he was somewhat surprised that they did not manifest their wrathful and malicious aspects as he had expected. Urgyen is depicted as a place as flat as the palm of one's hand, covered by a grey-blue sky. The place was laid out as 32 crossed arrows in a swastika-shape, with the overall effect of a chequer-board. He noted bearded *ḍākinī* girls everywhere, graced with ornaments of goat hair, flashing their clear, golden eyes and wearing only hair down to their hips. They held *ḍamaru* drums and leaned on tridents. Clearly at this stage, Kṛṣṇācārya had met the 32 *karma ḍākinīs* who surround the central Great Bliss figure in the *Cakrasaṃvara maṇḍala*. The very layout of Urgyen reflects the layout of the divine space itself, based as it is upon 32 crossed arrows, each delineated area representing one of the palaces within the *maṇḍala* of each *karma ḍākinī*.

> Upon opening the doors of each of the 32 *ḍākinī* palaces, he was held in awe of their glorious ornaments, their sensuous dances and the wondrous melodies to which they danced, the like of which he had never heard before (Kun dga' grol mchog 1982:4B–5B).

As Kṛṣṇācārya entered the main, central temple, that is the central Great Bliss locus at the very heart of the *maṇḍala*, he was amazed by the effulgence of the light as well as by the enigmatic songs the *ḍākinīs* sang. He realised that their songs contained secret symbolic content and were, therefore, a key to understanding the content of the *maṇḍala* itself. He saw that here the *ḍākinīs* appeared somewhat different, adopting the guises of repulsiveness and enigma, as well as charm and sexuality, both hallmarks of their *cultus*. Kunga Drolchog says,

> Some of the *ḍākinīs* who had gathered together had very old bodies and their masses of white hair were streaked with blonde, and were decorated with nits, like salt sprinklings. One of the latter *ḍākinīs* even had a beard and eyebrows of the same colour as her hair...he saw the *maṇḍala* of the mighty and youthful-bodied *ḍākinīs* who were arrayed around, and when he saw their bodily parts, he became completely fascinated by their great beauty, and especially the nipples of their huge, firm and heavy breasts, their tawny hair (and) their many glistening decorations pendant and lustrous... They were bedecked, all of them, most beautifully in sparkling white human bone ornaments, six in number...The sky-bodied girls, all of them naked, had hanging from them whole flayed human skins which they wore as aprons (Kun dga' grol mchog 1982:5B–6A).

Clearly we can see that Kṛṣṇācārya had entered the central part of the architectonic *maṇḍala* and had seen the *ḍākinīs* in their role as exemplifiers of Absolute Truth—their nakedness symbolising a complete absence of dualistic thought (*vikalpa*), their combination of menace and sensuality showing that all human senses are to be employed on the path, their lack of attention to personal pleasantness demonstrating their having died to the world, and their use of human skin and bone as decoration showing complete mastery over the realms of life and death.

It is at this stage that the *ḍākinīs* allowed him to witness their Chief engage each of them in turn in a debate. Both the questions and the responses were couched in an enigmatic language (*saṃdhyābhāṣā*), employing secret *ḍākinī* language, signs and secret gestures, and the responses were discussed by the assembled rows of *ḍākinīs*. Although no details of the language and symbols in this context are given, we have several examples of the genre from other sources. For example Tāranātha writes in his work of 1601, the *bKa' babs bdun ldan gyi brgyud pa'i rnam thar ngo mtshar rmad du byung ba rin po che'i lta bu'i rgyan,* (Tāranātha 1985a:547–689 (translation in Templeman 1983:26–8)) of precisely such symbolic communication.

Saroruha, a Royal priest, was preaching Buddhism to large numbers of people when he saw an old lady wood-gatherer collecting firewood. She was alternately laughing and weeping and this perplexed Saroruha who asked her what she intended. Her explanation was that she laughed because his preaching was in the very style of Vajradhāra himself but wept because he was unable to express the profundity of Vajradhāra's understandings. She then recommended that he apprentice himself to a swineherd, Anaṅgavajra, known as 'Adamantine Pigsty', which he attempted to do. Sometime after he saw a person whom he thought to be Adamantine Pigsty leading a herd of swine, accompanied by an old, low-born woman who was lugging a huge load of wood. He then realised that the load of wood was a symbol of the mental states he had to abandon and that the woman was a symbol of the passion he had to engender to work on the tantric path. Even the swine were symbols of the fundamental purity of ignorance. When he asked her for instruction she claimed to be unworthy to teach him and struck him, whereupon he laid his head on the threshold of the pig pen and slept. At night the pigs were restless and ruined all of Saroruha's possessions and, in a rage, he struck out at them. The old woman turned him out, but through his stubbornness he refused to leave, remaining there with his head resting on the threshold where he was seen by Anangavajra. At that stage his teaching process commenced, involving a scandalous 'relationship' with Adamantine Pigsty's daughter which nearly ruined the country because of the perceived pollution caused by his cohabitation with her (Templeman.1983:26–7). We may note in this brief account not only the almost classical manifestation of the *ḍākinī* as both hag and *agent provocateur*, but also the purposive function of symbolic instruction as it was employed in medieval India. This is only one example of many which could be cited, but its importance is clear.

There is a story related by Professor Giuseppe Tucci, for which I am unable to give exact citations, in which he recalls a discussion he had in the 1930s with a Tibetan hermit who had spent more than three years in solitary isolated meditation in a mountain hermitage. Tucci asked him if he ever became bored in his cell and the monk replied that he was never at a loss for company. When asked further about this the monk said that he could always 'listen in' on the *ḍākinī* chatter which was going on in the *maṇḍala* he was using as his meditation tool and that each of the *ḍākinīs* had become for him a living, talking being. We can take it that Kṛṣṇācārya had so completely entered the *maṇḍala* that it too had become a vivified entity into which he had completely entered, rather than remaining a mere painted or fabricated object of contemplation.

In Kṛṣṇācārya's case at the *ḍākinī* assembly, Kunga Drolchog notes that the final layout of the rows and the debate 'became rather like the manner of the layout of the deities in a *maṇḍala*' (Kun dga' grol mchog 1982:6B–7A). The reader of the hagiography is fully aware that it was not so much a layout 'in the manner of…' but it was in fact the *actual maṇḍala* itself that he had entered. This is evident because at this stage 37 *ḍākinīs* arose from the ten directions and performed a dance that implicitly gave him the permission to perform the meditations on the *Cakrasaṃvara maṇḍala* itself. There are precisely 37 *ḍākinīs* present in the most basic form of the *Cakrasaṃvara maṇḍala* within the inner circles including the Great Bliss circle. This may be elaborated into the 61 deities (62 in Luipa's vision of it) in the more complex form of the *maṇḍala*.

The *ḍākinīs* then go on to make certain predictions, the most important of which being that Kṛṣṇācārya must avoid frequenting places where the local deity lived, especially where that deity was unconverted to Buddhism. The word 'unconverted' meant that the local site deity was, in some manner, antithetical to Buddhism and 'held' the land thereabouts firmly in its control against alien religious encroachment. Clearly, here, we are entering into an entirely different area, that of contested sites within Indian religions. This may indeed become the topic of a later paper. However the point is of great importance in this context, as Kṛṣṇācārya ignored that warning and the mistake cost him his life prematurely at the hands of precisely such a *ḍākinī*.

Over a lengthy section of the narrative, the assembled *ḍākinīs*, together with their chief, explain to Kṛṣṇācārya the superiority of the *maṇḍala* of *Cakrasaṃvara* over that of *Guhyasamāja* and confirm him on that practice path. This instruction takes the form of a series of profound songs, which have already been the subject of a paper (Templeman 1992–3).

Kṛṣṇācārya, who, after receiving the initiation, refers to the collection of *ḍākinīs* as his mother(s), is the first recipient of these teachings, according to the chief. She says that they have, in fact, never been written down and that they are best exemplified by dance, which is precisely the mode the *ḍākinīs* then used to communicate them to Kṛṣṇācārya. The choice of dance as a medium of communicating the ultimate truth possibly has to do with it being unable to be polluted by the dual interpretation of words and with its utterly direct form of authentic impartment. As the *ḍākinīs* said (Kun dga' grol mchog. 1982:9A–9B):'...this, our vajra-song...is a song which has never left our lips before—we sing it then today!'

The chief of the gathering bestowed the blessings on the bone ornaments, thereby making them ready to be worn in rituals as signifiers of the wearer's readiness to practise the *caryās,* that is, the Perfection of Wisdom exemplified in all actions. Kṛṣṇācārya was deemed by his master as not being ready to employ the bone ornaments in practice, and he intended that they be brought to him, blessed but unused. However, being headstrong, Kṛṣṇācārya succumbed to their temptation. After they had been blessed by the *ḍākinīs*, he broke their seals while on the road home and donned them. He had a brief moment of spiritual glory and then, with pangs of guilt, he re-sealed the knots and offered them somewhat shamefacedly to his master who knew exactly what he had done. Finally, after further work, Kṛṣṇācārya was eventually granted the ornaments. However, contrary to the previous warning by both the *ḍākinīs* and his guru, he failed to demonstrate his complete mastery of the *caryās* in this life.

Ḍākinīs and Kṛṣṇācārya's death

A very important theme within Vajrayāna Buddhism is that of the contest between two sets of inimical forces, the non-Buddhists on one side and Buddhists on the other. Its most spectacular version deals with the conquest of Bhairava and his consort by the Buddhist deity Heruka (a form of Cakrasaṃvara) and his consort Vajravārāhī. The account tells us that Shiva and Umā adopted the form of Bhairava and Kālaratri and, conquering all 24 sacred sites of Buddhism, polluted them by their erection of *liṅga* and *yoni*. Moreover, the behaviour of the pair was offensive to Buddhists, as the couple allowed themselves to become slaves to their lusts at inappropriate times and encouraged animal sacrifices. The Buddhist supreme deity Vajradhāra transformed himself into Heruka, the Blood Drinker and his consort, who trounced the Bhairava pair. This defeat is clearly noted in iconographic terms where Heruka/Cakrasaṃvara and Vajravārāhī trample the Bhairava pair underfoot.

This theme of the contest between rival forces is also found in the account of Kṛṣṇācārya's death, but in his case it is Buddhism that loses, temporarily at least. History also tells us that Buddhism in fact never made any progress at all in the area of north-eastern India where the events are said to have taken place. Of interest is the viewpoint of the Tibetans for whom this area is believed to have been one of the strongholds of Buddhism in India. This view is still current in the 21st century. Whether the *ḍākinī* represented the local autochthonous tradition or some form of tantric religion is not discovered from the text. However, a reference to the *ḍākinī* placing her emblem, a *yoni*, atop a Buddhist *stūpa*, would suggest that she possibly belonged perhaps to a Saivite tradition.

It will be recalled that the chief *ḍākinī* at the *gaṇa* ceremony had warned Kṛṣṇācārya against ever going to tantric sites where the local deity lived and this was amplified by his guru, Jālandharipa, who said,

Inasmuch as you have performed the requisite ascetic deeds already, you may visit the other twenty three lands as you wish, with the express exception of Devīkoṭṭa. In Devīkoṭṭa there are very many wild *ḍākinīs* who bring ruin to people by snatching away their lives, and the whole place is unfit for humans to live in (Kun dga' grol mchog 1982:13B).

Devīkoṭṭa, said in ancient times to have been located near modern day Assam, was a *Tīrthika*, or non-Buddhist site and, according to Jālandharipa, not yet ready to be 'colonised' by Buddhists. There are two major accounts of the events surrounding Kṛṣṇācārya's death, one of them, the briefer of the two, by Kunga Drolchog and the other, vastly expanded, by Tāranātha (1575–1634), also a lineal descendent of Kṛṣṇācārya.

For a variety of reasons discussed elsewhere (Templeman 1994) Tāranātha was at some pains to make the hagiography he wrote a vast, seamless eulogy containing absolutely no material that could in any manner besmirch the dignity and enlightened activities of Kṛṣṇācārya. Kunga Drolchog, on the other hand, felt it was impossible to explain these 'enlightened activities', some of which appeared to be quite willful and possibly self-indulgent. His hermeneutic device was to explain them away as being utterly beyond our limited, relative levels of comprehension. He found an event such as the untimely and rather 'messy' death of Kṛṣṇācārya under these circumstances to be in this category. Tāranātha on the other hand discussed this event in terms of a miraculous series of ongoing after-death manifestations in which Kṛṣṇācārya became gradually 'perfected', making the whole narrative of events into something approaching an apotheosis. It is from Tāranātha's version of events that I draw a portrait of Kṛṣṇācārya's demise, because he gives us the best information about the role of the local *ḍākinī* in the narrative.

Despite his guru's and the *ḍākinī*'s warning, Kṛṣṇācārya, having performed his *caryā* meditation practices in all of the eight great charnel-grounds of India, decided that he would go to the forbidden site of Devīkoṭṭa. Tāranātha says that his reason for going was to stay there and engage in the *caryās* for the rest of his life, as he had already visited all the other *yogic piṭha*s, or pilgrimage power-places. It is also possible to infer from Tāranātha's text that Kṛṣṇācārya also wanted to 'convert' the site to Buddhism once and for all. Legend tells us that Virūpa, one of his predecessors, had only partially succeeded before him. However, another tradition says that the Devīkoṭṭa, which Virūpa himself had visited, was in South India, thereby suggesting that the site in Assam was still strongly under the sway of the local *ḍākinīs* and was therefore extremely dangerous. If the latter were the case, Kṛṣṇācārya was attempting precisely what the Buddhist *ḍākinīs* of Urgyen had warned him against.

Kṛṣṇācārya received a serious warning that something wrong was about to occur as he approached the place. On his way to Assam, and while in Varendra in Bengal, he engaged in a contest of *siddhi* powers with a beautiful local *ḍākinī* who trounced him, and yet he seems to have been so focused on his journey that he completely ignored his defeat and the explicit meaning it contained.

After Kṛṣṇācārya had spent some time at Devīkoṭṭa, the chief *ḍākinī* of the site manifested herself. Tāranātha records her name as Kāladāndibhartakālī, which contains reference to her holding a black cudgel. The Tibetan refers to her specifically as 'a great Tīrthika *ḍākinī* witch' (Tibetan—*phra men ma chen mo mu stegs kyi mkha' 'gro ma*) which covers a lot of possibilities for interpretation! For Kṛṣṇācārya the site was inalienably in the tenure of the *ḍākinī* by virtue of the *yoni* she had placed atop the Buddhist *stūpa*, presumably erected there previously as part of an unsuccessful attempt to convert the area, possibly even in Virūpa's time. The *ḍākinī* made a ritual gesture towards the *stūpa* and its alien *yoni* finial, and Kṛṣṇācārya realised that, were the *yoni* to remain there, it would do irreparable harm to the further propagation of Buddhism in the area. Having asked his disciples to remove the *yoni*, Kṛṣṇācārya then met with the *ḍākinī* who was holding a pestle and was pounding rice. She made a disrespectful gesture towards him and with a 'gaze', Kṛṣṇācārya smashed her mortar and pestle into pieces. The pair then engaged in ritualised warfare. In the ensuing exchange of wrathful, destructive 'gazes' (Sanskrit—*dṛṣṭi*; Tibetan—*lta stangs*), some bystanders had their clothes scorched and others fell into a swoon, so powerful was the ritual struggle. Kṛṣṇācārya wounded the *ḍākinī* so badly that he felt momentary compassion for her and it was in this very moment he allowed his protective shield to wane; with his guard temporarily down, the *ḍākinī* gave him a lethal wound. He retired to his shelter and his disciples went to search for an appropriate medicine to cure him. On their way back to Devīkoṭṭa, they were waylaid by a group of sensuous maidens in various states of undress, bathing in a lotus lake. They assured the disciples that their master had made a full recovery and that there was no need for them to rush back. Putting down their medicaments, the disciples prepared for dalliance, but immediately the maidens carried off the medicines and vanished. The girls were in fact transformational forms of that malicious *ḍākinī* and Kṛṣṇācārya eventually died, as he said, from 'the punishment of breaking the Guru's injunction' (Tāranātha *Slob dpon chen po spyod 'chang dbang po* 1985b:619, line 7 (translation in Templeman 1983:39)).

In this lengthy incident we can see not only the basic tensions which lay between existing and proselytising religions but also the manner in which the *ḍākinīs* may be said to act as protectors of their own sites, particularly in marginal areas. I have discussed the liminal nature and the possible origin of the model underlying the Buddhist idea of the *ḍākinī* in another paper and will not expand on that theme here (Templeman 2002). It is of interest, however, that both Urgyen and Devīkoṭṭa, in the west and the east respectively, were considered to be marginal areas of Buddhism in the 11th century CE. The activities of the *ḍākinīs* in Devīkoṭṭa are remarkably similar to the activities of the Iranian *peri* or *pairika*. These so-called 'fairies' have been referred to by Mary Boyce as, 'a class of female supernatural beings of malicious character, who seek to beguile and harm mankind—some of them are witch-like in character…(whereas) other *pairikas* it seems took on human form, and some made themselves enchantingly beautiful' (Boyce 1975:5ff). Both these characteristics have been noted in the account of the *siddha* Kṛṣṇācārya above.

The literary continuity of the *ḍākinī* presence in Urgyen is maintained by descriptions of Urgyen recorded by Tibetan pilgrims who visited the place in the 13th century. Among these is Urgyenpa (1230–1309 CE), named after the site he recorded in such detail. Urgyenpa also noted many of the aspects of the *ḍākinīs* there, such as their ability to change form at will, their maliciousness and their penchant for devouring meat and blood. However, we must also note that there is one major difference in that Urgyenpa's descriptions almost entirely omit mention of his initiation into any sort of *maṇḍala* at all. Although he travelled there ostensibly as a pilgrim, he seems not to have met *ḍākinīs* of the 'gnosis-bestowing' type but rather those belonging to the type far closer to the older Indian descriptions of women of 'suspect character' (Zla ba seng ge 1997).

An even later experience of the *ḍākinīs* of Urgyen is recorded in Tāranātha's biography of Buddhaguptanātha, an Indian Buddhist *yogin* who wandered the Indian subcontinent, Southeast Asia, Central Asia, Madagascar and Tibet in the 16th century and who later became Tāranātha's teacher. He describes Urgyen as being located in the area of present-day Ghazni in Afghanistan and notes that, unlike previous times in which there were Buddhist monks there, the order of monks had completely vanished and, in their place, a curious mixture of *yogins*, lay monks (*upāsaka*), *tīrthikas* and Muslims were living there. Buddhaguptanātha said that all the women of Urgyen were of the family of *ḍākinīs* and that they were fully accomplished in the art of mantras, both of the helpful and the hindering kinds. Furthermore, he said, they were able to 'shape shift' as well as being skilled in the art of working with mystic 'gazes' of the type that finally harmed Kṛṣṇācārya. While there, he saw various miracles such as a *ḍākinī* who parted the waters of a river to allow her to cross and another who transformed herself into a bat. The *siddha* also saw a partial manifestation of the *maṇḍala* of Vajravārāhī which lasted for three days and nights (Tāranātha 1987:539 line 6–542, line 2). This account seems to me to be quite important as it confirms the continuity of *ḍākinī* activity, at least until the relatively late date of about 1540, the period in which I believe that Buddhaguptanātha was in Urgyen.

Ḍākinīs: from 'nuisance' to 'powerful woman'

The reader will have noted that in certain cases some *ḍākinīs* may appear to be almost entirely 'Buddhicised' while others remain somehow more 'primitive' and dangerous in character. I suggest that the idea of the *ḍākinī*, wherever it may have ultimately had its origins, has sat comfortably within tantric Buddhism for a variety of reasons. Perhaps the foremost of these may be due to the character of these women, potentially capricious and yet, at the same time, positive and purpose-filled, encapsulating something of the mystery and unpredictability of the enlightenment process itself.

It is a commonplace observation that in Tibetan hagiographical writings the *ḍākinī* may appear in a profound and lengthy relationship with the practitioner, a relationship which may appear to eclipse much of the other content of the account of the progress towards Liberation. This relationship is often between the two of them, *siddha* and *ḍākinī*, with the *ḍākinī* fulfilling her role both as temptress, and as exemplifier of *avikalpa* or non-conceptualisation. An example of this is the detailed relationship between Ratnadāsa, the seventh incarnation of the deity Avalokiteśvara in India, and the *ḍākinī* 'Secret Knowledge' (Guhyajñāna, gSang ba ye shes) recorded by the fifth Dalai Lama's Regent, Sangs rgyas rgya mtsho in the late 17th century (Ahmad 1999:57, 65). The *ḍākinī* demonstrates to Ratnadāsa the essential emptiness of his self-nature and acts in a largely one-to-one relationship with him, with the circle of other *ḍākinīs* taking on a relatively minor supportive role. We remain relatively uncertain, in fact, of the role the *ḍākinīs* actually play in the creation of a *maṇḍala* in the initiation of Ratnadāsa. It is the relationship between them that is of prime importance in this account.

In other hagiographical writings the circle of *ḍākinīs* is entirely absent and the relationship appears to be brief and singular (Templeman 1983:25, 66). Frequently a *ḍākinī* in an entirely unlikely guise will attempt to make the *sādhaka* break caste rule or flout a monastic rule and, at the slightest hesitation by the *sādhaka*, will transform herself into Vajrayoginī and deny him initiation for a period of time.

Whatever their role within later Buddhism, the Buddhist *ḍākinī* would only be partly recognisable to earlier Indians of the period up to the fourth or fifth century CE, as they more frequently regarded the *ḍākinī* as a purely malevolent creature with an extremely limited soteriological role (Hermann-Pfandt 1992–3:46–7). Both the appearance and the function of the *ḍākinī* changed in their transition to Tibet, their soteriological role being greatly expanded and their wrathful aspect becoming at the same time, if anything, more explicitly grotesque. Exactly how much this was due to the Tibetan ability to express Indian tantric ideas in a far more graphic mode than Indians ever apparently conceived them is a matter for art historians to debate.

What remains for us is to make more use of a large number of wonderful Tibetan hagiographical accounts of *ḍākinīs* in their role as intimate and indispensable parts of the process to enlightenment, rather than as merely cemetery-haunting ghouls out to create trouble.

Notes

1 These examples give the account of the dancing girl Śrīsukha, a transformational form of a *ḍākinī* who acted without a troupe of assistant *ḍākinīs* (p. 25) and the account of the *siddha* Kukuripa and his beloved dog, a *ḍākinī* who had transformed herself into both puppy and the deity Vajrayoginī (p. 66–7).

2 Perhaps the best example of this is the account of Abhayākaragupta (Templeman 1983:70–2). This monk, born a Brāhmin and brought up a Hindu, was tempted by Vajrayoginī to engage her as a sexual consort which he refused. He later became a Buddhist and yet maintained the same levels of dualistic thought (*vikalpa*). Vajrayoginī again tempted him inside the temple, having adopted the guise of a *caṇḍāla* woman carrying blood-dripping beef for him to eat in a *gaṇa* ceremony with her. Having rejected the *ḍākinī* again he was unable to realise *siddhi* in that life and was relegated to being a scholar. He is perhaps best known as a masterly systematiser of *maṇḍalas* in his *magnum opus* the Niṣpannayogāvalī.

chapter eight

Devī's lion herders: bards and bardic goddesses and the moral regulation of power in late-medieval Rajasthan

Max Harcourt

The importance of the worship of the Devī in the warrior-clan conquest states of medieval Rajasthan has long been recognised by Indological scholars. (My use of the term 'medieval' is not to imply any close European parallels but to indicate the period between the Islamic invasions of the 11th century CE that ended the relative isolation of the classical Hindu/Buddhist ecumene, and the imposition of British colonial rule. Therefore, 'late medieval' signifies1600–1800 CE). From James Tod, writing in the 1820s, down to the impressive contemporary schools of Rajasthani studies in India, continental Europe and the United States, scholars have analysed the central role of Śākta religion and, particularly, the Kuldevī cults of the Rajput clans, in the warrior-clan polity (Tod 1987; Harlan 2003). Others have examined the Devīs of lineage, locality and disease in peasant, pastoralist and, especially, tribal society, while one of the contributors in this volume has investigated a remarkable *nirguṇa bhakti* Devī sect in the neighbouring Saurashtrian region of Rajput culture. The focus of this chapter, however, will be a distinctively Rajasthani variant of Devī religion that has only very recently come to the attention of modern scholars—the cult of the Cāraṇī Devīs (Harcourt 1993; Paul 1993, 1995; Tambs-Lyche 1999). What I argue in the following pages is that these Devīs and the living goddess institution associated with them played an important role in validating the moral regulatory function exercised by the Cāraṇa, or bard caste, in the warrior-clan conquest states of Rajasthan and northern and peninsular Gujarat.

Structural conflicts within the Rajput polity

The bardic moral regulatory role in late-medieval Rajasthani society arose out of certain structural features of the Rajput political system. Since the waning of the sterile debate over the 'feudal' or 'tribal' nature of Rajput society, a new generation of scholars, most notably Norman Ziegler, Henri

Stern and Denis Vidal, have greatly improved our understanding of the warrior-clan conquest polity of late-medieval Rajasthan (Stern 1971; Vidal 1997; Ziegler 1976). These states were formed by the conquest of territories previously under the control of tribal or other autochthonous communities by clans of Rajputs, a new category of warrior that emerged in north India in the early medieval period. At the time of the conquests—between the 9th and 15th centuries CE—the Rajputs were a comparatively open-status group of diverse origins with a strong propensity to use hypergamous marriage as an instrument of alliance-building (Kolff 1990). By the second half of the 16th century these conquest states were firmly entrenched in the region and began to evolve into more bureaucratised, hierarchical polities with the ruling Rajput warrior estate becoming more of a closed-status group based on strictly endogamous marriage patterns.

The military idiom of politics that characterised the Rajput clan-kingdoms resulted in high levels of culturally sanctioned armed conflict. This conflict ran along three major fault lines. The first lay within the ruling Rajput clan. At the heart of Rajput political culture there was a permanent tension between countervailing imperatives of kinship and monarchy. Thus a Rajput polity was at once a monarchy ruled over by its Raja and the collective patrimony of the ruling clan. The Raja asserted his royal authority by seeking to reduce his Thakurs (clan-nobles with hereditary *thikana* estates) to the status of dependent feudatories, holding their domains as royal land grants awarded on the basis of a military service obligation. To achieve this objective he would recruit dependent retinues of non-kin warriors to coerce the Thakurs. The latter, for their part, defended their untrammelled possession of their *thikanas* as their share of the original joint conquest enterprise and vigorously asserted their rights of sub-infeudation, constructing local war-bands of their own to resist the Raja's forces. Conversely if the clan monarch was weak, the Thakurs might seek to exercise their own kingship vocation by constructing new dynastic states at the expense of the ruling dynasty or even usurping the throne. This kingship imperative of the Thakurs, however, also limited the possibility of the clan-aristocracy coalescing against their Raja on a long-term basis and made conflict between Thakurs as much a characteristic feature of the Rajput polity as was conflict between them and royal authority.

The second of these major fault lines lay between the Rajputs of the conquest clan and unsubdued segments of the previous ruling communities, whether these were indigenous tribal polities or remnants of earlier warrior incursions into the territory. The limitations of the Rajput heavy cavalry military system, combined with the extreme nature of the topography and climate of the region, meant that the total subjugation of these autochthonous land-controllers was unrealisable. Hence in every Rajput clan-kingdom there were autonomous or semi-autonomous armed enclaves of displaced former ruling communities. They periodically launched plundering raids into the conquered and settled lands of the clan-kingdom, while land-hungry clan warriors often sought to complete the conquest by invading the tribal enclaves and attempting to reduce their populations to dependence (Tod 1987:793–4, 1429–30, 1715–6).

The third fault line along which armed conflict occurred lay between the conquest states. Since territorial expansion was a central obligation of Rajput kingship, warfare between the clan-kingdoms was chronic throughout most of the medieval era, save for the period 1570–1670 CE when the great Mughal emperors were able to impose a precarious peace. There was considerable overlap between this inter-clan warfare and the intra-clan and clan-kingdom/tribal conflicts. Internal dissent was recognised as providing an opportunity for a rival clan-kingdom to invade and inter-clan conflict often stimulated rebellion by the Thakurs or the tribal communities.

These conflicts not only periodically imperilled the survival of the warrior participants in the formal political system, but also constantly threatened to spill over into the productive economy that sustained the whole edifice of the Rajput clan kingdom. The basis of this economy, which was largely in civilian hands, was peasant agriculture, pastoralism and local and long-distance commerce—the region formed part of the southern extension of the Silk Road. In accordance with classical Hindu political theory, the Rajputs as Kṣatriyas had the right to rule and tax this civil population in return for safeguarding them against external threats and administering justice. A major problem for a social order with a military ruling class is the protection of the civilian economic producers from arbitrary violence and excessive taxation at the hands of the warriors. This is particularly the case when the warrior estate is racked by segmental conflicts that are constantly generating crises for the political actors that require the urgent mobilisation of cash or credit resources. In such circumstances the temptation to violate the levels of exaction considered acceptable in the societal 'moral economy' can be overwhelming. Moreover, the rapid changes in fortune characterising such conflicts can also result in the civil population often being subjected to multiple exactions by rival warlords as in medieval Rajasthan.

Since Frederick Barth's pioneering work on the Swat Pathans in the 1950s, political anthropologists have recognised that hierarchical societies with a military idiom of politics, like medieval Rajasthan, need 'moral regulators' to set limits to culturally sanctioned violence (Barth 1959). The honour/shame value system characterising such societies can give rise to self-destructive levels of conflict that threaten the wider social order. Typically the regulators who are called upon in such situations are associated with religious power which is seen as transcending the worldly power embodied in the political/ military system. This invests them with personal inviolability and enables them to impose negotiated settlements on the warring parties.

The role of the Cāraṇas in the moral economy of late-medieval Rajasthan.

In the Rajasthani case the most distinctive moral regulators were the Cāraṇas or bards. While the word itself and the concept of the bard are of great antiquity in Hindu culture, the Cāraṇa caste of the Rajput world is of more recent and obscure origin. They first appear in the early medieval period as a pastoral tribe with the subsidiary occupation of celebrating the exploits of the local warriors in oral narrative poetry. From the 16th century they underwent a major transformation, bifurcating into two streams, one evolving into a sedentary, literate, high-status service-caste of the Rajput aristocracy, the other remaining a semi-nomadic pastoralist community (Campbell 1918:219–20). This development was linked to changes in the nature of Rajput identity—the switch from an open to an endogamous caste status-group model during the period of the partnership with the Mughal Empire (Kolff 1990:72–3). The new Cāraṇa elite validated this transformation by developing written bardic literary genres. Borrowing elements of Muslim historiography encountered at the Mughal court, they transformed their traditional oral narrative genres, the Bhansavali, Khyat and Vigat, into more rigorously documented and chronologically precise clan and lineage histories that invested the claims of exalted ancestry associated with the new Rajput identity with a flavour of authenticity (Kathuria 1987:189). In return, the Rajputs lavished patronage on them, granting them tax-exempt Sāsan tenure landed estates, rewarding their versification with gifts of cash and kind and attaching them to their families as feudal retainers. They were thus incorporated into the circle of castes accepted as being of Kṣatriya *varṇa* and accompanied their Rajput patron into battle, motivating his retinue and taunting his enemies with the appropriate verses (Tod 1987:1654–5).

Although there is still no comprehensive historical study of the Cāraṇas in a Western language, most general historians of the Rajasthan region, from Tod onwards, have acknowledged their role as moral regulators of power. They have, however, universally depicted that regulatory agency as a function of the bardic vocation of the male members of the caste. This is seen as the crucial factor in the two distinct techniques Cāraṇas employed to exert moral pressure on a transgressor: literary censure and the performance of *trāga*, a unique repertoire of self-sacrificial rituals. That the former was a function of their vocation as poet-chroniclers is fairly self-evident, but it is my contention that the self-sacrificial behavioural response was linked with a popular perception of the caste as a religious community standing in a unique relationship to the Devī.

Their regulatory role through literary censure grew out of certain paradoxical features of their vocation as poets. For, if the Cāraṇa was to be fully effective as 'Fame-Spreader' and chronicler, he needed to be perceived as a 'Truth Teller' as well (Vidal 1997:85–108). The corollary of this was that he must be free to expose infamy as well as praise heroism and generosity in his verses. So the reverse side of the Cāraṇa's role of validator of the Rajput clan or lineage's good fame was his role as moral censor, employing the *bhūmd* (lampoon, though the word is stronger, implying a curse) to defame the transgressor. The Cāraṇa was expected to exercise this critical function on his own initiative in circumstances of intolerable violation of the moral order, and there are numerous examples in Rajput history of bardic moral censure of even the most formidable rulers. But he could also be engaged to perform it on behalf of third parties that perceived themselves as having been subjected to illegitimate levels of oppression. Although it is not easy to gauge the deterrent value of the Bardic imprecation in checking the excesses of the warriors (or other social categories of wealth or power, for the Cāraṇas did not restrict their lampoons to Rajputs), one should never underestimate the power of public obloquy with a social order that subscribed to an extreme ideology of honour and shame. Certainly British observers of the colonial period thought it made a material difference:

> They (the Cāraṇas) are credited with being very outspoken and the fear of being portrayed as inverse, cruel or unjust to future generations has often deterred many chiefs from acts of injustice (Shering 1881:133).

Trāga: restoring the moral order by the gift of flesh

The concern of this chapter, however, is chiefly the Cāraṇas' use of distinctive forms of self-sacrificial behaviour to protest against violations of the moral order by the powerful.

According to a Hindu story, the first Cāraṇa was created by Lord Śiva to tend his herd of four animals of incongruous disposition—a lion, a serpent, a cow and goat. The lion attacked the cow and the serpent attacked the lion, but the herdsman by the gift of some of the flesh of his arm quieted them and brought them safe to Mahadev who, in reward, gave him the name of Cāraṇa (Grazier).

According to the court Cāraṇa of Lunavada state, the Cāraṇas were originally superhuman spirit beings ranking 'with the Siddhis and the Vidyadharis'. In time, like certain other angelic classes, the Cāraṇas settled on earth and became bards of kings and chiefs (Campbell 1918:214).

The complex of Cāraṇa acts of self-harm, collectively known as *trāga*, was arguably the most extreme expression of the central Hindu and Jain belief in the efficacy of self-suffering as a means of redressing moral anomalies in the public and private realms. Unlike the passive techniques of self-suffering employed by Brāhmans, *sannyasis* and Jain monks—mainly variants of fasting—*trāga* involved a direct, physically active approach to the process, in keeping with the Cāraṇa claim to Kṣatriya status. Individuals or communities subjected to violence or economic oppression transgressing societal moral limits at the hands of a ruler or magnate could engage a Cāraṇa to intercede for them. The Cāraṇa would present their grievances to the offender, accompanied by a demand for redress. If this were not forthcoming, the Cāraṇa would begin to perform *trāga* outside the transgressor's residence. In the first stage the Cāraṇa would either seek to intercede or slash his own forearm with his dagger. This was usually enough to produce a settlement, but, if the transgressor remained obdurate, he would proceed to slicing off parts of his body—fingers, toes, ears etc—which would be flung into the grounds of the target's residence. Continued recalcitrance would lead to the infliction of ever more serious wounds and ultimately to self-slaughter, accompanied by a curse (the Cāraṇa's dying curse was greatly feared as it included a threat to return as a malevolent ghost to haunt its target.) Then other members of the dead Cāraṇa's family would continue the *trāga* until the offender capitulated. In cases where Cāraṇas were performing *trāga* to defend their own community, the response could be overwhelming, with whole families or lineages killing their children and old people and stabbing themselves to death. Sir John Malcolm, who served in Rajput Malwa in the early 19th century, wrote of

> collecting a number of well authenticated cases not only of individuals but of families (performing *Trāga*); and in two instances I found that the Cāraṇa inhabitants of a village had sacrificed themselves. On one occasion there was a string of four people with a spear through their necks. Instances of people dipping their clothes in oil, setting fire to them and dancing in the flames until they were burnt to ashes were not uncommon (Campbell 1918:17).

The target of most of the cases of *trāga* that we have information about was a ruler or his deputy, but it could be directed against a Thakur, a tribal or bandit chief or a great merchant or banker—anyone with power that could be abused. While it is not clear whether all social categories could engage the services of a Cāraṇa for *trāga,* the example of the Valivas, the Cāraṇa caravan escorts mentioned below, suggests that the transaction was fairly widely available in the Rajput world. The Valivas were quite prepared to hire out their services 'which included an implicit undertaking to perform *trāga* if the caravan was attacked', even to Muslim and European merchants travelling in Rajasthan (Vidal 1997:94). As the latter indicates, there was clearly a cash nexus in the arrangement, perhaps in the form of a gift like that applicable to bardic poetic services.

The Cāraṇas' capacity for *trāga* spawned a multitude of ancillary intercessional services. They became the preferred guarantors of political settlements, safe conduct arrangements (a very common transaction, given the nature of the Rajput political process), business deals and personal loans. In a particularly bizarre spin-off, some Cāraṇas became Valivas, professional caravan escorts. If a caravan was threatened by bandits—whether of the authentic criminal variety or Thakurs, Jagirdars or tribal bands exercising the brigandage idiom of feudal politics—the Cāraṇa escort would take his knife to his arm and threaten *trāga* (Tod 1987:1654–55; Campbell 1918:217). Indeed, in some parts of Rajasthan, the Cāraṇa pastoralist communities took advantage of this capacity to deter banditry through *trāga* to become important goods and grain carriers in their own right. They were also much in demand as messengers and go-betweens, practically monopolising communications between Rajas and Thakurs and tribal chiefs.

Another dimension of their intercessory function was their use of their *sāsan jagirs* and *orāns* (sacred grounds of the temples of Cāraṇī Devīs), as sanctuaries for individuals or communities in conflict with the ruler. Besides providing asylum, these enclaves doubled as safe storage centres for the moveable property of fugitives. Bardic landed estates and temples were not the only such extra-judicial sites, but they were regarded as the safest places of refuge because their custodians could defend them by performing *trāga* (Paul 1993:58–60).

The Cāraṇas' capacity to exert moral pressure through *trāga* has generally been associated with their bardic vocation. While not seeking to dispute that this made a contribution, I believe that the main source of their self-sacrificial power lay elsewhere. Studies of the practice of exercising moral authority through self-suffering behaviour portray it as the province of religious specialists like the Brāhmans, *bhakti* sectarians or Jain monastics and *sannyasis*. Their ritually pure or world-renunciatory lifestyles validate their claim to act on behalf of a higher religious power that has priority over secular political power. At first sight it would seem incongruous for Cāraṇas to be in this company since they are meat-eaters and warriors like their Rajput patrons. Nevertheless, it is quite clear that in Rajasthan, Rajput Gujarat and Malwa they were perceived as having a religious status. This can be seen from the fact they shared the legal privileges of the religious specialists. Their landed estates, like Brāhman landholdings, were tax-exempt and outside the ruler's jurisdiction. At court they were absolved from presenting *nazrana*, the feudal cash offering incumbent on all secular courtiers (Kathuria 1987:189). Above all they shared the Brāhman's privilege of personal inviolability, save for when they were fulfilling their warrior role on the battlefield.

But in the Rajput world ritual purity was not the only basis of religious status. In the Śākta religious culture prevalent amongst the crucial Rajput and tribal segments of that society, the sanctity of a community was defined by its relationship to the goddess, not the avoidance of ritual pollution. Thus the Cāraṇas were perceived as a sacred caste because they were believed to enjoy the Devī's special esteem, a connection that was aptly summed up by the title they gave themselves—Devīputras (literally, Sons of the Devī). It was this religious status of the Cāraṇas that gave *trāga* its moral force. To cause injury or death to people of such sanctity by remaining obdurate in the face of their demands for moral redress was a particularly gross form of sacrilege. It is important to emphasise that all Cāraṇas were regarded as Devīputras, not just those who served as bards. Significantly participation in *trāga* was also not confined to them; all members of the caste were eligible for the ritual.

What I want to argue in the concluding section of the paper is that the Cāraṇas' capacity to exercise the moral regulation of power through the practice of *trāga* stemmed from the belief, in traditional Rajasthani religious culture, that it was the Cāraṇa incarnations of the Devī who were the guardians of the moral order in the western region of Śakti (Śaktipīṭha), a territory roughly coterminous with the Rajput world.

The Cāraṇī Devīs in the Rajput world of Śakti

> Lord Śiva decided to send his Cāraṇa herdsman into the world to teach justice to the unruly Kṣatriyas. But the bard was a devotee of Pārvatī and was reluctant to leave her. On learning this, Pārvatī promised that if he complied with Mahadev's command, she would always be born into his race when she chose to enter the world as an *avatāra*. Since then there have been incarnations of the goddess in every generation of Cāraṇīs (Cāraṇa story related to the author by Professor Sohan Dan Cāraṇa (1987)).

The Cāraṇas' status as Devīputras derived from the remarkable theophany encapsulated in this traditional account of the origins of the Cāraṇī living goddess institution. It endowed Cāraṇa women with the unique privilege of being the chosen vehicles for the Devī's periodic human incarnations. This belief in a particular caste being the natural site for the incarnation of the Goddess is not, to my knowledge, found anywhere else in the Hindu world. It is certainly not the case in Nepal, the other region in the Indian subcontinent with a prominent living goddess institution. What is equally remarkable is that the belief is given credence by most Hindus involved in the worship of the Devī, not just by the Cāraṇas, though the Cāraṇas subscribe to it with especial vehemence. Indeed tribal villagers do not confine their reverence to the acknowledged living goddesses and the historical *Pūrṇa Avatāras*, but view all Cāraṇīs as potential Devīs (Tambs-Lyche 1999:64). As a British scholar official in Gujarat early in the last century observed:

> They (Cāraṇīs) are supposed to have supernatural power and in Kachh are even now addressed by the lower classes as Mother or Goddess Mother (Campbell 1918:216).

But it was not just the fact that they were members of a caste peculiarly favoured by the Devī that gave the Cāraṇas the religious status that underpinned their use of *trāga* as an instrument for restoring the moral order. The nature and function of the Goddesses incarnated amongst their womenfolk also contributed to the perception that they were uniquely suited to the role of moral regulators.

In Rajasthani Devī religion the Cāraṇī goddesses, popularly called Sagats, occupy an intermediate space between the great tradition Purāṇic Devīs that the region shares with the rest of Hindu India and the goddesses specific to particular communities like the Kuladevīs of the Rajput clans and the Devīs of 'lineage, locality and disease' of the tribal villages. While the latter are acknowledged to be emanations of the universal *śakti* principle, they only become alive and active in the world when they respond to an invocation from an individual or group associated with a kin-body or localised community bound to them by specific ties of tutelage. The Cāraṇī Devīs, by way of contrast, transcend the boundary between the private and public realms. Although they can be invoked by individuals and families for aid in personal crises, they also play a role in the wider political and social order and are accessible to the Hindu community as a whole, not just to particular local or kin constituencies. There are two categories of Cāraṇī goddesses: Khan Avatāra Sagats (limited incarnations); and Pūrṇa Avatāra Sagats (incarnations with the full powers of the Devī). The former are expected to occur in every generation of Cāraṇīs and thus constitute a living goddess institution comparable with the *kumāri* phenomenon in Nepal. But, whereas the Kumāris are prepubescent girls who lose their divine status with the onset of puberty, the Khan Avatāra Sagats are adult women who remain goddesses across their lifetime. Moreover, they are expected to assert their own divinity in contrast to the Kumāris who are usually selected by their relatives. While they are sometimes recognised as children, the Sagat's actual assumption of her divine status generally occurs around the time she becomes eligible for marriage. This is, of course, a problematic occasion as the Devī is both divine mother and virgin. So recognition as a Sagat commits the new goddess to a lifetime of celibacy, a state which is, however, not necessarily incompatible with a form of ceremonial marriage. In exchange, she is released from the restrictions of *purdah* and can now participate in the public 'male' realm, a transition that is sometimes marked by her adopting male dress and becoming, in Marwari vernacular, a Mardana Sagat. Once her divinity is acknowledged, the Sagat sets up, or is set up in, a shrine and commences her mission. This involves granting *darśan* to pilgrims and performing spiritual services for petitioners. The services performed by the current Khan Avatāra Sagats (there can be multiple incarnations per generation) are mostly concerned with healing and counsel, such as those performed by the Rajput Kuladevīs and the tribal lineage and locality Devīs, and not with the moral regulation of power in the formal political system (Paul 1993:50–2). But the power dynamics of the contemporary democratic political system are so different to those of the medieval Rajput polity that this may not tell us very much about the way Khan Avatāra Sagats functioned in the past. It is certainly not unknown, even today, for politicians and social reformers to solicit their endorsement (Sohan Dan Cāraṇa 1987).

With the other category of Cāraṇī Devī, the Pūrṇa Avatāra Sagats, there is no doubt whatever about their involvement in the moral regulation of power. Indeed it could be said to be their principal function. They are messianic incarnations, the *śakti* counterparts to the Vaisnavite *avatāras*, and, like them, they appear only when the moral order is profoundly threatened. Their advents are recorded in the Lok Devī, a chronological *avatāra* sequence that resembles the better known Daśa Avatāra of Vaisnavism. As in Vaisnavism, the very early incarnations are located in such a remote and shadowy chronological epoch that they can be safely relegated to the mythological rather than the historical realm, but the majority appeared in the period between the 9th and 16th centuries CE when the Rajput clan conquest states were established. Significantly there has been no advent of a Pūrṇa Avatāra in recent centuries, a fact that explains, perhaps, why one

European scholar actually categorises them as 'Medieval Devīs' (Tambs Lyche 1999/2004:60).

The crisis in the moral order that each of these messianic Cāraṇī Devīs is depicted as resolving invariably relates to a conflict between a transgressive warrior ruler and his subjects. Often the ruler is characterised as a demonic, recalcitrant figure that has to be destroyed by the goddess in order to restore the moral order. In other instances she affects reconciliation between the warrior chieftain and his subjects, conferring divine legitimacy on his dynasty in return for his acceptance of specified moral restraints on the exercise of his power. A third scenario involves her mediating a peace settlement in a protracted, self-destructive armed conflict between warrior states.

A useful illustration of these moral regulatory activities associated with the Pūrṇa Avatāra Sagats is provided by the career of Karṇī Mātā, a Devī who was active in the arid north-west of Rajasthan in the 15th century CE Arguably the most widely venerated of all Cāraṇī Devīs, she founded a temple complex 30 kilometres south-east of Bikaner, at Deshnoke, which has become one of the most important sacred centres in the Marwari linguistic-culture region. The narrative of her life intersects in so much detail with the key events in the formative period of the two great Rathod warrior-clan states, Jodhpur and Bikaner, that we can fairly safely infer that she was a real historical personage, unlike some of her more historically remote precursors perhaps. There is a strong moral regulatory flavour to both the *dicta* and the miracles attributed to her. Thus one of her earliest statements of her mission, delivered when she was still a child (but already recognised as a goddess by some of her co-villagers), announced that

> she had come into the world to apprise the rulers and Jagirdars of their duty which is presently being neglected by them, and as a result of that they are engaged in torturing their innocent public (Ghadavi 1983:165).

Her first major *parcha* (miracle, an act that defined a Pūrṇa Avatāra's unlimited power) was, appropriately enough, the miraculous slaying of Rao Kanha, the tyrannical Rathod overlord of the Sankla territory in the Jangal Desh region in the north-western corner of Rajasthan. His offence was to attempt to bar her congregation from watering their livestock at the public wells in the Deshnoke sub-region that she had divined as the site for her temple complex (Ujwal 1972:45–7). This was an act that could be seen as symbolic of the predatory disdain initially displayed by the Rathod conquerors towards the autochthonous communities of the Thar desert margin. In a second miracle she secured a peace settlement between the formidable Rathod adventurer, Rao Bika, who was seeking to construct a kingdom encompassing the entire Jangal Desh, and Rao Sekha, the ruler of the native Bhatti Rajput principality of Pugal in the western extremity of the region. The keystone of the arbitration was a marriage between Bika and Sekha's daughter which Karṇī Mātā was able to facilitate by miraculously rescuing the Bhatti chief from sultanate captivity (Ujwal 1972:87–91). She is also credited with presiding over the moral-cum-legal arrangements that secured the peaceful submission of the Jat pastoralist clans, the dominant indigenous land-controllers, to Bika's suzerainty. Finally, it was her personal demarcation of the contested frontier between Bikaner and the parent Bhatti kingdom of Jaisalmer that brought to an end the long cycle of ruinous warfare between the Rathod invaders and the native Rajputs (Tambs-Lyche 1999/2004:71).

The alternation of retributional violence with peacemaking and even marriage-broking in these miracles demonstrates the aptness of Tamb-Lyche's observation that the Pūrṇa Avatāra Sagats embody both the terrible and the benign aspects of the Devī Māhātmya version of the goddess (Tamb-Lyche 1999/2004:64). This duality is as essential to their role as guardians of the moral order in the Rajput world as it is to her role as defender of the cosmic order. Their terrible guise is necessary to deal with warriors, like Rao Khana, who refuse to accept any moral limitations on their exercise of their military power. But the Sagat's destructive power is always deployed in the service of the wider moral order and never selfishly. So Karṇī, for example, does not destroy Rathod warlords like Rao Bika and Rao Jodha who are prepared to subordinate their power to moral imperatives. On the contrary she displays her benign side to them, assisting their legitimate Kṣatriya empire-building ambitions, in return for their respect for the dignity and economic subsistence of the conquered population. It is instructive to contrast this moral regulatory role of the Sagats with the modus operandi of the Rajput Kuladevīs. The latter rewards the clan warriors for their sacrifice in battle and the clan womenfolk for their sacrifice for the family (Harlan 2003). But, although this may serve the interests of the particular warrior-clan, it does not contribute to the welfare of the wider society.

It was their kinship with these formidable Cāraṇī Devīs, identified with the preservation of the moral order in the heroic, semi-legendary historical epoch when the Rajput warrior-clan kingdoms came into being, that made the Cāraṇas the natural moral regulators of power in the subsequent late medieval period. As mentioned earlier, there are no advents of Pūrṇa Avatāra Sagats after the 16th century CE, though the appearance of Khan Avatāra

Sagats has continued down to the present. Despite the high incidence of internal conflict analysed in the first section of this chapter, the Rajput clan kingdoms of the late medieval period were fundamentally stable entities; after 1700 CE no major new states emerged and nor were any expunged. Consequently the abuses of power generated by these conflicts were more quotidian than apocalyptic and could be regulated by the human descendants of the Cāraṇī Devīs, the bards. However, the relative importance of the religious status component in validating the bard's moral regulator function can be gauged from the fact that, amongst the members of the caste, it was the Cāraṇa *pujaris* of the temples dedicated to the Pūrṇa Avatāra Sagats who were regarded as the most effective intercessors for the oppressed. Even a ruler as powerful as the redoubtable Abhai Singh of Jodhpur could be discomfited by the censure of the Deepawat Cāraṇa *pujari* of Karṇī Mātā's temple at Deshnoke (Ujwal 1972:115).

It is paradoxical that it was the male bards who inherited the Cāraṇī Devī's moral regulatory function, not the Cāraṇīs who were the actual vehicles for the goddess's incarnation. The most likely explanation of this is that it reflects the patriarchalisation of bardic society that accompanied the adoption, by their Rajput patrons, of a strictly endogamous status group model in the late medieval period. This seems to have been the time when the Cāraṇa communities close to the courts of the major Rajasthani warrior clan kingdoms embraced *purdah*. Certainly when we look at those centres of bardic regulation, the great medieval Cāraṇī Devī temples, we find that there was still some female agency in the operational procedure of the earliest of them. In the Mewar Cāraṇī Devī temple at Nahra Magra, for example, the interpretation of the will of the goddess was determined by Cāraṇī oracular priestesses (Tod 1987:341). But in the Deshnoke Karṇī Mātā temple, one of the later centres to emerge, the interpretation of the Devī's will and the administration of the complex have, since her transfiguration, been firmly in the hands of the Deepawat Cāraṇa *pujaris*, the male descendants of Karṇī's husband through his co-wife. Of course this transference of the Cāraṇī Devīs' regulatory function to the Cāraṇas also owed much to the refinement and formalisation of the bardic literary vocation, which coincided with the patriarchal transformation of the caste. It is, nevertheless, entirely possible that the Khan Avatāra Sagats, whose incarnations have continued down to the present day, did sometimes act in the moral regulatory role in the late medieval period, but, to my knowledge, the only instances of such activities by Cāraṇī Devīs in that era are posthumous miracles of the Pūrṇa Avatāra Sagats.

Epilogue

The onset of colonial rule fatally undermined the intercessory role of the Cāraṇas in the Rajput world. In those parts of that world that were incorporated into British India, the decline was swift. *Trāga* was criminalised, the bards stripped of their religious privileges and tax-free landholdings. By the turn of the 19th century, British bureaucrats were describing the Cāraṇas, chillingly, as a 'failing caste' (Campbell 1918:222). In Rajasthan, where the Rajput kingdoms were not annexed but brought under indirect British control via hegemonic treaties of alliance, the decline was slower but just as inexorable. The British threw their unprecedented military power behind the Rajas enabling them to suppress local sovereignties. They also pressured the Rajas into adopting legal and tax regimes harmonising with those operating in British India. These developments led to a decline in the demand for bardic intercessory services, even where the rulers declined to outlaw *trāga* and abolish their privileges. The slow but steady indoctrination of the Rajas and Thakurs with Western cultural values, combined, of course, with the enforced peace, produced a waning of the demand for bardic heroic poetry. With the Rajput lions becoming tame bureaucrats and civilian landlords, there was no longer any need for their Cāraṇa 'herders'.

chapter nine

Songs in the presence of Mammai Mātājī

Effy George

The village of Ordar is situated half a kilometre from the Arabian Sea on the western coast of the Saurashtran Peninsula, in the state of Gujarat. On the western periphery of the village, nearest the sea, is the caste neighbourhood of about 100 Sorathiya Rabari families, a pastoralist Hindu community.[1] Sited amongst them is the Ordar Mādh, a distinctive flat-roof temple for the worship of Mammai Mātājī (figure 1). The Rabaris believe her to be the supreme deity, the beginning and end of the cosmos, a great goddess beyond space, time and all dualities (even gender). Since the establishment of the *mādh* in the late 18th century, it has also become a pilgrimage site for many individuals from other Hindu castes. They come to take *darśan* of the goddess, as well as to seek blessings from the Rabaris' spiritual patriarch and matriarch, the Bhuwa Atta and Bhuwi Ma.

Figure 1: Ordar Mādh.

The greatest homage (*mahāpūjā*) to Mammai Mātājī is the ten-day celebration called Punj, which coincides with the Gujarati festival of Nav Ratri (nine nights). Punj can occur annually, but is only ever held if the spiritual portents are favourable. In 1989 nearly 100,000 attended Punj at Ordar; almost all were Rabaris. It was the first Punj held at Ordar for 12 years. Women usually assemble around the periphery of the crowd, whilst the men occupy a central position closer to the *mādh*, the Bhuwa Atta, the Bhuwi Ma and the formal rituals. There are periods though when this geographical separation is substantially blurred by a cacophony of many thousand voices, Rabari men chanting *sarju*, a mantra to Mammai, and Rabari women singing songs in praise of her.

In this chapter I will discuss these devotional songs by Rabari women. I will focus on the dynamic contexts in which they are performed, especially at Punj, but also on the occasions of Chelāṇ and Kalaś, rituals performed by one or more patrilines in homage to Mammai Mātājī, or as fulfilment of a personal *māntā* (a vow). What is initially apparent in these contexts is that Rabari women's songs confirm the truism that Indian women express their deep religiosity in a very personal way. In fact, the singing of Mammai songs in a group adds to the spiritual ecstasy experienced by every individual, and a study of the lyrics and performances shows that they articulate far more than just patricentric notions of devotion. These songs are a deliberate means of effecting the presence of the sublime.[2]

The soundscape

> By shifting the voice, by introducing many voices we move from simple first person narrative to dramatic narrative, a hundred voices and perspectives on the same idea, note, pause, silence...(Rao 1990:34).

Vidya Rao's description of the musical textures created by women *thumri* singers resonates conceptually with those created by Sorathiya Rabari women during the performance of devotional songs to Mammai Mātājī. Referring to Victor Turner's concept of texturing (Turner 1974), Rao comments, 'all forms and styles of singing employ some degree of texturing which brings into play different "voices"—a kind of polyphony' (Rao 1990:33). The effects of such polyphony are intensely perceptible during the performance of Rabari religious rituals. In fact, the musical textures created by individual song leaders through subtle shifts of voice tonality, syllabic distortion and rhythmic improvisation connect melodiously with those created by other female singers and with those formed by Rabari men chanting *sarju*. The musical space woven by these textures is a 'field' within which Rabari women's *bhakti* (devotion) to Mammai Mātājī 'finds shape' (Sangari 1990:1464).[3]

The warp and weft of this musical space are akin to what Paul Stoller termed a phenomenology of space; 'observers and/or social actors are no longer in space, but constitute it through the dynamic actions of their consciousness' (Stoller 1989:62). In short, Rabari women's devotional songs and their experiential field as female *bhaktas* are the conduit for connecting to and summoning the goddess Mammai.

The words

Rabari women are deeply religious and express this disposition through 'active religious worship' (Wadley 1977:126). Rabari women regularly propitiate their conjugal *kuladevi* (lineage goddess), *pitru jute* (ancestors) and regionally prevalent gods and goddesses from the Hindu pantheon, as well as their own great *sants* (female saints). Their devotional singing (in chorus), however, is only for Mammai Mātājī and is performed only during rituals propitiating Her.

What is initially striking about these songs is that there is never a description of Mammai Mātājī. There is only a rare mention of her name. In this Mammai Mātājī as supreme deity remains nameless in a sacred space. Even so, it is common for Rabari women to utter Mammai Mātājī's name during the course of their day, something like Greek Orthodox women, who use the phrase 'praise the Virgin Mary' routinely throughout the day. Older Rabari women, especially, were of the view that good fortune for themselves[4] and their family was inextricably linked to the daily grace bestowed on them by Mammai. One can say that one grows into religion and, thereby, for elderly Rabari women, ever closer to the goddess. Nonetheless, this still does not explain why there is no mention of Mammai Mātājī in contemporary devotional songs.

Indeed, the following verses from a Rabari marriage song (not a devotional song), translated by the Indian sociologist BL Mankad during the 1930s, are from one of only two instances of the mention of Mammai Mātājī, both recorded by Mankad, that I have come across other than in my own field notes;

> I ask, what good deeds our bride must have done, due to which she has been fortunate to get such a father-in-law and mother-in-law.
>
> Yes she has been to worship Bileshwar in the Barda hills.[5]
>
> It is due to that that she has got such a worthy father-in-law and mother-in-law.

> I ask, what austerities she must have performed that she has been so fortunate to get a husband, Mesurbhai.
>
> She has been to worship Goddess Mammai. It is due to that she is able to secure him as her husband (Mankad 1939:66).

The narrative asks what has the bride done to marry into such a good family, and this is answered by mentioning some of the auspicious pilgrimages she has made. In this sense Mammai's name is a metonym for the *mādh* (temple). Other than this nothing is revealed except that her visit to the *mādh* has brought blessings from Mammai.

The song also highlights the great value placed on asceticism as a means of devotion, and that individual women can have a personal relationship with the goddess. However I do not wish to emphasise the presence of individualism, as requests to the goddess are more typically a desire for the good fortune of kin and others.

The action

The Rabaris' three major religious rituals (Punj, Kalaś and Chelāṇ)[6] involve some sort of austerity on the part of the devotee (expressions of adjustment, such as fasting or some other form of abstention from typical daily activity). More generally, austerities are undertaken as part of a *māntā*. The primary aim of *māntās* is to initiate a closer connection with Mammai Mātājī in order to fulfil a worldly desire.

Amongst older Rabari women, *māntās* involve lengthy periods of fasting and rigorous forms of self-sacrifice. For almost a month, Ramiben Kodiyatar, who is in her early 70s, performed the ritual *daṇḍavat praṇām*. Each day she made her way from her home to Mammai Mātājī's *mādh*, a distance of 400 metres, taking one step and then prostrating herself, bending on her knees and touching her forehead to the ground. This action is indicative of utter submission. She would do this until she reached the *mādh* (figure 2), which she would enter to take *darśan* in front of Mammai's *sthapna* (location).

Ramiben undertook this *māntā* with the hope of fulfilling her son's desire for a child and her desire to be a grandmother. When her *māntā* was fulfilled some months later, she and her son performed *nived* morning and night, offering fruit and sweetmeats at the *kuldevi mandir* (lineage goddess temple). For Mammai had granted a boon to the patrilineage.

Figure 2: Taking Darśan, Ordar Mādh.

Ritual Song 1, Punj

We have received sixteen head cloths from the great town.
They are not to be compared with others (head cloths),
For they are the best of their kind.
They are soft, so nice, so glossy, so well woven.
Mammai Mātā's names are woven in them.
Only the devotees can voice and decipher them.
We have received sixteen head cloths from the great town.
They are not to be compared with others (head cloths)
For they are the best of their kind.
One cannot say whether their warp and the weft
are of silk or cotton, gold, or silver.
Such dexterous hands and fingers weave them
that it is difficult for anyone to say for certain what it means.
Blessed are the cloth makers,
Blessed are those that bring them,
And blessed more blessed than all (Mephabhai) is Bhuwa,
who offers them to Mātājī (Mankad 1939:69)

Translated by Mankad in the 1930s and still sung today by Rabari women of the Ordar *parāṭh*,[7] this song differs only slightly from the version I recorded in 1991 and in 1998. The most important difference is that I never heard the use of Mammai's name, rather simply the less specific term Mātājī was always used. The song refers to the *pāghaḍi* (scarf) tied upon the head of the Rabari's *dharma guru* (spiritual leader), the Bhuwa Atta, prior to his performance of *pat chadwu* (to climb the sacred stool)[8] which he does at all three types of religious rituals. During the performance of this ritual, the Bhuwa is possessed by Mammai and radiates her divine presence to those gathered to receive her blessing (figure 3). Rabaris say the ritual *pāghaḍi bharavvu* (to give a *pāghaḍi*) signifies a gift of love to Mammai Mātājī. This helps contextualise the last lines of the song; 'and blessed more blessed than all (Mephabhai) Bhuwa who offers them to Mātājī'.

The literalness of the refrain tells us that the *pāghaḍi* came from great cloth makers and a great town, a place of status. However, these details become less concrete and dissolve under the weight of the coded descriptions of Mammai Mātājī in the other three verses. Rabari 'devotees only can voice them and decipher them' (Mammai Mātājī's name) and, even then, 'it is difficult for anyone to say for certain what it means'. This gives a glimpse of the nature of the devotional act, the drowning in the sublime, that which is 'beyond descriptive semantics' (Mishra 1998:20). But the quality of certitude does not extend to feeling and experiencing Mammai Mātājī during devotional acts. Devotees come ever closer to Mammai, but not in her entirety. For the absolute sublime 'remains a goal, a desired end rather than an experiential state' (Mishra 1998:21)—bliss, but not absolute bliss (*cidānanda*).

Rabari women's coded language, as well as the detail that Mammai Mātājī can only be embodied by name, suggests that she has no form and, therefore, that any attempt to anthropomorphise her leads the devotee to the indescribable. Much like the woven cloth referred to in the song, there is no definition to her 'warp and weft.' She has no *mūrti* (idol); just her name and her symbols (such as conch, peacock and swan) index the omnipotent.

Figure 3: The Bhuwa Atta and his son perform Pat Chadwu on the day of Punj, Ordar Mādh, 1989.

Rabari *Bhaktas*

The Rabaris consider themselves Mammai Mātājī *bhaktas* (devotees). Each *bhakta* has a particular experience of the goddess, 'which is incommensurate with that of others' (Hancock 1995:85). This 'personal encounter' with the goddess takes different forms, especially amongst Rabari *bhagats* (holy persons), like the Bhuwa Atta and his wife the Bhuwi, who are viewed as having a closer relationship with the goddess. For the Bhuwa Atta, this is a result of divine selection and, consequently, he is endowed with special capabilities (the ability to be possessed by Mammai Mātājī). By contrast the Bhuwi, by virtue of her marriage, symbolically occupies her position as a blessed consort. Even though the Bhuwa assumes supreme importance in formal public rituals and the administering of particular rites, in the event of his absence from the *mādh* the Bhuwi will receive visitors and conduct *darśan*. Most Rabaris also claim that the Bhuwi can become possessed and perform acts of divination, but I did not observe this.

In the Saurashtran region, most characterise Mammai *bhagats* by the austerities they practise in order to continue their life of devotion and service to other devotees as teachers or ritual celebrants. In a limited sense, and despite significant differences, the *bhagats*' devotion to Mammai Mātājī is evocative of the brahmanic conception of the *sannyāsin*, a renouncer.[9]

Rabari *bhagats* (and others) operate within *māyā*. In fact, this seemingly irreconcilable contradiction between the renouncer and the 'man [sic] in the world' in orthodox Hinduism is what characterised *bhakti* as a revolutionary religious movement after the 12th century.[10] For 'a personal encounter' between the devotee and god (Mishra 1998:106) was no longer the sole confine of the celibate ascetic, but accessible to all regardless of one's caste, gender or the degree to which they removed themselves from *māyā*.

In the region, there are no female Mammai *bhagats*, other than the Bhuwi, although there are female *bhagats* from other sects and castes. Female *bhagats* can also be referred to as Bhuwi Ma, a suffix denoting respect ('mother').

Rabari *bhaktas* such as Ramiben undertake great austerities and self-sacrifice, which, like those of Rabari *bhagats*, are directed towards a goal. A *bhakta*'s goal, however, is usually to affect something of this world, not to abandon it. Therefore, the austerities that a Rabari *bhakta* takes on as part of a *māntā*, be it for alleviating sickness afflicting their livestock or a suffering child, or (as in the case of Ramiben) for the birth of a grandson, entail the renunciation of worldly things in order to control or change this world (*māyā*). Rabaris also say that certain *sarjus* can effect change as well. The learning of *sarju* by male initiates also involves severe austerities and many personal sacrifices, but the act is undertaken without desire for things of this world.

The Bhuwa Atta and the Bhuwi, like other Rabari *bhagats*, do not abandon family and social life. Nevertheless, Rabaris invariably highlight the Bhuwa's and the Bhuwi's asceticism, which they see as characterised by long periods spent in religious devotion rather than familial affairs or the daily chores of ordinary Rabaris. This distinction signifies for them that Bhuwi Ma and the Bhuwa Atta are not only closer to Mammai, but also straddle this world and the heavens.

Rabari women's *Bhakti*: ascribed *dharma*

The nature of women's *dharma* is routinely narrated through the origin myth of the first Rabari man, Raykā. This myth also serves to situate the caste's genealogy, cosmology, social status, and *dharma*. In the myth, the divine protagonists are Lord Śaṅkara and the Goddess Sāmuṇḍā.[11] The narrative centres on an immediate earthly conundrum concerning a rogue camel wreaking havoc in a temple garden and a recalcitrant old ghost living in a dead tree trunk. Eventually Śaṅkara and Sāmuṇḍā resolve to create Raykā. Sāmuṇḍā created a male body from her own side, whilst Śaṅkara gave life to him by implanting the ghost's *jiv* (anima).[12] Raykā's *dharma* in *māyā* was to tame the rogue camel and to do likewise with other livestock—to be a shepherd. Śaṅkara also provided an *apsara* (celestial dancer) to be Raykā's wife.

The duty of the *apsara* (Rai, that is, the first Rabari woman) was to assure the continuity and wellbeing of the lineage while Raykā looked after the livestock. These worldly roles of Raykā and Rai parallel that of Śaṅkara and Sāmuṇḍā, both pairs symbolising the fundamental gendering of the cosmos and by extension the explicit duality of Rabari metaphysics.[13] Like Sāmuṇḍā, Rabari women are born to bear whilst in *māyā*.

At the end of the myth, Rai bears four daughters and they, in turn, enter into hypergamous marriages with four Rajputs. Their progeny (male sons) produced the first four *śākhā* (branches) of Rabaris. Hence, Rabaris believe they are born with the karmic qualities of Rajputs and it is this which characterises their *ātman*. However, a woman's body, the basis for her gendered *dharma*, does not prevent (although it constrains) either her communication with the divine or the ability to obtain *mokṣa*.

Punj

Rituals enact myth and, by participating in them throughout life, one is imbued with Mammai *dharma*, her stories and their philosophy. The force of this mode of participatory devotion becomes most evident prior to and during Mammai's *mahā pūjā* (greatest homage), Punj.

Ritual Song 2, Punj

Ordar *Mādh* has doors of gold.

Sarman Bhuwa is regally sitting on the silver *bajot*, *Manaraj*.

Sarman Bhuwa is possessed by Mātājī.

Give invitations to Ordar city, *Manaraj*.

Brave Chelāṇ men are decorated with *gulal*.[14]

Send a loping camel to Junagadh, *Manaraj*.

This song sung prior to the Bhuwa Atta's performance of *pat chadwu* invokes the participatory character of Rabari *bhakti*. Invitations are sent out, men's faces and clothes are sprinkled with *gulal*, messages are conveyed to other *parāṭhs* and preparations begin for the enactment of Mammai Mātājī's *pūjā*.

The celebration of Punj is initiated solely by Mammai Mātājī's desire to do so, and her will is conveyed to the Bhuwa Atta every year during *Aso Sud* (first half of October).[15] If celebrated, Punj corresponds with the festival of *Nav Ratri* (nine nights), which is auspicious to all Hindus and honours *śakti*, the feminine principle of the cosmos. During this ten-day period, all Hindus participate; thus towns and villages large and small become spectacular visual and auditory enchantments.

Amidst this communal celebration, it is not hard to notice the high presence of Rabaris (especially men). On buses, lorries or on foot, they stop at crossroads and roadside pavements to drink tea or to greet and chat with other Rabaris. Men in *chorano* (pantaloon trousers), *āṅgaḍi* (short waist coat) and *pāghaḍi*, and women in *kilkāpaḍu* (highly decorated backless bodice) and *perṇu* (red wrap skirt) with their luggage, are covered in *gulal*; all eventually to make their way to Ordar *Mādh* for the celebration of Punj (figure 4).

In years when Punj is to be celebrated in full, groups of four to five young male *samekhiyās* (Rabari messengers) head off on the first day (decision day) of Punj to inform other Rabaris. Covered in *gulal*, carrying a *morpicchi dhajā* (bundle of peacock feathers) and chanting *sarju*, *samekhiyās* travel on foot to regional villages or other *parāṭhs*, some covering a distance of more than 300 kilometres. The *samekhiyās* return to the *mādh* eight days later on the morning of Punj. In fact, their entrance through the gateway of the *mādh*'s compound with the Bhuwa Atta constitutes the start of the ritual of Punj. This ritual is called Welcoming the *Dhajā (*flag). Just prior to the arrival of the *samekhiyās*, groups of men representing the five other *mādhs*, each headed by a *dhol* (drum) player, enter the gateway waving a *morpichhi dhajā* and chant *sarju*, proceeding towards the *mādh* to take *darśan*. These groups are heralded by a Mir (a Muslim and a traditional musician who is paid for his services) playing *śaraṇai*.

Figure 4: Men and women arrive for Punj.

Already assembled in the *mādh*'s compound, a few older women join Bhuwi Ma in a room adjacent to the *mādh*, while young women, adolescent girls, and female children line the periphery of the buildings adjoining the *mādh*. Men converge closest to the *mādh*, whilst *agewans* (male elders), *kuldevi* Bhuwas, *padhiyārs* (ritual specialists who assist the Bhuwa), Rabari *bhagats* and important personages assemble on the *mādh*'s veranda. Children scale the gateway's parapet and their cries of excitement hint at the coming of the *samekhiyās*.

Apart from the excited sounds emanating from the awaiting crowd of thousands, it is the hundreds of women singing Welcoming the *Dhajā* songs that builds the anticipation of further events (figure 5). These songs speak of great respect for the emblems, that is the *dhajās*, the *samekhiyās* and the Bhuwa who are about to enter. They arouse a collective spirit, which Ramiben explained to me as an awakening to the presence of Mammai. This is literally illustrated in the following song.

Ritual Song 3, Welcoming the Dhajā

On the eastern gate there is (elder brother) Nathubhai's room

Mātājī's *sthapna* is on the interior back wall.

Brother Nathubhai requests (his) wife Parmi;

'Wake up Oh Beloved'[16] and welcome the flag!

Instruments are playing, instruments (the bells) will ring and the drum will sound,

On the eastern gate there is (groom) Khodabhai's room,

Mātājī's *sthapna* is on the interior back wall.

Brother Khodabhai requests (his) wife Sajan,

'Wake up Oh Beloved and welcome the flag! '

Instruments are playing, the instruments will ring and the drum will sound.

Welcoming the *Dhajā* songs and *pat chadwu* songs constitute the two major genres of Rabari women's devotional songs. The order in which they are sung is the same for Punj, Chelāṇ and Kalaś ceremonies, as the process of rituals is identical, though on vastly differing scales. The Welcoming the *Dhajā* song pre-empts the performance of *pat chadwu*. This one however was performed not at Punj, but for a Chelāṇ ceremony.

Figure 5: Welcoming the Dhajā.

Chelāṇ

A Chelāṇ ceremony typically is given as homage to Mammai Mātājī for the fulfilment of a *māntā* or simply to bring together her devotees. It is held in March or April, after the Rabari marriage season, which is also convenient for the Bhuwa Atta as he has fewer demands on his services. Rabaris say that Chelāṇ ceremonies are only for strict believers, 'authentic *bhaktas*', and as such, they are caste exclusive.

Rabaris explain Chelāṇ as a feast given to Mammai Mātājī's followers. They also conjoin the verb, *pava*, literally to drink Chelāṇ, to convey a metaphoric sense of imbibing Chelāṇ, or indeed Mammai. The term is also a collective noun, as *Chelāṇ* are persons who are followers of Mammai Mātājī. However, I heard this usage applied only to Rabari males. In a limited sense, a Chelāṇ can be likened to the orthodox Hindu ceremony, Brahm Bhojan (*bhojan*; feast). Brahm Bhojan is also exclusive, given only to Brāhmans. Rabaris say that a Chelāṇ gains for the giver Mammai's blessing and raises the social status not only of the host but also of his kin.

To hold a Chelāṇ, there must be at least five invited guests, each one from a different patrilineage. Rabaris consider this the minimum and any number above this must correspond with a multiple of five that is, 10, 15, 20, and so on. The significance of this number remained unclear, with most explaining that it corresponded with the number of ghee lamps lit in the *mādh* during the occasion. Typically, the Bhuwa Atta and a group of *sarju* singers with *morpichhi dhajā* (who will act as his *padhiyārs* also) attend Chelāṇ and the reverence inspired by the Bhuwa's presence is nothing less than that produced by royalty. It is only in very special circumstances that the Bhuwi will attend, and if she does attend, her arrival (typically after the Bhuwa) is no less significant, and Welcoming of the *Dhaja* songs signal her entrance as well. She is accompanied by *sarju* singers waving *morpichhi*, whilst older Rabari men and women gather prior to her entrance to perform *page lāgavun* (to bow down and touch the feet). Rabaris say this is recognition of her saintly presence, and unlike Rabari women who sit on the ground, a regal cot with the best *dharaniyo* (an embroidered quilt) is prepared for her (figure 6).

Figure 6: Bhuwi Ma with devotees performing Page Lāgavan.

In the above Welcoming of the *Dhajā* song, the persons mentioned are members of the Mori family, the sons and daughters-in-law of Mesurubhai Mori who held the Chelāṇ. The intent is to give praise to Mammai, but also to express publicly that all in the family are devoted *bhaktas*. Welcoming of the *Dhajā* songs performed at Punj are identical to Chelāṇ performances though there is no reference to a domestic *sthapna*.

Most frequently, Chelāṇ ceremonies are undertaken as fulfilment of a *māntā*, and the invited guests say they too partake in the joy of the boon granted. Ramiben held a Chelāṇ after her *māntā* was realised. Indeed Ramiben's action was unusual, as typically Rabari men host Chelāṇs. A Chelāṇ is also held in anticipation of a good outcome but without a formal *māntā*. In one particular case, a Chelāṇ was held for a boy in poor health. His parents hoped and believed that the collective gathering of Mammai's *bhaktas* and the divine intervention of Mammai would heal the boy.[17] In another case a Rabari shepherd whose livestock was being ravaged by disease and sickness held a Chelāṇ.

Kalaś

Ritual Song 4, Kalaś

It is true that border of the *sidi*[18] is made of gold;

(There is) an invitation for Jetha Bhuwa and Sarman Bhuwa.

Oh Kings, you are most welcome.

On Jetha Bhuwa's hand there is a gold ring;

Sarman Bhuwa's speech is sweet.

Oh Kings, you are most welcome.

It is true that the border of the *sidi* is made of gold;

There is an invitation for Punja Bhuwa and Vira Bhuwa.

Oh Kings, you are most welcome.

On Punja Bhuwa's hand there is a gold ring;

Cool, calm and steady[19] is Vira Bhuwa's *dharna*.[20]

Oh Kings you are most welcome.

The dominant theme expressed in Kalaś songs is veneration for the Bhuwas and, more generally, the naming of the individual *mādhs*. Kalaś songs reaffirm the political order of things, the attachment to an individual *parāṭh* and one's Rabari identity.

A *kalaś* is a pot-bellied water pitcher with a small narrow mouth. Architecturally a *kalaś* is mounted at the top of a *śikhara* (finial), characteristic of all Hindu temples, although this is not the case for a *mādh*, which is flat-roofed. Rabaris normally use the term *kalaś bharvo* metaphorically, that is, to fill the body with holiness.

A Kalaś is similar to a Chelāṇ, but more prestigious and typically more than one hundred guests attend. It also includes the rituals Welcoming of the *Dhajā* and *pat chadwu*. If the Kalaś is held at the home of an individual, Mammai's *sthapna* is made on the eve of the ceremony and five ghee lamps are lit.

A Rabari Kalaś is held more to express a philanthropic intent as well as the status aspirations of the host, rather than for the fulfilment of an individual *māntā*. Two brothers who wished to donate 10,000 rupees towards the rebuilding of the *mādh* hosted a Kalaś ceremony which I attended in the compound of Ordar *mādh* in 1991. Ramiben and other women I spoke to afterwards said that such an act was unusual because the brothers and their families would have had to endure great deprivation. In fact, most knew that the brothers were barely eking out a living and that such a material sacrifice represented further testament to their devotion.

Punj preparations

From the earlier discussion of Punj and its preparations, it seems clear that Rabari women's devotionalism cannot be distinguished from women's *dharma*. During Punj the 'home' (with its attendant concerns for the wellbeing of kin) becomes a place of reception for Mammai and the reproduction of women's *dharma*.

Here the term 'reception' attempts to invoke both the literal and the performative sense of the word, that is, hospitality. It is the dimension of giving welcome (*lābha* and *śubha*). Over the nine days that follow the decision to hold Punj, a woman's home becomes a place for receiving Mammai *bhaktas*. The great movement of Rabaris from different *parāṭhs* to the *mādh* hosting Punj invariably requires that those in the host village provide bedding and hospitality for many guests. It is in this domestic context that aspects of women's *bhakti* became most perceptible. In fact, this hospitality for guests is a fundamental preparation for the reception of Mammai Mātājī's blessing.

The first day of Punj, decision day, is attended by many Rabari *bhaktas*, many of whom will remain at the host *mādh* until Punj (tenth day). Rabari residents in the surrounding villages typically supply milk and other dairy products for the duration. Women, in the main, attend to guests' comfort, serve tea continuously and fetch water to fill 44-gallon drums from nearby wells. This and other arduous work is done as well as other daily household tasks.[21] The demands placed on women are enormous. In most *kedās* (the Rabari neighbourhoods of a village) I visited during this time, female relatives, much as for other events on the ritual calendar, pooled resources and labour to lessen the burden. This solidarity amongst women was expressed each morning over the nine days, as women of the same patrilineage, led by elder women, took *darśan* at Mammai's *sthapna*, returning to their *kedās* with *prasād* (blessed offerings) for guests and children.

Figure 7: Miniben Kodiyatar, resurfacing her veranda with cow dung plaster.

Among other things, 'reception' literally means opening to receive. *Padhiyārs* (the Bhuwa's attendants) prepare the *mādh*, replacing the *morpichhi* and cleaning the hundreds of *śaṅkhā* (conches) that constitute Mammai's *sthapna*. The Bhuwa and the Bhuwi undertake fasting, spending their time propitiating Mammai Mātājī (doing *pujā*) or in deep meditation. The Bhuwa

Atta ritually enacts this process of preparation through a bath in the ocean before being possessed by Mammai. This is done prior to Punj and again on Punj day, or indeed any occasion when *pat chadwu* is performed at the *mādh*.

For Rabari women, this ritualized purification takes place largely in the home, in the form of replastering walls, floors and verandas with cow dung (figure 7). Plastering the house with cow dung is clearly an economical way of keeping the house clean and free of insects. But many women emphasised the relation between the household's ritual purity and a woman's *dharma* to preserve it. Ramiben explained that the reason why cow dung was used, instead of mere water or anything else, was that it is one of the five purifying products produced by the holy cow.

For better-off Rabaris, the traditional limestone house rendered in cow dung has become synonymous with backwardness and want. 'How one can live like this these days?' Daeben Mori, a Rabari teacher from Porbandar, said to me. For her the use of cow dung seemed unnecessary. Her attitude towards the worship of Mammai and her notions of ritual purity were different. She felt it better simply to perform the regional practices of sprinkling water or placing a wick of cotton on or around the kitchen hearth (usually a gas stove) prior to doing *pūjā* at the *kuldevi* (family) temple.

Daeben's attitude is representative of other better-off Rabari women whose changed work patterns and education have altered traditional forms of status acquisition. More pertinent here, though, is the modernisation occurring in their religious practices. It is now not uncommon for such women to participate in the rituals and festivals of the wider middle classes, and even less in Rabari ones.

Punj Day: the poetics of devotional performance

> If we are to learn how songs...can stir human hearts we must inform interpretation with a grasp of the relationship between expressive forms and feelings, which themselves are culture bound and which derive their significance from their place within the life experiences of particular people in particular societies (Rosaldo 1980:22).

Punj rituals (and other formal religious rituals) give primacy to Rabari males. The Bhuwa Atta and Rabari elders are the ritual specialists, whilst male *bhaktas* are active participants who corporeally express their relationship with the divine in such rituals as Welcoming of the *Dhajā*. This is also the case during the Bhuwa's performance of *pat chadwu*, where divine ecstasy manifests in hundreds of Rabari males, who run frantically to and fro from the large banyan tree in front of the *mādh* towards the Bhuwa Atta hoisted up in the air.

Ritual Song 5, Chelāṇs during Punj

> Chelāṇ (devotee) climbs on the *champa* (tree) and descends onto the *marva* bush,
>
> Chelāṇ mounts the platform of the veranda and climbs down onto the steps,
>
> Chelāṇ climbs onto the upper storey and descends down to the terrace,
>
> Chelāṇ (you) have waited much time for our *padhiyārs,*
>
> People of this special occasion are happy and rejoicing.
>
> Chelāṇ (you) have waited much time for Jetha Bhuwa,
>
> People of this special occasion are happy and rejoicing,
>
> Oh Chelāṇ if Sarman Bhuwa will come then *pat chadwu* will happen.

The individualistic digression from normative social behaviour is a hallmark of the *bhakti* tradition. *Bhakti*'s emphasis on individual performance is what directly links a devotee to god and provides an avenue for personal salvation. Vijay Mishra (1998:82), in his analysis of the devotional poetry of Kabir, Namdev and other *sant*-poets, articulates this with the idea of 'the principle of communicability'. A 'sender' (the performative self) desires to send a 'message' to god (object of desire). In fact, this mode of worship usurps the traditional priest-mediated ritual and allows each *bhakta* to experience communion with Mammai.

It is clear that the Bhuwa Atta is the prime instrument for expressing the presence of Mammai and is the focus from which this collective relationship takes shape. Thus, this apparent male exclusivity serves to invert the 'principle of communicability' for Rabari women and reinforces patriarchal strictures. On this level, Mammai *dharma* sits comfortably with orthodox belief and reiterates AK Ramanujan's observation that

> ...*bhakti*-communities, while proclaiming anti-structure, necessarily develop their own structures for behaviour and belief, often minimal, frequently composed of elements selected from the very structures they deny or reject (Ramanujan 1973:35).

Women and Mammai Mātājī

The more corporeal conception of women's *bhakti* is better located in the offering of hospitality and the purification of the home than in formal public ritual. This field of structured gender roles (women's *dharma*) and the sheer weight assigned to women's responsibilities surface as one mode in which the 'principle of communicability' for women is accessed. In short, hospitality and the purification of the home function as invitations to receive Mammai Mātājī.

However, what remains unanswered is women's interpretation and expression of Mammai Mātājī's identity. Women's *māntās*, Chelāṇ and Kalaś clearly reveal that Mammai Mātājī operates in this world and that all Rabaris have direct access to her. In this sense, Mammai is in *māyā* (the phenomenal world), but Rabaris also claim she is beyond it. I suggest the absence of her name, both in Rabari myth[22] and in devotional songs, provides the key element for a fuller understanding of women's *bhakti* and, therefore, of Mammai's identity as the sublime, the meta-*māyā*. The following *pat chadwu* song was performed during Punj in 1991.

Ritual Song 6, Pat Chadwu

The entire caste and the sun god have stopped (refrain);

The entire caste and the sun god have stopped.

Sarman Bhuwa is wearing his ornaments resplendently.[23]

The sun god has stopped.

He is putting on ornaments, he is wearing a *bana*;[24]

He will take much time in tying his *sidi* (shawl).

The sun god has stopped.

Amresh Bhuwa[25] is wearing his ornaments and the sun god has stopped;

He is putting on ornaments, he is wearing a *bana*.

He will take much time in tying his *sidi*,

The sun god has stopped.

The Bhuwi

The performance of this *pat chadwu* song begins just prior to the Bhuwa's emergence from the *mādh* and continues throughout his performance of *pat chadwu* directly outside. In other words, it is sung throughout the time he is possessed by Mammai.

During this liminal epoch of divine presence, the Bhuwi is also in the *mādh* bowed before Mammai's *sthapna*. She remains in deep meditation, unconcerned with the events surrounding her. For she also plays a role in

Mammai's drama, becoming the vessel that receives the Bhuwa's spirit, which is in limbo due to his possession (being filled up) by the spirit of Mammai. The Bhuwi, like Sāmuṇḍā's relationship to Śaṅkara, hosts his *śakti* (is embodied as an emanation of him), whilst he is possessed by something greater.

During Punj the focus of the formal rituals is on the males near the *mādh*, but on the periphery, Rabari women envelop the ritual space, physically and with the sung aesthetic of the sacred. They define the exteriorisation of this sacred body and they also 'texture' its interior sanctity.[26] Women from every *parāṭh* are present, but the regional variations that typically distinguish the styles of women's marriage songs are absent (George 2004:60–5). Punj songs do not vary, other than in their reference to individual Bhuwas. This gives a further dynamic to the performance as the individual song leaders (representing each *parāṭh* and most *kedās* in them) bring into play different 'voices,' a 'polyphony', which constructs the density and range of the musical texture.[27] Whilst hidden from view in the *mādh* the Bhuwi embodies the purificatory rebirth of the patriarch, the patriline and Rabari karma.

Rabari women 'send' the message that 'the entire caste and the sun have stopped', that the laws of *māyā* have been suspended. The delusions of *māyā* have been removed in order to glimpse the divine, to host momentarily the grace of the goddess, to 'know' the Real and rehearse *mokṣa*.

The Bhuwa like Jalan Bapu is the mediator of the Real and, as such, becomes the object of devotion. The Bhuwa is Mammai, becoming the *saguṇa* form necessary for Mammai's presence to 'appear'.[28] Time has stopped; the space between worlds has been warped.

Wearing his ornaments and tying his *sidi*, the Bhuwa is a vision of pure resplendence, but, as Rabari women reminded us earlier, the accoutrements of his resplendence are ill-defined—fabric without the definition of 'warp' or 'weft', gold so luminous that it becomes unclear from where it emerges.

Poetics in the presence of the divine

In many ways a Rabari woman's religious practices are no different from those of other Hindu women within patriarchy, for her *bhakti* incorporates the wellbeing of her household, her husband, her children and her husband's kin. Nevertheless, by bracketing Rabari women's relation to the divine, I have indicated that their performative actions, both in the home and through their songs, in fact point beyond this confining gendered archetype. Women's actions are integral to the performance of Rabari rituals and, most significantly, their songs provide the sequencing to individual rites, such as the Welcoming of the *Dhajās* or the enactment of *pat chadwu*. Ostensibly women sing in praise of the Bhuwa, whom they regard as the custodian of the ritual aspects of Mammai *dharma*.

Also implicit in my discussion is the obvious parallel with the singing of *sarju*, within which there is also a marked rarity, if not absence, of Mammai's name, although she is, nonetheless, expressed in the void of direct praise. This rarity can be partly explained by the secrecy of Rabari religion generally and the need to shroud the intricacies of Mammai *dharma* from non-believers, non-initiates and, indeed, researchers such as myself.

Beyond this there is a mystery which is only accessible at an experiential level, although it is hinted at in the fabric without warp and weft. More so it is expressed in the mystery of the sounds, which even Rabaris themselves must grow into understanding.

Notes

1 I did anthropological fieldwork in the region during 1989–91, 1992–3 and 1998.

2 I discuss the limits of prior patricentric scholarship on subaltern women's songs in my doctoral dissertation (George 2004) with regard to both devotional and marriage songs. Unfortunately most feminist scholarship in India has only concentrated on the latter. In the chapter on marriage songs in my dissertation, I engage most decisively with the theoretical insights offered by the feminist anthropologists Gloria Raheja and Ann Gold (1994).

3 In analysing the works of the *bhakti* poet Mirabai, Kumkum Sangari argues that *bhakti* can be neither understood solely in terms of its social content nor evaluated separately from the social practices in which it is implicated.

4 Often, this good fortune was the ability to rise each morning and to be still physically capable of performing a few basic household tasks without pain.

5 A regionally renowned temple in the Barda Hills, northwest of Porbandar.

6 Here I am only referring to the rituals performed as group homage to Mammai Mātājī. In general, the Rabaris consider all rituals, be it the various rites of passage, marriage or death rituals, as sacred.

7 A *parāṭh* is a territory serviced by a *mādh*, a jurisdiction comprising a number of villages and *neses* (remote settlements) wherein Sorathiya Rabari reside. The songs in this chapter were mainly collected in the Ordar *parāṭh*, which is territorially equivalent to the Porbandar *zilla* (district). The *mādh* is located in Ordar village, some ten kilometres south of Porbandar. In western Saurāshtra, there is a total of six *parāṭhs* (and six *mādhs*).

8 For a detailed account of this ritual and transliteration of the Jalan myth, see George (1992:13–6; 2004:53–64) and also Maddock (2006:100–126).

9 For the renouncer, 'there is indeed only one goal, *mokṣa* (liberation from rebirth) which will suffer no dissipation of attention and efforts' (Biardeau 1989:67). According to Biardeau, a precondition that made this possible in orthodox Hinduism was chastity, an asceticism based on the renunciation of the married state and the social world, especially with its attendant pleasures, desires and illusions. In orthodox Hinduism the phenomenal world is typically referred to as *māyā* (the world of illusion and incessant dualities), which is inclusive of more cosmic illusions and is itself characterised by changeability and impermanence.

10 Mishra (1998:106–7) notes that by the 12th century the *bhakti* tradition was characterised by an 'intense emotionalism' where the renouncer (as a *bhakta*) ceases to function in the binary of the renouncer and the 'man in the world'.

11 There is no Purāṇic evidence to suggest that Sāmunḍā (Cāmunḍā) was Śaṅkara's wife, but it is generally understood that she is a tantric version of Durgā, the great mother.

12 This act of creation of the human being accords well with the physiological understanding of the genesis of life. By contrast, Judaic myth creates the woman

out of the man's side. In both, the male is primal, but more so in the Judaic myth. In the Rabari's case, the mother's act of creating the body albeit of a male, constitutes the initial action, Śaṅkara only contributing the vital elements. The point is that both myths are patricentric but perhaps the Rabari one less so.

13 It is Sāmuṇḍā and Śaṅkara who are conceived anthropomorphically through their cosmic role. In this context Sāmuṇḍā is a consort goddess, not an independent *śakti*. Mammai seems to be the latter.

14 A red coloured food dye, which is sprinkled over each male devotee.

15 Mammai Mātājī's decision is conveyed to the Bhuwa Atta during *chapṭī vagādvi*, a divination ritual performed in the *mādh* while he is possessed by Her.

16 The feminine noun *gori* used in this line refers to a beloved bride, a wife or a lover. But it also denotes a woman of fair complexion. There is a further association, however, that is derived from the Sanskrit word *gaurī*, which is one of the names of Pārvatī who lives in Kailāsa.

17 The cost of hosting a Chelāṇ typically can exceed more than 10,000 rupees.

18 *Sidi*, or alternately *sini*, are the Rabari words for a white and red shawl, half a metre wide by one and a half metres long, with a highly ornate border pattern made with gold thread. Most Rabaris hold the cloth to be sacred and, therefore, it is worn only by the Bhuwa Atta who ties it around his waist before commencing the ritual of *pat chadwu*.

19 The word *dhiri* also means steady, which is the virtue of a hero. A hero type is a *dhir* and *uddat* meaning steady and noble.

20 The term *dharna* refers to the Bhuwa Atta's state of being prior to his possession by Mammai Mātājī. It has two nuances, one of which suggests a state of deep meditation and the other when combined with the last word of this line, *dhiri* (steady), indicates a calm deep prayer-like trance.

21 During this period, Rabari women also continue to work as wage labourers and volunteer their labour for the preparation of the host *mādh*'s compound, which is typically resurfaced in fine sand to cushion the area for Rabari guests to sit or sleep on.

22 In the Rabari myth of Jalan Bapu, the *āchariya* who brought Mammai *dharma* to the Rabaris of Sorath, the main protagonists are dualistic divinities, the goddess Sāmuṇḍā (*prakṛti*, female) and Śankara (*puruṣa*, male). Mammai is not present in the story, and the only reference to her occurs in the gifts Sāmuṇḍā gave to Jalan in remembrance of her.

23 The translation of *sangar* as ornaments falls short of the meaning here. What is implied is a sense of resplendence that comes from adorning oneself with precious jewels and fabrics.

24 A silver bracelet worn by Rabari men.

25 After the death of his father, Sarmanbhai, Amresh will be inaugurated as the next Bhuwa.

26 Like the symbolic opposition of the peacock (*prakṛti*) and the swan (*puruṣa*), Sāmuṇḍā and Śaṅkara, the Bhuwi and the Bhuwa, women's colourful costumes complement the sartorial white of Rabari men.

27 Polyphonic texture consists of more than one line moving independently in a different melodic unit. These lines reference the same text, but are different in terms of melodic gestures.

28 *Saguṇa* divinities are part of the dualist framework of the cosmos and, as such, are represented anthropomorphically. In opposition to this, Mammai Mātājī is a *nirguṇa* divinity. She has no form, image or qualities.

chapter ten

The Khāḍādevī Temple of modern Mumbai: communal harmony and the koḷī goddess[1]

Marika Vicziany and
Jayant Bhalchandra Bapat

The Koḷī villagers residing in the middle of Cuff Parade are internationally renowned for living on one of the world's most highly prized pieces of real estate—a thin strip of land that connects the luxury districts of the Oberoi and the Taj Presidency hotels in south Mumbai. This village constitutes one of the 23 remaining Koḷī villages of Mumbai city. The Koḷīs are the original inhabitants and have villages stretched along the northern coast-line as far as Karachi, in Pakistan. Our interest in the Koḷīs began with research on the temple of Mumbādevī, located today at Bhuleshwar on one of Mumbai's important commercial sites. The city itself is said to derive its name from Mumbādevī, the patron goddess of Mumbai. In an earlier paper we have described how the temple of Mumbādevī probably predates European settlement in western India (Vicziany & Bapat 2008). It is a widely held belief that, in the beginning of the modern era, Mumbādevī was the favoured mother goddess of the indigenous Koḷīs. That paper also explained how the temple of Mumbādevī today has largely lost its old connections with the Koḷīs and is now patronised by Bombay's Gujarati community; it is located in the Gujarati cloth market area and the temple trustees are Gujarati. We argued that Mumbādevī—both the temple and the worship around her—have been Sanskritised[2]; in other words, that since the early 20th century the temple of Mumbādevī has become increasingly disconnected from the Koḷī communities and tied more intimately to the higher-caste communities of Mumbai. So what do the indigenous Koḷīs of Mumbai worship? Does the Sanskiritisation of the Mumbādevī temple mean that they have abandoned the mother goddess and turned to popular Hindu gods such as Gaṇeśa, Rāma or Mārutī? Or have the Koḷīs become atheists or communists? Alternatively, have the Koḷīs become entrapped in the religious politics of the Hindu fundamentalist Shiv Sena (Mumbai's right wing communal party) which has promoted increasingly narrow definitions of Hindu religious belief and practice? We were certainly worried about this latter issue when large posters carrying the image of Bal Thackeray, leader of the Shiv Sena party, started to appear next to some of the Koḷī villages of Mumbai from 2000 onwards.

This chapter extends the work we have been doing during the last four years by focusing on perhaps the oldest and most important Koḷī temple in Mumbai—that of Khāḍādevī. As a typical example of the complex history of Mumbai, the Khāḍādevī shrine is located in the Kolaba police station, next to the central business district and within a short 15-minute walk from the Gateway of India and the Taj Intercontinental Hotel. The image of the goddess that appears in the Khāḍādevī shrine is different from the other 22 Koḷī temples; it is not a sculptured image, but rather a *swayambhū* stone (self-arising stone) on which the etched image of the goddess Khāḍādevī is accompanied by seven eyes and seven mouths representing the *āsarās* or water spirits. The parallel appearance of both Khāḍādevī and the seven *āsarās* makes this particular shrine the only one in Mumbai that is directly connected to the ancient Koḷī myth of the origins of the first temples of Mumbai. Further, the Khāḍādevī temple manifests few signs of Sanskritisation, also suggesting that both the temple and rituals practised there today are probably survivals of the earliest religious system of Mumbai, stretching far into the pre-British history of that island. This chapter describes the Khāḍādevī temple, its history, its images, its management and, above all, its location in the modern belief systems of India's largest commercial city. We argue that the age-old worship of Khāḍādevī brings together some of the disparate communities of Mumbai and in doing so facilitates social cohesion and mutual respect.

Koḷī goddesses in the villages of Mumbai

Modern Mumbai is one of the largest cities in the world—it has a population of at least 20 million and rising. It remains the commercial heart of India, with the Bombay Stock Exchange dominating the skyline of downtown Bombay. Behind its financial vibrancy lies a recent history of inter-community violence, some of which has been drummed up by fundamentalists of all persuasions and some by criminal elements who thrive on the city's capacity for excitement by selling and smuggling prostitutes, guns, narcotics, explosives and terrorists (Vicziany 2007). In the midst of this vast metropolis are some 23 Koḷī localities, perhaps more (we cannot pretend to have undertaken a systematic survey of their number). Of these, at least five localities, Harbādevī (at Madh), Golphādevī (at Worli), Mumbādevī (at Bhuleshwar), Hirādevī (at Erangal) and Ekavirā Devī (at Karle) have temples containing iconographically similar images of the mother goddess accompanied on either side by two minor goddesses or sisters. Each of these mother goddesses has a different name depending on the locality and the associated history of that area. But none of them features the *āsarās* (see figure 3 below) that are unique to the Khāḍādevī shrine in the Kolaba police station.

The island of Mumbai was created by a process of landfill and siltation that caused the seven original islands to merge: Kolaba, Smaller Kolaba (Dhakta Kolaba), Mazgaon, Worli, Parel, Matunga and Mahim. Legend has it that each of the islands housed a goddess shrine erected by the Koḷīs. As the islands merged and Bombay developed as a major international trading port, the population was redistributed to make way for new infrastructure, including the port, roads, bazaars, housing and other religious shrines. As we noted in our earlier paper, the temple of Mumbādevī, located for a long time in the area where the Victoria Train Terminus currently stands, was moved to Bhuleshwar to make way for urban expansion. This was the beginning of a Sanskritisation process, which increasingly brought about a separation between the Koḷī people and worship of Mumbādevī during the 20th century. However, there are other shrines that appear to have a long Koḷī heritage and remain places of worship today—for example the shrines of Harbādevī at Madh island and Golphādevī at Worli.

The uniqueness of Khāḍādevī arises from the self-arising sacred stone that represents the Devī in all her power. The temple was built much more recently to encase the image of Khāḍādevī. The stone itself may well be one of the original stones that 'emerged' from the seas and that the Koḷīs have worshipped for so long. The Koḷīs themselves say that the name Khāḍādevī derives from the devī of the Khāḍī or the bay. Today the stone is dressed in many layers of red lead (Marathi: *shendur*) that conceals the pristine stone beneath. We know nothing of the relationship of the Khāḍādevī temple to that of Mumbādevī or any of the other Koḷī goddess temples, but what we do know is that the Khāḍādevī temple remains one of the most active Koḷī shrines in south Mumbai. It is also the only Koḷī temple that provides a visual manifestation of the Koḷī myth of the seven divine sisters which we describe next.

The myth of the Seven Divine Sisters

The number seven plays an important role in the mythology of Mumbai. Mumbai began as seven islands and the image of the Devī in the Khāḍādevī temple is accompanied by a distinctive group of seven eyes and seven mouths (Figure 1). Khāḍādevī is also flanked by two further sets of eyes which are discussed later. The seven eyes resonate with the myth about the origins of the Koḷī goddesses as explained to us by the temple *pujārī*:[3]

> God had seven daughters and one son. One day these eight divine children decided to go on a boat trip. Because of a storm, their boat capsized in the middle of the ocean. However all of them swam ashore and each of them found a place at one of the seven islands of Mumbai and stayed there. The brother, Vetāldev, decided to stay on the seashore to protect the seven sisters. These goddesses appeared in the dreams of the local inhabitants and directed them to construct shrines for them and worship them. Since the islands were inhabited mostly by Koḷī fishermen, the sisters became the patron goddesses of the Koḷīs.

Vandana Kshirsagar, the female *pujārī* at the temple, told us that the seven eyes were *āsaras*[4] or female water spirits who, when propitiated, protect fishermen and their boats. She also described them as goddesses but was unsure of the connection between these *āsarās* and the seven sisters of the myth. However she told us that

> When a fisherman or his boat is missing at sea, or when the weather looks ugly and threatens their safety, the Koḷīs come to the Khāḍādevī temple with pots which they fill with water, milk, yoghurt, and *supari*—a betel nut. They then toss into the pot one rupee and a quarter. A *puja*-worship of this pot is then performed.[5] They then return to the foreshore where the water is disbursed into the ocean to please the goddesses.

To us, the relationship between the myth and the iconography of the Khāḍādevī temple is obvious. The Koḷī myth of the seven *āsarās* is shared by all Koḷīs today, even though the iconography of the other Koḷī temples does not typically include them. Our interpretation is that the Khāḍādevī temple in Kolaba serves the function of being a historical repository; here is the only extant iconographic representation of the *āsarās*, an image that integrates the myth, history and beliefs of the Koḷīs. What the myth does not explain is the relationship of the seven *āsarās* to Khāḍādevī . Could it be that Khāḍādevī, as a manifestation of the supreme Devī, incorporates the seven *āsarās* with the result that in the other Koḷī temples of Mumbai the seven *āsarās* are implied by a single iconic representation of the Devī? This sounds logical given the *pujārī*'s description of the seven spirits as goddesses—perhaps they were once minor goddesses ultimately incorporated into the supreme Devi? In this way, the temple in Kolaba does indeed represent the memories of the community by visually establishing the original link between the supreme Devī and the seven *āsarās.* We put this forward as a working hypothesis to be tested against further research.[6]

The Khāḍādevī temple and the Kolaba police station

The Kolaba police station has acquired some notoriety since the publication of a novel by an Australian fugitive in 2004 (Roberts 2004:405–413; Ghosh 2004). What is less well appreciated about the police station, a ten-minute walk down the Kolaba causeway away from the Regal Cinema, is that it houses the oldest Koḷī temple of Mumbai. The present police station building was constructed in 1906 on land sold to the British government by Mr Gotankar, the great-grandfather of Vandana Kshirsagar, the present *pujārī*. The origin of the temple is not known, but legends say that it all began when fishermen discovered a crop of rocks on the seashore. They started worshipping these, associating particular rocks with particular deities. In this way, Khāḍādevī, the *āsarās* and Jari-Mari were identified. The Koḷīs and the other people living nearby started believing in the power of this autochthonous goddess and her fame soon spread. Mr Gotankar was the Collector of the district at the time. His wife, Vandana's great-grandmother, was very religious and persuaded her Collector husband to buy the piece of land and erect a shrine to honour the Devī.[7] Initially, the temple had four brick walls around it but the roof consisted of galvanised iron sheets. This was later replaced by the present structure (*śikhara*).[8]

The couple had no male issue so that generations after the great-grandfather saw the temple pass down the line through the daughters. That is how the land and the temple came into the possession of the current family. The temple has, therefore, had female *pujārīs* for the last 100 years. Vandana does have a brother, but he is younger than she, so, as the eldest sibling, she has inherited the mantle of temple priest. On the other hand, her brother Gotankar is still the owner of the temple.

The land on which the temple sits, with its surrounds, was sold to the government during the British Raj. The Government needed land to build a police station, and the sale was effected on the understanding that the temple and the adjacent house would remain in the possession of the *pujārī*'s family. Moreover, the family was shielded from land tax inflation; in the 19th century the family paid a token one rupee in taxes to the municipality and still pays the same amount today.

The *mandir* (temple) is located to the back left-hand side of the main building that constitutes the police station. Just outside the temple, to the right, is a large circular area covered by concrete; it is said to be the original well which drew water from a creek that flowed here separating the island of

Bombay from Old Woman's Island. Beneath the concrete seal are a number of coloured stones representing the Devī of the well and water. Behind this now disused well and adjacent to the temple is the *pujārī*'s home. In front of the well stands a black, undated marble stone on which are carved the following words:

> This tablet marks the site of the former crossing of about 300 yards of creek that separated the island of Bombay from Old Woman's Island. The creek was filled in 1838.

To the far side of the water tank is an open yard; here animal sacrifices are still performed on especially auspicious occasions. In our earlier paper on Mumbādevī we noted that animal sacrifices used to be conducted at the Mumbādevī temple on behalf of the Koḷīs in the early 20th century, but this has long since stopped.

The shrine of Khāḍādevī was originally located at the edge of the sea.[9] As more and more land was reclaimed, the waters moved further away from the shrine. Today, the Koḷī village is located on Cuff Parade, over a kilometre away from the shrine. In the village, however, there is a permanent reminder of the connection with the temple; a wooden post and a small stone representing the goddess have been implanted in the sandy shore to represent the main image of Khāḍādevī in the Kolaba police station.[10] Early in the morning, before the men embark on their fishing trips, they offer prayers to this icon.

The inner sanctum of the Kolaba *mandir* is approached through an open, three-sided area covered by the main roof. Under the roof of the temple, on entering the front room, are two rows of cast-iron bells, which look old and may indeed be the original ones. Within the inner sanctum, the central, dominant place is given to a long *swayambhū* (autochthonous) stone that represents a number of gods and goddesses worshipped here. Moving from the left-hand side of the stone, there is an etched representation of Mahiśāsura,[11] Khāḍādevī and her companions, and the seven *āsaras* (see figure 1 below). On the left-hand side of the image of Khāḍādevī is an image of Mahiśāsura (the Buffalo Demon), also in the form of a face. Behind the main stone stands a vertical stone representing Śitalāmātā (the smallpox goddess). To the right-hand side of the main tablet is a second, smaller stone with two sets of eyes, representing Jari-Mari (the cholera goddess). Khāḍādevī is the main goddess here; there is no representation of Mumbādevī.

Diagram of the inner sanctum showing main shrines

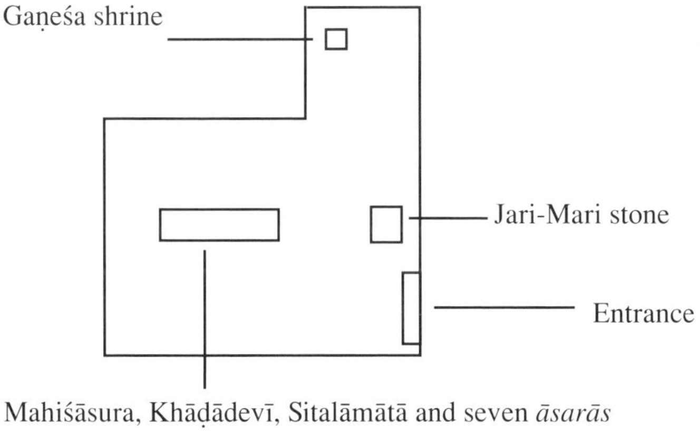

There is marked differentiation in the representations of Khāḍādevī and the seven *āsarās* at this shrine. While the Khāḍādevī and Mahiśāsura images are shown with both eyes and a mouth, the seven *āsarās* each have only a single eye and a mouth. Two possible alternative explanations for this unusual iconography of the *āsarās* follow. Although nowadays the Koḷīs do not distinguish the *āsarās* from other goddesses and worship them as such, there is an implicit hierarchical ordering between Khāḍādevī and the *āsarās*. For the Koḷīs, the *āsarās* are unpredictable and potentially malevolent spirits who are, nevertheless, more relevant in their vexatious seagoing lives. Khāḍādevī, on the other hand, is relevant in a general way for the wellbeing of the community and for its unity. It is also possible that the stone is a composite representation of two distinct divinities. In that case, Khāḍādevī represents the emblematic 'Hinduness' of the Koḷīs who are basically a tribal group. One would not be surprised if the arrival of a Hindu ruler in the past may have prompted the Koḷīs to accept the chief's own family goddess and to incorporate it in their iconography. Although this last is but speculative and the Koḷīs have no memory of such token genuflexion focusing on an incoming overlord, it is both logically and historically feasible. That is one way of explaining the present identification of Khāḍādevī with Durgā-Mahiśāsuramardini in the Koḷī psyche.

When we saw the temple in 2005, we noticed 17 minute, ornamental silver swings and three silver umbrellas suspended between Khāḍādevī and the right-hand edge of the large stone. We were told that all of these were offerings to Khāḍādevī. The 20 ornaments were suspended from the ceiling;

three of the swings had tiny model houses moulded into one corner and the others were plain without any objects. According to the *pujārī*, the umbrellas are offerings from believers whom the Devī has favoured with good fortune in the form of wealth or promotion. The plain swings are offerings from parents blessed with children after they prayed to the goddess; and the swings with tiny model houses are 'thank you tokens' from followers who asked the Devī to intervene with difficult building contractors or settle other matters related to their homes.

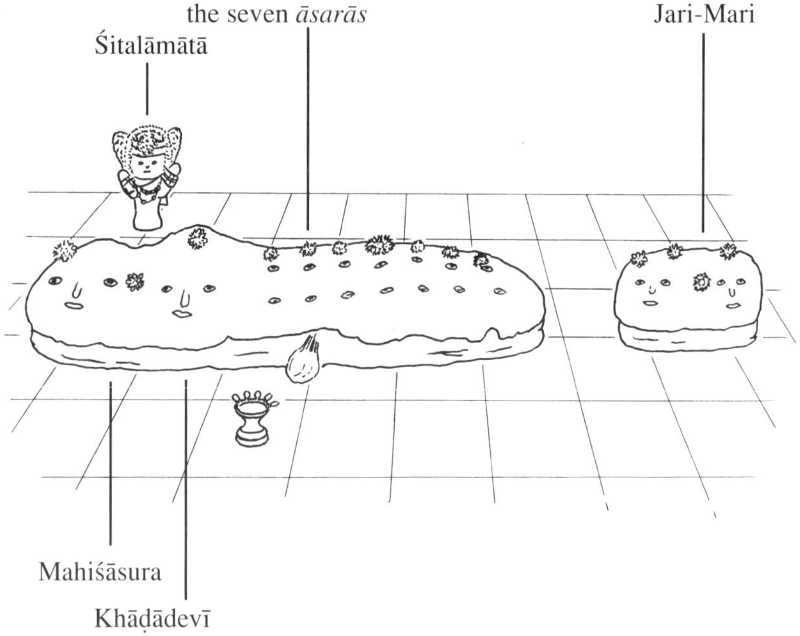

Figure 1: Khāḍādevī and other goddesses.

On the floor in front of the images etched into the main rock, there are picture frames and statuettes of many other gods and goddesses, left there in respect by recent worshippers. There is also a small bronze statue of Buddha given to the temple by an Englishman during the Raj. To the far right of this central stone is a second stone representing Jari-Mari, an incarnation of Kālī, which is commonly worshipped in order to ward off cholera. Again, before her lie various objects offered in veneration. Above the deity are two large drums.

Figure 2: Khāḍādevī stone with swings above.

The power of the goddess

The special power of Khāḍādevī derives from the origin of this shrine. According to oral tradition, as told to us by the current *pujārī*, Khāḍādevī is derived from the Marathi words *khadak* (rock) and *devī,* so literally means 'rock-goddess'. This name refers to her status as a *swyambhū* object, or a self-arising sacred image. The Cuff Parade Koḷī fishermen gave us another etymology for the word Khāḍādevī. In Marathi, *khāḍī* means 'a bay'. Therefore, the goddess that resides in the proximity of the bay was known as Khāḍīdevī, and eventually changed to Khāḍādevī.

By observing the gods and goddesses on and around the two self-arising sacred stones within the inner sanctum of the Kolaba temple, it is clear that, although Khāḍādevī is the main goddess, the temple's patrons do not worship her to the exclusion of others in the Indian pantheon. The walls and niches of the inner sanctum contain further images that expand the sphere of worship inside this precinct. Behind Khāḍādevī and on the left-hand side of the wall is a shrine to Lakṣmī. On the opposite wall, in the far left-hand corner of the room, is a shrine with two statues of Gaṇeśa followed by a colourful print of Maruti, the monkey god, which hangs on the wall, and a second shrine to Sai Baba and Gaṇeśa. In front of the Gaṇeśa shrine is a large table on which are placed images and symbols of Rādhā and Kṛṣṇa, Mahalakṣmī, a triśula (trident), Saraswati, Mahākalī, and a large bunch of peacock feathers.

In other words, although Khāḍādevī dominates this *mandir*, she is worshipped in a manner that does not exclude homage to other *devīs* and *devas*. This intermingling of the gods and goddesses of India (and even the non-god Buddha) is a characteristic feature of religious worship in western India and one already stressed in earlier work by us. At the same time, it is the worship of Khāḍādevī that is central to the life of this shrine. The Koḷīs pray for her protection against rough weather and storms before the men go fishing—frequently they are at sea for prolonged periods in order to collect a bumper catch. They offer *kauls* to ensure the safe return of the fishermen—this is a ritual that involves the *pujārī* placing two flower buds to the left and right of the image. Whichever bud falls first is then interpreted by the *pujārī* as a sign of future good luck or bad luck. They pray to her for a male heir and they pray to her during their rites of passage. Koḷī women visit the shrine and pray while their husbands are away and the men join the women at the shrine when the fishing season is over.

For both Koḷī men and women, it is the mother that is the most important support in their hard and uncertain life. The mother goddess is the supreme mother. During *pūjā* it is not uncommon to see both men and women constantly uttering words to this effect: 'Mother! Look after me, protect me. Everything around me is your *māyā*. You are the one who knows everything and understands my shortcomings'. In Kakar's words, the goddess acts as 'a nurturing, fear-dispelling presence'. This is described as 'a fundamental quality of the good mother' (Kakar 1996:84). Khāḍādevī has a pervasive presence in the psyche of the Koḷīs but is also a force that is respected by the other communities in Mumbai. Her many powers are symbolised by the silver swings, and the stories surrounding the origins of these swings provide further testimony of her wider community relevance.

During the life of the *pujārī*'s grandfather, a childless Parsi couple prayed to the goddess and eventually a boy was born. They offered the boy to the goddess and left him behind to be reared by the *pujārī*'s family. The boy grew up and married, but shortly after marriage he went mad and was confined to an asylum. The *pujārī*'s family decided that the madness was in some way linked to the goddess. From then on, they forbade any more people placing babies before the goddess or to dedicate them to her. Instead, the goddess is thanked in the form of a silver swing or umbrella that is suspended over the image. This is a sad tale, but one full of humanity and wisdom. It reflects the Koḷīs' pragmatic attitude to life. Living the life of a full human being, especially as a member of a family, is more important to them than sacrifices to the goddess. Indeed, their goddess is a benevolent one; she does not want to steal the children from the parents and sent this harsh incident as a powerful sign of the appropriate way of venerating her.

The humanity of Khāḍādevī sits comfortably alongside the alleged 'blood thirst' of the goddess. If blood is understood as a metaphor for the spirit of life, then the assumed brutality of the goddess vanishes. Live animal sacrifices in the manner reported in 1900 continue to be practised at the Kolaba shrine on special festive occasions in the month of Āṣādha (July–August). Sheep and poultry are sacrificed not only by the Koḷīs but also by the local police who show their respect for the Devī by this means.

From the viewpoint of life in the modern cauldron of Mumbai, Khāḍādevī is important to the wider community. She attracts followers with diverse beliefs and in so doing provides a place of common worship, peace and shared respect for people of different religions. About 80% of the people who worship at the Khāḍādevī temple are Koḷīs; the rest come from other Hindu communities, the local police force and the Parsis. The most popular days of worship are Tuesday, Thursday and Friday when about 100 people a day come at various times to do *pūjā*. During the monsoon, however, the daily attendance can rise to some 500, largely because the Koḷīs do not fish during the wet season, so they have extra time for worship and other things. During times of intensive worship, the *pujārī* will receive between 600 and 2,000 rupees per day as donations to the Devī.

The inter-religious importance of the Khāḍādevī shrine is reinforced by the oral traditions of the Koḷīs that refer to the values of the 'good Samaritan'. Legends amongst the Koḷīs today continue to speak of the many shipwrecked visitors that the Koḷīs rescued when European, Arab and other boats crashed into the western coast of India. Tales are still told in modern Mumbai about the Koḷīs nursing Portuguese, Jewish, Parsi and Arab traders long before the British took control of the seven islands in 1760. Many Koḷīs today point out that Koḷī surnames are to be found amongst these diasporic communities (Warhaft 2003: 55–8).[12] Survivors took on Koḷī names as they sought the protection of the goddesses and as a way of thanking her for her divine intervention.

Each year, the power of Khāḍādevī is renewed during the monsoon when the temple mysteriously floods with waters that rise up from below the stone floor; the water does not rush into the temple from outside, even though the main room of the temple lies much lower than street level. Some years ago the stone floor was repaired but this has not prevented the waters from rising some two feet, well above the image of the Devī, during the monsoon season.

The goddess and the police

As the patron deity of the Kolaba neighbourhood, the power of the Devī also manifests itself in the relationship between the temple and the Kolaba police force. When a policeman has a personal problem, he is likely to make an offering to the goddess. When the problem is resolved, or when the policeman is promoted, he will leave some rupees on the tray before the image. In 1994, when the present *pujārī* began to officiate at the shrine, there were only two female constables on the day shift and another two on the night shift. Sometimes the policewomen were away from the station when problems arose with female detainees. There had been many occasions when the *pujārī*'s mother was called to calm the female prisoners who typically claimed to be possessed by demons. Hysterical women were dragged to the temple by the police so the *pujārī* could determine whether their possession was real or a special drama that had been put on for the purposes of avoiding prosecution.

Some years ago, a female criminal attacked the *pujārī*'s mother with a knife, making a small cut on her arm. Since then the number of female constables attached to the Kolaba police station has been increased to ten or 12, but hysterical women are still brought before Khāḍādevī to calm them, exorcise evil spirits or figure out whether they are genuinely ill or faking it.

The relationship between the temple and the police has not always been so smooth. During the time of the *pujārī*'s grandfather, the police wanted to take control of all the temple land in order to build a road through the property so that the Kolaba Causeway could be linked to the parallel road behind the police station. The policeman who announced this plan dropped dead from a heart attack as he left the shrine but before he reached the front gate of the police station. His sudden death was seen as a sign of the Devī's anger. Since then nobody has dared to suggest that the Devī should be disturbed or that any development encroach on her temple.

The goddess and the Gurav *Pujārī*[13]

As is usual in the non-Vaisnavite temples of western India, particularly in Maharashtra, the current *pujārī* is called a *gurav*. The *gurav* at this temple, Vandana Kshirsagar, is a married woman who belongs to the Maratha caste. The manner in which the Maratha caste came to service the religious practices of the Koḷīs is not known. But it does represent some early Sanskritisation amongst the Koḷīs who clearly accepted the interventions of the *pujārī*. Perhaps the greater wealth of the *gurav* provides the key, as the grandfather of the current *pujārī* was willing to build a shrine to house the image.

Vandana Kshirsagar looks after the Devī every day. She is 34 years old and educated up to ninth standard. There are three boys in the family in grades 10, 7 and 6. Her husband (educated to tenth standard), now unemployed and aged 45, used to work in the laundry of the Oberoi Hotel. Although the property of the temple runs through the male line, she is the main breadwinner earning money through offerings and fortune telling. When asked what her sons were planning to do, she said she did not know, but that they would not listen to any of her suggestions. The Kolaba temple is not famous she volunteered and as there is no trust to manage the temple, fund-raising is difficult. She and her family manage the temple on their own, but she prefers this to having a trust. Her control over this special Koḷī temple was more important to her than any other consideration. The *pujārī*'s family get by on temple contributions. Although she pays only one rupee per annum in municipal taxes, the costs of water and electricity are much larger expenses.

Conclusion

The Koḷī temples of Mumbai have been one of the enduring characteristics of this multicultural city for hundreds of years. Despite this, very little scholarship has focused on the Koḷīs and we are not aware of any work on their mother goddess temples. Raghunathji provides one of the few accounts of the Koḷī temples at the turn of the 20th century. His inventory of the Hindu temples of Bombay, published in 1900 and recently reprinted by Phiroze Ranade, identifies 12 temples which have some association with the Koḷis. This information is summarised in Appendix 1, which shows that nine of the temples were dedicated to the Devī and three to male Gods. Raghunathji's information about the relationship between the temples, the Koḷis and Mumbai society is based on a mixture of local myths, rumours (*kiṁvadanti*) about the buildings and observations by the author.

As Mumbai continued to expand its physical dimensions with land reclamations and landfills, the original seven Koḷī temples spoken about in the myths also increased in number. We have located 23 of these, the most important being the Khāḍādevī temple inside the Kolaba police station. The long-established customs surrounding the image of Khāḍādevī and its self-arising sacred origin has provided it with a lasting divine power that has attracted many worshippers, Koḷī and non-Koḷī, for many centuries, even though the shrine housing the image dates from the early 20th century. As one Mumbai resident recently noted, 'Ever since I have been told about the origins of this *mandir,* I have made it a point to visit it every Saturday' (quoted in Khergamker 2006).

Khāḍādevī has attracted devotees without any urging or political campaigns. She, like the other Koḷī goddesses of Mumbai, remains a powerful presence despite the growing competition from other gods, in particular Gaṇeśa. At the same time the annual Gaṇeśa, or Gaṇapati, festival has become one of the most important festivals for the Koḷis today (Warhaft 2003:52).[14] This has happened as the Koḷis have become more integrated into the popular culture of Mumbai, a process accelerated by the political campaigns of the Shiv Sena. It is sad to reflect on the large number of Koḷīs who have been mobilised by the ultra-right-wing parties of Indian politics to support the cause of Hindutva (Hindu fundamentalism). The popularity of Khāḍādevī's competitors, Gaṇeśa in particular, is based on the free public events that the Shiv Sena organises. Being tribal people, typically treated as marginal subordinates by the rest of Bombay society, the Koḷīs feel especially comforted by the opportunities which the Shiv Sena provides for interacting with the rest of society on these festive occasions. Whether these new political and cultural forces have taken the Koḷī youth away from the veneration of Khāḍādevī and the many other Koḷī goddesses in the 23 shrines we have found is a question that we will engage with in a future research paper. Certainly employment diversification amongst the Koḷīs[15] has contributed to weakening the protection that the goddess gave to the fisherfolk for so many centuries.

Despite this, we have sufficient evidence to suggest that the relentless impact of modernisation has not overthrown Khāḍādevī yet, as she remains a vibrant presence in Mumbai, especially in Kolaba. In addition to the Koḷī fisher people, the worshippers include policemen, housewives, professionals and people of many different religious persuasions—especially Parsis. In this way, the goddess brings together the disparate communities of Mumbai at a time when the work of political parties such as the Shiv Sena has sought to separate them. Hindu nationalism does not appear to us to have a strong future amongst the Koḷīs. We say this because the Koḷīs have not only given spiritual ideas to the non-Koḷīs but have themselves incorporated into their own belief systems elements of Christianity, Hinduism and even Islam. Throughout western India and into coastal Pakistan, we can find Koḷīs who represent strong syncretic traditions which at census times become over-simplified into categories that describe these Koḷīs as Hindu, Muslim or

Christian. For us the Koḷīs represent a unique and living reflection of Indian history and culture.

Appendix 1: Temples associated with the Koḷī Communities of Mumbai in 1900

Derived from Raghunathji's *The Hindu temples of Bombay* (1900).

Serial no/Page no.*	Name of temple	Images/icons of goddesses and gods in the temples	Koḷī association
16/29	Mumbādevī	Next to the Mumbādevī shrine is the physically linked shrine to Gaṇeśa with images of Gaṇeśa, Hanumān, Kālabhairava, and, in the main shrine, Mumbādevī as Durgā and Annapūrṇā. Other rooms/temples to Gaṇeśa, Mahādeva or Śivaliṅgam, Indrāyaṇī	Koḷī origins
64/59	Mahālakṣmī	Mahālakṣmī, Mahāsarāswatī, Mahākālī; Durgā riding on a tiger, with Mahiśāsura at her feet, Gaṇeśa	One of three local *dharmashalas* was built by a Koḷī fisherwoman; in 1854 animal sacrifices here were discarded by the temple authorities; Koḷī amongst the first to worship here before upper castes
123/106	Kalkādevī	Kalkādevī, Mārutī, Śāḷunkā, Pinḍī of Mahādeva, Nandī	Founded by a Koḷī who installed the stone images of Kalkādevī, Mārutī and Śāḷunkā
152/117	Cedyādevī	Devī; a male god; Caṇḍikā, the main goddess of the fishermen	Koḷī shrine to Caṇḍikā, on the road to Koḷī village at Shivri
182/125	Cedyādevī	Cedyādevī at Worli. After worshipping here, Koḷīs go to worship at the Golbadevī temple	Based at Koḷīwādā in Worli and belongs to the Koḷī caste; worship of both Cedyā and Golbā *devīs*

194/128	Jari-Mari	Jari-Mari	Koḷī temple founded by Agris and Koḷīs of Navroji Hill; annual goat sacrifice
232/150	Golbādevī	Three stone images of the Devī worshipped by fishermen	Based in Koḷī *wadi*; founded and managed by Koḷī caste
255/161	Lakṣmī Nārāyaṇa	Devī, Lakṣmī Nārāyaṇa, Ṛṣis, Gaṇāpatī, Viṭhobā, Rakhmāi, Mahādeva, Marutī, Pārvatī	Founded by a Koḷī fisherwoman 12 years ago
189/126	**Mhasobā		On the road to Koḷī *wadi* near Sivri; managed by Koḷī-Patel; animal sacrifice once a year. Koḷīs visit each day to bathe the stones; all Koḷīs visit on Jatra day
26/36	**Walkeshwar (Valukeśvara)	Walkeshwar = Lord of the Sand; Mahādeva, Rāma, Gaṇapatī, Pārvatī, stone *liṅgam*	Koḷī worship the sand version of the temple *liṅgam* that jumped back into the sea, at the exact spot on the beach
58/54	**Bhuleshwar	Self-arising *liṅgam*, Pārvatī, Nandī, Śitalā Devī	One of five legends says temple built by Koḷī woman

* The temple number given by Raghunathji and page number in his inventory.

** The last three temples are not male temples but have been included here because they all had a special relationship with the Koḷī community of Mumbai.

Notes

1 The authors wish to thank Ms Kavita Rane, our research assistant in Mumbai, for her support to this project. Ms Rane was completing a Masters thesis comparing the employment opportunities of the Koḷīs and Bihari communities in Mumbai when she agreed to help us. Sanjay Ranade, Head, Department of Mass Communications, University of Bombay, was the supervisor of this thesis and assisted our research in innumerable ways for which we thank him. We are also grateful to Kannan Srinivasan, doctoral candidate, Monash Asia Institute, for his advice and support, particularly for his assistance in finding a copy of one of the oldest maps of Mumbai.

2 Sanskritisation is a concept coined by the noted sociologist, MN Srinivas. He identified two main strands in Hinduism: Brahmanic Hinduism and folk religion. Brāhmans worship iconic images of gods and goddesses through the medium of Sanskrit. Their rituals are performed as laid down in the Vedas and other religious books. Folk religion, on the other hand, depends on local traditions that have survived for many hundreds of years; it exists in the local oral traditions and vernacular languages. Folk deities are often worshipped in the form of self-arising stones; these rituals help to ward off evil spirits. Both these traditions borrow extensively from each other. When a folk practice is adopted by the higher-caste Brāhmans, changes occur in the practice of the local ritual. The language of the ritual also changes and, together, these shifts were described by Srinivas as the process of Sanskritsation.

3 These paragraphs and the subsequent section are based on a series of on-site interviews with the current *pujārī* (temple priest) of the Koḷī temple in the Kolaba police station, Vandana Kshirsagar, on 10 February and 14–17 December 2006.

4 In Hindu mythology, *āsarās* are underworld water spirits who have their kingdom deep down below the surface of the water in the rivers and the seas. They are generally malevolent in nature and are often held responsible for whirlpools that drown people and capsize ships. However, properly propitiated, they assume a benign character and protect people from drowning.

5 This is the classical Brahmanic *pūjā* procedure for the worship of Varuṇa, the god of water. However, the worship of a pot full of water has been a part of many Hindu rituals for a very long time and the practice seems to have originated from the Dravidians. It is therefore difficult to know if this is a process of Sanskritisation or the reverse.

6 A fascinating aspect of the representation of Khāḍādevī and the seven *āsarās* is clearly seen at this shrine. While Khāḍādevī and Mahiśāsura are shown with two eyes and a mouth each, the seven *āsarās* have been shown only with one eye and one mouth each. A possible explanation for this rather unusual iconography may be that although the Koḷīs worship the *āsarās* as goddesses, to them, they are obviously minor goddesses and not as important as Khāḍādevī. Secondly, the *āsarās* have an ambivalent character as against the benign boon-giving Khāḍādevī.

7 Vandana has been the *pujārī* since 1996. Before that, her mother and aunt were responsible for the *pūjās*. Her aunt decided not to marry, because she thought that her marriage would result in the division of the temple estate between her and her sister, thus destroying the sanctity of the shrine. Vandana's mother predeceased her sister. After the aunt had also died, the property had to be transferred into her brother's name and many difficulties were created by Indian bureaucracy in the process. Vandana at one stage got so concerned that she approached Khāḍādevī and begged the goddess to ensure the smooth passage of the transfer. She firmly believes that it was the desire of the goddess that Vandana should continue doing the *pūjās* and, consequently, the transfer went through without too many hitches.

8 The *śikhara* is the typical dome-like spire of a Hindu temple.

9 According to the President of Cuff Parade Koḷī village in an interview on 18 January 2005.

10 In folk Hinduism, posts are often used to represent goddesses. See Biardeau (2004).

11 Mahiśāsura, the Buffalo Demon, was killed by Durgā and so is often depicted sitting beneath the goddess, in this case Khāḍādevī, who also represents the power of Durgā.

12 Many of the Bene Israeli Jewish community of western India carry Koḷī names.

13 The following paragraphs use information gathered in interview with the current *pujārī* of the Koḷī temple in the Kolaba police station, Vandana Kshirsagar, 14–15 December 2006.

14 This was confirmed also in an interview with a Koḷī immigrant in Melbourne, July 2006. The authors befriended this young Koḷī woman who had a degree from Mumbai, a Masters degree in IT systems from an Australian university and was working for an Australian IT firm. She had become an Australian citizen, having migrated on her own from a Koḷī village near Bandra, in Mumbai.

15 Sally Warhaft mentions the following occupations of Koḷī living in the village that was the subject of her doctorate: dental assistant, taxi driver, postman, mechanic, port authority; confirmed in interview with Koḷī immigrant in Melbourne, July 2006.

Bibliography

Abhinavagupta 1985, *Parātriṃśikāvivaraṇa, Il commento di Abhinavagupta alla Parātriṃśikā*, translated by Raniero Gnoli, Istituto Italiano per il Medio ed Estremo Oriente, Roma.

—— 1987, *Tantrāloka* 1987, with the commentary of Jayaratha, re-edited by RC Dwivedi and Navjivan Rastogi, enlarged with an introduction by Navjivan Rastogi, 8 vols, Motilal Banarsidass, Delhi.

—— 1990, *The Dhvanyāloka of Anandavardhana with the Locana of Abhinavagupta*, translated by Daniel HH Ingalls, Jeffrey Moussaieff Masson and MV Patwardhan; edited with an introduction by Daniel HH Ingalls, Harvard University Press, Cambridge, Mass.

Agrawal, Dileep P 1982, *The archaeology of India*, Curzon, London.

Agrawala, Prithvi Kumar 1983, *Mithuna. the male female symbol in Indian art and thought*, Munshiram Manoharlal, New Delhi.

—— 1984, *Goddesses in Ancient India*, Abhinav Publications, New Delhi.

—— 1993, *Ancient Indian mother-goddess votive discs*, Books Asia, Varanasi.

Agrawala, Vasudeva S 1970, *Ancient Indian folk cults*, Prithivi Prakashan, Varanasi.

Ahmad, Zahiruddin 1999, *Saṅs-rGyas rGya-mTsho: life of the Fifth Dalai Lama*, International Academy of Indian Culture and Aditya Prakashan, New Delhi.

Allchin, Bridget and Frank Raymond Allchin 1982, *The rise of civilization in India and Pakistan*, Cambridge University Press, Cambridge.

Allchin, Frank Raymond 1995, 'Mauryan architecture and Art' in Allchin, FR, *The archaeology of Early Historic South Asia*, Cambridge University Press, Cambridge.

Amiet, Pierre 1986, *L'âge des èchanges inter-iraniens 3500–1700 avant J-C*, Editions de la Réunion des musées nationaux, Paris.

Apte, VS 1979, *The student's Sanskrit English dictionary*, Motilal Banarasidass, New Delhi.

Ardeleanu-Jansen, Alexandra 1992, 'New evidence on the distribution of artifacts: an approach towards a qualitative-quantitative assessment of the terracotta figurines of Mohenjo-Daro' in Catherine Jarrige, John P Gerry, and Richard H Meadow (eds), *South Asian archaeology 1989*, Prehistory Press, Madison.

Arts Council of Great Britain, 1971, *Catalogue of the exhibition on Tantra*.

Atre, Shubhangana 1998, 'The high priestess: gender signifiers and the feminine in the Harappa context', *South Asian Studies* 14.

Babb, LA 1970, 'The uses of sexual opposition in a Hindu pantheon', *Ethnology* 9(2).

—— 1975, *Popular Hinduism in Central India*, Columbia UP, New York.

Bailey, Greg 1995, *The Gaṇeśa Purāṇa, Volume One: Upāsanā Khaṇḍa*, Otto Harrassowitz, Wiesbaden.

—— 2008, *The Gaṇeśa Purāṇa, Volume Two: Krīḍā Khaṇḍa*, Otto Harrassowitz, Wiesbaden.

Banerjea, Jitendra Nath 1956, *The development of Hindu iconography*, University of Calcutta, Calcutta.

—— 1966, *Purāṇic and tāntric religion*, University of Calcutta, Calcutta.

Banerji, Arundhati 1994, *Early Indian terracotta art*, Harman Publishing House, New Delhi.

Barth, F 1959, *Political leadership among the Swat Pathans*, Athlone Press, London.

Bhāgavata Purāṇa 1950, NR Acarya, (ed), Bombay.

Bhattacharyya, Narendra Nath 1996, *History of the Śākta religion*, Munshiram Manoharlal, New Delhi.

—— 1999, *The Indian mother goddess*, third enlarged edition, Manohar, New Delhi.

Biardeau, Madeleine (ed) 1981, *Autour de la déesse hindoue*, Ecole des hautes études en sciences sociales, Paris.

—— (trans R Nice) 1989, *Hinduism: the anthropology of a civilisation*, Oxford University Press, New Delhi.

—— 2004, *Stories about posts: Vedic variations around the Hindu Goddess*, translated by Alf Hiltebeitel, Marie-Louise Reinike and James Walker, University of Chicago Press, Chicago.

Boyce, Mary 1975, *A history of Zoroastrianism* Vol 1, EJ Brill, Leiden.

Brahmānda Purāṇa 1993, Vol 23 Part I in Shastri, JL (ed), *Ancient Indian tradition and mythology*, Motilal Banarsidass, Delhi.

Brooks, DR 1990, *The secret of the three cities, an introduction to Hindu śākta tantrism*, Chicago UP, Chicago.

Bruckner, Heidrun 1994, 'Divinity, violence, wedding and gender in some South Indian cults' in Schwartz, AM et al (eds), *Wild goddesses in India and Nepal: proceedings of an international symposium, Berne and Zurich, November 1994*, Peter Lang, Bern.

Bryant, Edwin 2001, *The quest for origins of Vedic culture*, Oxford University Press, Oxford and New York.

Bryant, Edwin and Laurie L Patton (eds) 2005, *The Indo-Aryan controversy: evidence and inference in Indian history*, Routledge, London and New York.

Bühnemann, Gudrun 2000-2001, *Iconography of Hindu tantric deities*, 2 vols, Egbert Forsten, Groningen.

Byron, John 1987, *Portrait of a Chinese paradise*, Quartet Books, London.

Caldwell, Sarah 2005, 'Margins at the center: tracing Kālī through time, space and culture' in McDermott, Rachel Fell and Jeffrey J Kripal (eds), *Encountering Kālī: In the margins, at the center, in the West*, Motilal Banarsidass, Delhi.

Campbell, James 1884, *Gazetteer of the Bombay Presidency*, vol 23, Bijapur.

Campbell, JM (ed) 1918, *Hindu tribes and castes of Gujarat*, Bombay Presidency Gazetteer.

Campbell, June 2002, *Traveller in space: gender, identity and Tibetan Buddhism*, Continuum, London.

Chakrabarti, Dilip 2001, 'The archaeology of Hinduism' in Insoll, Timothy (ed) *Archaeology and world religion*, Routledge, London, New York.

—— 2004, 'Introduction' in Chakrabarti, DK (ed), *Indus Civilization sites in India: new discoveries*, Marg Publications, Mumbai.

Chandra, Pramod 1971, 'The cult of Śrī Lakshmī and four carved discs in Bharat Kala Bhavan', *Chhavi Golden Jubilee Volume*, Bharat Kala Bhavan, Banaras Hindu University, Varanasi.

Choudhary, Radakrishna 1964, *The Vrātyas in Ancient India*, Chowkhamba Sanskrit Series Office, Varanasi.

Clark, Sharri R 2003, 'Representing the Indus body: sex, gender, sexuality, and the anthropomorphic terracotta figurines from Harappa', *The Journal of Archaeology for Asia and the Pacific* 42(2).

Codrington, K de B 1935, 'Iconography, Classical and Indian', *Man* 35(70).

Coomaraswamy, Ananda Kentish 1971 [1928 & 1931], *Yakṣas*, Munshiram Manoharlal, New Delhi.

Courtright, Paul B 2001 (1985), *Gaṇeśa: lord of obstacles, lord of beginnings*, Motilal Banarsidass, Delhi.

Crooke, William 1907, *Natives of Northern India*, Constable & Company, London.

Czuma, Stanislaw 1985, *Kushan sculpture: images from early India*, Cleveland Museum of Art in association with Indiana University Press, Bloomington.

Dani, AH 1999 [1992], 'Pastoral-agricultural tribes of Pakistan in the post-Indus period' in Dani, AH and VM Masson (eds), *History of civilizations of Central Asia*, Vol 1, *The dawn of civilization: earliest times to 700 BC*, Motilal Banarsidas, Delhi.

Dani, AH and BK Thapar 1999 [1992], 'The Indus civilization' in Dani, AH and VM Masson (eds), *History of civilizations of Central Asia*, Vol 1, *The dawn of civilization: earliest times to 700 BC*, Motilal Banarsidas, Delhi.

Daniélou, Alain 1994, *The complete Kāma Sūtra*, Park Street Press, Rochester.

Das Gupta, Charu Chandra 1961, *Origin and evolution of Indian clay sculpture*, University of Calcutta Press, Calcutta.

de Mallmann, Marie-Thérèse 1963, *Les enseignements iconographiques de l'Agni-Purāṇa,* Presses Universitaires de France, Paris.

de Sade, le Marquis 1969, *Justine, ou les malheurs de la vertu,* Union Générale d'Edition, Paris.

Dehejia, Vidya 1986, *Yoginī cult and temples: a tantric tradition*, National Museum, New Delhi.

—— 1999, *Devi: the great female divinity in South Asian art*, Arthur M Sackler Gallery, Smithsonian Institution, Washington, Mapin Publishing, Ahmedabad & Prestel Verlag, Munich.

Desai, Devangana 1975, *Erotic sculpture of India: a socio-cultural study*, Tata McGraw Hill, New Delhi.

Dexter, MR (ed) 1990, *Whence the goddesses. a source book*, Pergamon, New York.

Dhavalikar Madhukar Keshav 1977, *Masterpiece of Indian terracottas*, Taraporevala, Bombay.

—— 1985, 'Chalcolithic cultures: a socio-economic perspective' in Dikshit, KN (ed), *Archaeological perspectives of India since Independence*, Books and Books, New Delhi.

—— 1987, 'Śakaṃbharī—the headless goddess', *Annals of the Bhandarkar Oriental Research Institute* 68.

—— 2002, *Environment and culture: a historical perspective,* Bhandarkar Oriental Research Institute, Pune.

Dhere, RC 1988 (1978), *Lajjagauri*, Shri Vidya Prakashan, Pune (Marathi).

Di Castro, Angelo Andrea 1998, *L'archeologia dell'Uttarāpatha tra il V e il III sec. a. C.*, Istituto Universitario Orientale, Naples (unpublished doctoral dissertation).

Dimmit, C and JAB van Buitenen 1978, *A Reader in the Sanskrit Purāṇas,* Temple University Press, Philadelphia.

Donaldson, Thomas 1975, 'Propitious-apotropaic eroticism in the art of Orissa', *Artibus Asiae* 35(1–2).

Doniger, Wendy 1995, 'Introduction' in Eilberg-Schwartz, Howard and Wendy Doniger, *Off with her head!: the denial of women's identity in myth, religion and culture*, University of California Press, Berkeley and Los Angeles.

Dupuche, John 2003, *Abhinavagupta, the Kula ritual as elaborated in Chapter 29 of the Tantrāloka,* Motilal Banarsidass, Delhi.

Eilberg-Schwartz, Howard and Wendy Doniger (eds) 1995, *Off with her head!*, University of California Press, Berkeley and Los Angeles.

Eisler, Riane 1992, 'La Dea della natura e della spiritualità: un ecomanifesto' in Campbell, Joseph & Charles Musés (eds), *I nomi della Dea: Il femminile nella divinità* , Ubaldini Editore, Rome (translation of *In All Her Names: Explorations of the Feminine Divinity*, 1991), Harper and Row, San Francisco.

Eller, Cynthia 2000, *The myth of matriarchal prehistory: why an invented past won't give women a future*, Beacon Press, Boston.

Erdosy, George (ed) 1995, *The Indo-Aryans of Ancient South Asia: language, material culture and ethnicity*, Walter de Gruyter, Berlin, New York.

Erndl, Kathleen 1993, *Victory to the Mother: the Hindu goddess of northwest India in myth, ritual and symbol*, Oxford University Press, New York.

Faust, B 1982, *Women, sex and pornography,* Penguin, London.

Fleet, JF 1881, 'Sanskrit and Old Canarese inscriptions', *Indian Antiquary* 10.

Foulston, Lynn 2002, *At the feet of the goddess: the divine feminine in local Hindu religion*, Sussex Academic Press, Brighton.

Francfort, Henri-Paul 1992, 'Dungeons and dragons: reflections on the system of iconography in Protohistoric Bactria and Margiana' in Possehl, Gregory (ed), *South Asian archaeology studies*, Oxford & IBH Publishing, New Delhi.

—— 1994, 'The Central Asian dimension of the symbolic system in Bactria and Margiana', *Antiquity* 68(259).

Freed, Stanley A and Ruth S Freed 1998, *Hindu festivals in a North Indian village* (Anthropological papers of the American Museum of Natural History, no 81), University of Washington Press, Seattle.

Führer, Alois 1897, *Monograph on Buddha Sakyamumi's birth place in the Nepalese Tarai* (Archaeological Survey of India, new imperial series 26, Northern India, 6), Allahabad.

Gail, AJ and GJ Mevissen (eds) 1993, *South Asian archaeology*, Stuttgart, GJR Verlag.

Gaṇeśa Purāṇa 1892, Gopal Narayan & Sons, Bombay.

George, E 1992, 'A background to the uneven development amongst the women of one caste in Western Saurashtra', Unpublished MA Prelim, Latrobe University.

—— 2004, *The Sorathiya Rabari: women's instrumentality in the culture of a pastoral caste*, Unpublished PhD thesis, Latrobe University, Bundoora.

Ghadavi, LP 1983, *Cāraṇa ni Asmita*, Jamnagar (Gujarati).

Ghosh, A (ed) 1989, *An encyclopaedia of Indian archaeology*, 2 vols, Munshiram Manoharlal, Delhi.

Ghosh, Avijit 2004, 'Catch me if you can', *The Telegraph* 23 May, www.telegraphindia.com, accessed 24 February 2007.

Gimbutas, Marija 1974, *The gods and goddesses of Old Europe 7000 to 3500 BC: myths, legends and cult images*, University of California Press, Berkeley.

—— 1999, *The living goddesses*, University of California Press, Berkeley.

—— 2001a, *The language of the goddess*, Thames & Hudson, London.

—— 2001b, *The living goddesses* (edited and supplemented by Miriam Robbins Dexter), University of California Press, Berkeley, Los Angeles, and London.

Giri, Gitu 2003, *Art and architecture remains in the Western Terai region of Nepal*, Droit Publishers, Delhi.

Goldman, Robert P 1999, 'God in hiding: the *Mahābhārata*'s Virāṭa Parvan and the divinity of the Indian epic hero', *Purāṇa* XLI/2:95–131.

Guha, R 1985, 'The career of an anti-god in heaven and on earth' in Mitra, Ashok (ed), *The truth unites: essays in tribute to Samar Sen,* Subarna Rekha, Calcutta.

Gupta, Swarajya Prakash 1980, *The roots of Indian art*, BR Publishing, Delhi.

Gyatso, Janet 1998, *Apparitions of the self: the secret autobiographies of a Tibetan visionary,* Princeton University Press, Princeton.

Hall, Fitz-Edward 1859, 'The Śrīsūkta or litany to fortune', *Journal of the Asiatic Society of Bengal* 28.

Hamilton, Jennifer 1998, 'Reclaiming the goddess: feminist spirituality and the use of symbols' in Casey, M, D Donlon, J Hope and S Wellfare (eds), *Redefining archaeology: feminist perspectives*, ANH Publications, The Australian National University, Canberra.

Hancock, M 1995, 'The dilemmas of domesticity: possession and devotional experience among urban Smārta women' in Harlan L and P Courtright (eds), *From the margins of Hindu marriage: essays on gender, religion and culture*, Oxford University Press, New York.

Harcourt, MV 1993, 'The Deshnoke "Karni Mata" temple and political legitimacy in medieval Rajasthan' *South Asia* 16 (supplement 1).

Harlan, L 2003, *The Goddesses' henchmen,* Oxford University Press, New York.

Harper, EB 1959, 'A Hindu village pantheon', *Southwestern Journal of Anthropology* 15(3).

Hawley, John S 1996, 'Prologue' in Hawley, John S and Donna M Wulff (eds) *Devī: goddesses of India*, University of California Press, Berkeley, Los Angeles, and London.

Heesterman, JC 1962, 'Vrātya and sacrifice', *Indo-Iranian Journal* 6(1).

Hermann-Pfandt, Adelheid 1990, *Ḍākinīs: zur Stellung und Symbolik des Weiblichen in tantrischen Buddhismus,* Indica et Tibetica Verlag, Bonn.

—— 1992–3, '*Ḍākinīs* in Indo-Tibetan Tantric Buddhism: Some Results of Recent Research', *Studies in Central and East Asian Religions* 5/6.

Hiltebeitel, Alf 1981, 'Draupadī's hair' in Biardeau, Madeleine (ed), *Autour de la déesse hindoue*, Ecole des hautes études en sciences sociales, Paris.

Hobsbawm, Eric 1983, 'Introduction: inventing traditions' in Hobsbawm, Eric and Terence Ranger (eds), *The invention of tradition*, Cambridge University Press, Cambridge.

Hodder, Ian 1986, *Reading the past*, Cambridge University Press, Cambridge.

—— 1993, 'Social cognition', *Cambridge Archaeological Journal* 3(2).

—— 1998, 'The goddess and leopard's den: conflicting interpretations at Çatalhoyuk' in Casey, M, D Donlon, J Hope and S Wellfare (eds) *Redefining archaeology: feminist perspectives*, ANH Publications, The Australian National University, Canberra.

—— 1999, *The archaeological process: an introduction*, Blackwell Publishers, Malden.

Humes, Cynthia Ann 1996, 'Vindhyavāsinī: local goddess yet great goddess' in Hawley, JS and DM Wulff (eds), *Devī goddesses of India*, University of California Press, Berkeley.

—— 2005, 'Wrestling with Kālī: South Asian and British constructions of the Dark Goddess' in McDermott, Rachel Fell and Jeffrey J Kripal (eds), *Encountering Kālī: in the margins, at the center, in the West*, Motilal Banarsidass, Delhi.

Insoll, Timothy 2004, *Archaeology, ritual, religion*, Routledge, London, New York.

Jamkhedkar, AP 2004, 'Symbols, images and rituals of the mother in Vakātaka period', *Lalit Kala* 30.

Janssen, Frans HPM 1991, 'On the origin and development of the so-called Lajjāgaurī' in Gail, AJ, and GJR Mevissen (eds), *South Asian Archaeology,* FS Verlag, Stuttgart.

Jarrige, Catherine 1984, 'Terracotta human figurines from Nindowari' in Allchin, Bridget (ed), *South Asian archaeology 1981*, Cambridge University Press, Cambridge.

Jarrige, Jean-Francois 2000, 'Mehrgarh Neolithic: new excavations' in Taddei, Maurizio and Giuseppe De Marco (eds), *South Asian Archaeology 1997*, Istituto Italiano per l'Africa e l'Oriente, Rome.

Jayakar, Pupul 1989, *The Earth Mother*, Penguin, New Delhi.

Joshi, NP 1986, *Mātṛkās: Mothers in Kuṣāna art*, Kanak Publications, New Delhi.

Jung, CG 1938, 'Psychological aspects of the mother archetype' in Jung, CG, *The archetypes and the collective unconscious*, RFC Hull (trans), Princeton UP, Princeton.

Kakar, Sudhir 1991, *The analyst and the mystic*, University of Chicago Press, Chicago.

—— 1996, *The Indian psyche*, Oxford University Press, Delhi.

Kalff, Martin 1979, *Selected chapters from the Abhidhānottara-Tantra: the union of female and male deities,* Unpublished PhD thesis, Columbia University, New York.

Kathuria, RP 1987, *Life in the courts of Rajasthan,* New Delhi.

Kelkar, Kamal 2002, *Vidharbhātīla Prācīna Mūrtī* [Old sculptures in Vidharbha], Shri Mangesha Prakashan, Nagpur.

Kenoyer, Jonathan Mark 1993, 'Socio-ritual artifacts of Upper Paleolithic hunter-gatherers in South Asia' in Possehl, Gregory (ed), *South Asian archaeology studies*, Oxford & IBH Publishing, New Delhi.

—— 2000, *Ancient cities of the Indus Valley Civilization*, American Institute of Pakistan Studies, Oxford University Press, Oxford, New York.

Kenoyer, Jonathan Mark, JD Clark, JN Pal and GR Sharma 1983, 'An Upper Palaeolithic shrine in India?', *Antiquity* 57(220).

Khan, Gulzar Muhammad 1973, 'Excavations at Zarif Karuna', *Pakistan Archaeology* 9.

Khergamker, Gajanan 2006, 'Goddess of the sea polices over Kolaba cop station', *Downtown plus Times of India* 26 June.

Kinsley, David 1986, *Hindu goddesses: visions of the divine feminine in the Hindu religious tradition*, University of California Press, Berkeley, Los Angeles, London.

Kolff, DHA 1990, *Naukar, Rajput and Sepoy: the ethno-history of the military labour market in Hindustan, 1450–1850*, Cambridge University Press.

Kosambi, Damodar Dharmanand 1962, *Myth and reality: studies in the formation of Indian culture*, Popular Prakashan, Bombay.

Kovacs, Anja 2004, 'You don't understand, we are at war! Refashioning Durga in the service of Hindu nationalism', *Contemporary South Asia* 13(4).

Kramrisch, Stella 1956, 'An image of Aditi Uttanapad', *Artibus Asiae* 19.

Kun dga' grol mchog 1982, 'Nag po spyod pa'i rtogs pa brjod pa'i yal 'dab' in *The Autobiographies of Jo-nang Kun-dga' grol mchog and his Previous Embodiments*, Tibet House Publishers, New Delhi.

Kūrma Purāṇa 1972, (edited and translated into English by AS Gupta et al), Kashiraj Trust, Varanasi.

Kurtz, Stanley 1992, *All the mothers are one: Hindu India and the cultural reshaping of psychoanalysis*, Columbia University Press, New York

Lalye PG 1973, *Studies in Devāī Bhāgavata*, Popular Prakashan, Bombay.

Lele-Trymbakkar, Ganesha Shastri 1964, *Trīthayātrāprabandha* (2nd edn), Deshmukh Prakashan, Pune.

Lerner, Martin and Steven Kossak 1991, *The lotus transcendent. Indian and Southeast Asian art from the Samuel Eilenberg Collection*, Metropolitan Museum of Art, New York.

Lohuizen-de Leeuw, Johanna Engelberta van 1972, 'Gandhara and Mathura: their cultural relationship' in Pal Pratapaditya (ed), *Aspects of Indian art*, Brill, Leiden.

Mabbett, IW 2006, 'L'indologie de Paul Mus: sociologie ou cosmologie?' in Chandler, DP and C Goscha (eds), *Paul Mus (1902–1969): L'espace d'un regard*, Les Indes savantes, Paris.

Mackay, Ernest 1931, 'Household objects, tools and implements' in Marshall, John H (ed), *Mohenjodaro and the Indus Civilization*, Arthur Probsthain, London.

—— 1948, *Early Indus Civilization*, Luzac, London.

Mackenzie Brown, C 1991, *The triumph of the Goddess: the canonical models and theological visions of the Devībhāgavata Purāṇa*, State University of New York Press, Albany.

Maddock, P 2006, 'Mammai Mataji: a contemporary Indian great goddess,' *Fieldwork in religion*, 2(2).

Mahadik, Krishnaswami A (ed) 1952, *Śarabhendra bhūpālakṛta tristhalī yātrecyā lāvṇyā aṇi Śarabhendra tīrthāvaḷi,* Saraswati Mahal Granthalaya (Marathi).

Malcolm, J 1832, *A memoir of Central India*, London.

Mankad, BL 1939, 'Rabaris of Kathiawar (a social study)', *Journal of the University of Bombay* 7(4).

Marglin, FA 1985, Wives of the god-king: the rituals of the devadasis of Puri, Oxford University Press, Delhi.

Marshall, John H 1931, 'Religion' in Marshall, John H (ed), *Mohenjodaro and the Indus Civilization*, Arthur Probsthain, London.

—— 1951, *Taxila*, Cambridge University Press, Cambridge.

Maula, Erkka 1984, 'The calendar stones from Moenjo Daro' in Jansen, Michael and Gunter Urban (eds), *Interim reports vol. 1: Reports on field work carried out at Mohenjo-Daro, Pakistan 1982–83 by the IsMEO-Aachen University Mission*, RWTH/IsMEO, Aachen, Rome.

McDermott, Rachel Fell and Jeffrey J Kripal (eds), *Encountering Kālī: In the margins, at the center, in the West*, Motilal Banarsidass, Delhi.

Mehta, Rustam J 1976, *Masterpieces of Indian sculpture*, Taraporwala and Sons, Bombay.

Menzies, Jackie 2006, 'Concept of the goddess' in Menzies, Jackie (ed), *Goddess divine energy*, Art Gallery of New South Wales, Sydney.

Meskell, Lynn 1998, 'That's capital M, capital G' in Casey, M, D Donlon, J Hope and S Wellfare (eds), *Redefining archaeology: feminist perspectives*, ANH Publications, The Australian National University, Canberra.

Mishra, Tara Nanda 1996, 'The archaeological activities in Lumbini', *Ancient Nepal* 139.

Mishra, V 1998, *Devotional poetics and the Indian sublime*, State University of New York Press, Albany.

Misra, Baba and Pradeep Mohanty 2002, 'Headless contour in the art tradition of Orissa, Eastern India', *Bulletin of the Deccan College Post-Graduate and Research Institute* 62–63.

Mitra, Debala 1972, *Excavations at Tilaura-Kot and Kodan and explorations in the Nepalese Terai*, Department of Archaeology, Kathmandu.

Mode, Heinz 1960, *L'antica India* (translated by G Gentili and L Petech), Le Grandi Civiltà del Passato, Editrice Primato, Rome.

Moffat, Michael 1979, *An Untouchable community in South India: structure and consensus*, Princeton University Press, Princeton NJ.

Monier-Williams, Monier 1986, *A Sanskrit–English dictionary*, Motilal Banarasidass, New Delhi (originally published by Oxford University Press, 1899).

—— 1993, *Sanskrit–English Dictionary,* Motilal Banarsidass, Delhi.

Mukherji, Purna Chandra 1901, *A report on a tour of exploration of the antiquities in the Tarai, Nepal, the Region of Kapilavastu; during February and March 1899, with a prefatory note by Vincent A Smith* (Archaeological Survey of India, imperial series 26, part I), Calcutta.

Murray, MA 1934, 'Female fertility figures', *Journal of the Royal Anthropological Institute of Great Britain and Ireland* 44.

Narasimhaswami, HK 1952, 'Nagarjunakonda image inscription', *Epigraphica Indica* 29 (5).

Nasim Khan, M 2002, 'Lajjāgaurī seals and related antiquities from Kashmir Smast-Gandhāra', *Journal of the Society for South Indian Studies* 18(8).

—— 2003, 'Kashmir Smast (Gandhara) and its religious significance: study based on epigraphic and other antiquities from the site' in Franke-Vogt, Ute, and Hans-Joachim Weisshaar (eds), *South Asian Archeology,* LindenSoft Verlag, Aachen.

Nath, Amarendra 1990, 'Lajjā Gaurī and her possible genesis', *Lalit Kala* 25.

Nelson, Sarah Milledge 1997, *Gender in archaeology: analyzing power and prestige*, AltaMira Press, Walnut Creek.

O'Flaherty, WD 1981, 'The shifting balance of power in the marriage of Śiva and Pārvatī' in Hawley J, and D Wulff (eds), *The divine consort: Rādhā and the goddesses of India*, Graduate Theological Union, Berkeley.

Obeyesekere, Gananath 1984, *The cult of the goddess Pattini*, University of Chicago Press, Chicago.

Obeyesekere, Gananath 1990, *The work of culture: symbolic transformation in psychoanalysis and anthropology*, University of Chicago Press, Chicago.

Parpola, Asko 1994, *Deciphering the Indus script*, Cambridge University Press, Cambridge.

—— 1995, 'The problem of the Aryans and the Soma: textual-linguistic and archaeological evidence' in Erdosy George (ed), *The Indo-Aryans of Ancient South Asia: language, material culture and ethnicity*, Walter de Gruyter, Berlin, New York.

—— 2002, 'Pre-proto-Iranians of Afghanistan as initiators of *śākta* tantrism: on the Scythian/Saka affiliation of the Dāsas, Nuristanis and Magadhans', *Iranica Antiqua* 37.

Paul, K 1993, 'Negotiating sacred space: the Mandir and the Oran as contested sites,' *South Asia* 16(supplement 1).

—— 1995, *Constituting Cāraṇa,* unpublished PhD thesis, Anthropology Dept Sydney University.

Piggott, Stuart 1950, *Prehistoric India*, Penguin, Harmondsworth.

Pintchman, Tracy 1994, *The rise of the goddess in the Hindu tradition*, State University of New York Press, Albany.

Possehl, Gregory L 2002, *The Indus Civilization: a contemporary perspective*, Vistaar, New Delhi.

Poster, Amy J 1986, *From Indian earth: 4,000 years of terracotta art,* Brooklyn Museum, New York.

Prabhudesai, PK 1968, *Ādiśaktīce viṣvasvarūpa (Devikośa),* Tilak Maharashtra Vidyapeeth, Pune (Marathi).

Radcliffe-Bolon, Carol 1997 (1992), *Forms of the goddess Lajja Gauri in Indian art*, Motilal Banarasidass, Delhi.

Raghavan, V 1956, 'Variety and integration in the pattern of Indian culture', *Far Eastern Quarterly* 15.

Raghunathji 1900, *The Hindu temples of Bombay*, Fort Printing Press, Bombay (Reprinted in 2004 by Mumbai philanthropist and scholar, Phiroze Ranade.)

Raheja, Gloria and Ann Gold 1994, *Listen to the heron's words: reimagining gender and kinship in North India*, University of California Press, Berkeley, Los Angeles, London.

Ramanujan, AK 1973, *Speaking of Śiva*, Penguin, Harmondsworth.

—— 1986 'Two realms of Kannada folklore' in Blackburn, SH and AK Ramanujan (eds), *Another harmony: new essays on the folklore of India*, OUP, Delhi.

Rao, Vidya 1990, '*Thumri* as feminine voice', *Economic and Political Weekly* 28 April.

Renfrew, Colin 1994, 'The archaeology of religion' in Renfrew, Colin and Ezra BW Zubrow (eds), *The Ancient mind: elements of cognitive archaeology*, Cambridge University Press, Cambridge.

Renfrew, Colin and Paul Bahn 1991, *Archaeology, theories, methods and practice*, Thames and Hudson, London.

Rijal, Babu Krishna 1996, *100 years of archaeological research in Lumbini, Kapilavastu and Devadaha*, with the reprint of '*A report on a tour of exploration of the antiquities in the Tarai, Nepal (1901)*' by PC Mukherji, SK International Publishing House, Kathmandu.

Roberts, Gregory David 2004, *Shantaram*, Scribe Publishers, Melbourne.

Roerich, George 1959, *Biography of Dharmasvāmin, Chag lo-tsā-ba Chos-rje-dpal, A Tibetan monk pilgrim*, KP Jayaswal Research Institute, Patna.

Rolland, Pierre 1973, 'Le Mahavrata. Contribution à l'étude d'un rituel solonnnel védique', *Nachrichten der Akademie der Wissenschaften in Gottingen, Philologisch-Historische Klasse.*

Rosaldo, M 1980, *Knowledge and passion: Ilongot notions of self and social life*, Cambridge University Press, Cambridge.

Roscoe, Will 1996, 'Priests of the goddess: gender transgression in ancient religion', *History of Religions* 35(3).

Sanderson, Alexis 1985, 'The category of purity and power among the Brahmins of Kashmir' in Carrithers, M, S Collins and S Lukes (eds), *The category of the person: anthropology, philosophy, history*, Cambridge University Press, Cambridge.

—— 1988, 'Śaivism and the tantric traditions' in Sutherland, S, L Houlden, P Clarke and F Hardy (eds), *The World's Religions*, Routledge, London.

—— 1995, 'Meaning in tantric ritual' in Blondeau, AM and K Schipper (eds), *Essais sur le rituel III: colloque du centenaire de la section des sciences religieuses de l'Ecole pratique des hautes études*, Peeters, Louvain-Paris,

Sangari, K 1990, 'Mirabai and the spiritual economy of *bhakti*', *Economic and Political Weekly* 7 July.

Sankalia, HD 1960, 'The nude goddess or "shameless woman" in Western Asia, India, and South Eastern Asia', *Artibus Asiae* 23(2).

Sankalia, Hasmukh Dhirajlal, Shantaram Bhalachandra Deo and Zainuddin Dawood Ansari 1971, *Chalcolithic Navdatoli: The excavations at Navdatoli 1957–59*, University of Baroda Press, Poona, Baroda.

Sarohamāhātmya, included in *Vāmana Purāṇa* 1968.

Sax, WS 1991, *Mountain goddess: gender and politics in a Himalayan pilgrimage*, Oxford University Press, New York.

Schopen, Gregory 1997, 'Archaeology and Protestant presuppositions in the study of Indian Buddhism' in *Bones, stones, and Buddhist monks: collected papers on the archaeology, epigraphy, and texts of monastic Buddhism in India*, University of Hawaii Press, Honolulu.

Sen, Amartya 2005, *The argumentative Indian*, Penguin, London.

Shanks, Michael and Christopher Tilley 1987a, *Re-constructing archaeology*, Cambridge University Press, Cambridge.

—— 1987b, *Social theory and archaeology*, Polity Press, Cambridge.

—— 1989, 'Archaeology into the 1990s', *Norwegian Archaeological Review* 22(1).

Shastri, Hariprasad 1982, *Lokayata and Vratya*, Firma KL Mukhopadhyay, Calcutta.

Shastri, JL (ed) 1983, *Manusmṛti, with the Sanskrit commentary Manvarthamuktāvali of Kullūka Bhaṭṭa*, Motilal Banarsidass, Delhi.

Shering, MA 1881, *The castes and tribes of Rajasthan*, London.

Shulman, David 1980, *Tamil temple myths*, Princeton University Press, Princeton NJ.

—— 1984,'Die Integration der hinduistischen Kultur durch die Brahmanen, "Große", "mittlere" und "kleine" Versionen des Parasurama-Mythos', in Schluchter, Wolfgang (ed), *Max Webers Studien über Hinduismus und Buddhismus. Interpretation und Kritik,* Suhrkamp, Frankfurt .

Silburn, Lilian 1983, *La kuṇḍalinī, l'énergie des profondeurs.* Les Deux Océans, Paris.

Simmer-Brown, Judith 2002, *Ḍākinī's warm breath: the feminine principle in Tibetan Buddhism,* Shambhala, Boston.

Sinha, Amita 2006, 'Cultural landscape of Pavagadh: the abode of Mother Goddess Kalika', *Journal of Cultural Geography* 23(2).

Sjöö, Monica and Barbara Mor 1991, *The great cosmic mother: rediscovering the religion of the Earth*, Harper, San Francisco.

Sohan Dan Cāraṇa 1987, Interviews with Professor Sohan Dan Cāraṇa, Hindi Deparment, University of Jodhpur, February 1987.

Sonawane, VH 1988, 'Some remarkable sculptures of Lajja Gauri from Gujarat', *Lalit Kala* 23.

Srinivas, MN 1952, *Religion and society among the Coorgs of South India*, Clarendon, Oxford.

Srivastava, Mahesh Chandra Prasad 1979, *Mother goddess in Indian art, archaeology and literature*, Agam Kala Prakashan, Delhi.

Staal, JF 1963, 'Sanskrit and Sanskritization', *Journal of Asian Studies* 22(3).

Stern, H 1971, 'Power in traditional India: territory, caste and kinship. A study of the Rajasthan region' in Fox, R (ed), *Kin, clan, raja and rule: state–hinterland relations in pre-industrial India*, University of California Press, Berkeley.

Stoller, P 1989, *The taste of ethnographic things: the senses in anthropology*, University of Pennsylvania Press, Philadelphia.

Stutley, Margaret 1985, *Hinduism*, The Antiquarian Press, Wellingborough.

Sukhthankar (ed) 1942, *Mahabharata* (Bombay edition) vol 3 Bhandarkar, Oriental Institute, Poona.

Tambs-Lyche, Harald 1999, 'Introduction' in Tambs-Lyche, Harald (ed), *The feminine sacred in South Asia*, Manohar, New Delhi.

—— 2004, *The feminine sacred in South Asia,* Manohar, Delhi.

Tāranātha, 1985a, 'bKa' babs bdun ldan gyi brgyud pa'i rnam thar ngo mtshar rmad du byung ba rin po che'i lta bu'i rgyan' in Namgyal, C and T Taru (eds), *The collected works of Jo-Nang Tāranātha* Vol 16, Smanrtsis Shesrig Dpemzod, Leh.

—— 1985b, 'Slob dpon chen po spyod 'chang dbang po'i rnam par thar pa ngo mtshar snyan pa'i sgra dbyangs' in Namgyal, C and T Taru (eds), *The collected works of Jo-Nang Tāranātha* Vol 12, Smanrtsis Shesrig Dpemzod, Leh.

—— 1987, 'Grub chen Buddha gupta'i rnam thar rje btsun nyid kyi zhal lung las gzhan du rang rtog gi dri mas ma sbags pa'i yi ge yang dag pa'o' in Namgyal, C and T Taru (eds), *The collected works of Jo-Nang Tāranātha* Vol 17, Smanrtsis Shesrig Dpemzod, Leh.

Templeman, David 1983, *The seven instruction lineages by Jo Nang Tāranātha,* Library of Tibetan Works and Archives, Dharamsala.

—— 1989, *Tāranātha's Life of Kṛṣṇācārya/Kāṇha,* Library of Tibetan Works and Archives, Dharamsala.

—— 1992–3, 'A narrative account of a Gaṇacakra, and the fulfillment of Guhyasamāja through Cakrasaṃvara', *Studies in Central and East Asian Religions* 5/6.

—— 1994, 'Reflexive criticism: the case of Kun dga' grol mchog and Tāranātha' in Kvaerne, Per (ed), *Tibetan studies: proceedings of the 6th Seminar of the*

International Association for Tibetan Studies, The Institute for Comparative Research in Human Culture, Oslo.

—— 2002, 'Iranian themes in Tibetan tantric culture: the *ḍākinī*' in Blezer, Henk (ed), *Religion and secular culture in Tibet, Tibetan studies II*, EJ Brill, Leiden.

Thapar, Romila 1963, *Aśoka and the decline of the Maurya*, Oxford University Press, Oxford.

—— 1984, *From lineage to state: social formations in the mid-First Millennium BC in the Ganga Valley*, Oxford University Press, Delhi.

—— 2002, 'The Rgveda encapsulating social change' in Pannikar, KN, Terence L Byres and Utsa Patnaik, *The making of history*, Anthem, London.

Tiwari, JN 1985, *Goddess cults in Ancient India*, Sundeep Prakashan, Delhi.

Tiwari, Sudarshan Raj 1996, 'Mayadevi temple: recent discoveries and its implications on history of building at Lumbini', *Tribhuvan University Journal* 19.

Tod, J 1987, *Annals and antiquities of Rajasthan*, Motilal Banarsidass, Delhi.

Townsend, Joan B 1990, 'The goddess: fact fallacy and revitalization movement' in Hurtado, Larry W (ed), *Goddesses in religions and modern debate* Scholars Press, Atlanta.

Trigger, Bruce G 1989, *A history of archaeological thought*, Cambridge University Press, Cambridge.

Tripathi, Vibha and K Srivastava Ajeet 1994, *The Indus terracottas*, Sharada Publishing House, Delhi.

Turner, V 1974, *Dramas, fields and metaphors: symbolic action in human society*, Cornell University Press, Ithaca NY.

U rgyan Ghuru n.d. *U rgyan Ghuru Padma 'byung gnas kyi skyes rabs rnam par thar pa rgyas par bkod pa padma bka'i thang yig,* Shes rig par khang, Dharamsala.

Ujwal, KS Dan 1972, *Bhagwati Shri Karṇīji Maharaj*, Jaipur.

Urban, Hugh B 2003, *Tantra: sex, secrecy, politics and power in the study of religion*, University of California Press, Berkeley.

Urban, Hugh B 2005, 'India's darkest heart: Kālī in the colonial imagination' in McDermott, Rachel Fell and Jeffrey J Kripal (eds), *Encountering Kālī: in the margins, at the center, in the West*, Motilal Banarsidass, Delhi.

Vāmana Purāṇa 1968, (edited and translated into English by AS Gupta et al), Kashiraj Trust, Varanasi.

Van Buitenen, JAB (ed and trans) 1975, *The Mahābhārata: the book of the forest*, Chicago University Press, Chicago.

Verardi, Giovanni 1996, 'Religions, rituals, and the heaviness of Indian history', *Annali dell'Istituto Universitario Orientale di Napoli* 56(2).

—— 2003, 'Images of destruction. an enquiry into Hindu icons in their relation to Buddhism' in *Buddhist Asia 1*, Papers from the First Conference of Buddhist Studies held in Naples in May 2001, Italian School of East Asian Studies, Kyoto 2003.

Verhoeven, Marc 2002, 'Ritual and ideology in the pre-pottery Neolithic B of the Levant and Southeast Anatolia', *Cambridge Archaeological Journal* 12(2).

Vicziany, Marika 2007, 'Understanding the 1993 Mumbai bombings: madrassahs and the hierarchy of terror', *South Asia* 30(1).

Vicziany, Marika and Jayant Bapat 2008, 'Mumbādevī and the other mother goddesses in Mumbai', *Modern Asian Studies,* Cambridge University Press (43)1.

Vidal, D 1997, *Violence and truth: A Rajasthani kingdom confronts colonial authority*, Oxford University Press, Delhi.

Wadley, Susan S 1977, 'Women and the Hindu tradition' in Jacobson, D and Susan S Wadley (eds), *Women in India: two perspectives*, South Asia Books, Columbia MO.

Warhaft, Sally 2003, *Fishing in the City of Gold: an ethnography of the Koḷīs of Mumbai*, PhD thesis, La Trobe University, Bundoora, Australia.

White, David Gordon 2003, *Kiss of the yoginī: tantric sex in its South Asian contexts*, University of Chicago Press, Chicago and London.

Wilson, HH (ed and trans) 1961, *The Vishnu Purāṇa: a system of Hindu mythology and tradition*, Punthi Pustak, Calcutta.

Winkelmann, Sylvia 2000, 'Some new ideas about the possible origin of the anthropomorphic and semi-human-creature depictions on Harappan seals' in Taddei Maurizio and Giuseppe De Marco (eds), *South Asian Archaeology 1997*, Istituto Italiano per l'Africa e l'Oriente, Rome.

Witzel, Michael 1995, 'Early Indian history: linguistic and textual parameters' in Erdosy, George (ed), *The Indo-Aryans of Ancient South Asia: language, material culture and ethnicity*, Walter de Gruyter, Berlin, New York.

Wood, Juliette 1996, 'The concept of the goddess' in Billington, Sandra and Miranda Green (eds), *The concept of the goddess*, Routledge, London, New York.

Ziegler, NP 1976, 'Marwari historical chronicles: sources for the social and cultural history of Rajasthan', *Indian Economic and Social History Review* 12(2).

Zla ba seng ge (ed) 1997, *Grub chen U rgyan pa'i rnam par thar pa byin rlabs kyi chu rgyun*, Vol 32 of series, *Gangs can rig mdzod*, Bod ljongs bod yig dpe rnying dpe skrun khang, Tibet Autonomous Region.

Index

Abhidhānottara–Tantra, 216
Allāmmā (goddess), 68
Allchin, R, 35
Amarnath, 86, 87
Ambikā (a name of Pārvatī), 51
Anugraha, 125
apotheosis, 142
archaeology
  of goddess cults, 21–42
  cognitive 23
Aryanisation, 22
āsarā, 190, 191, 192, 193, 195, 196
Aśoka (emperor), 31
āśramas, 47
Assam, 17, 141, 142
asura, 48, 53, 55
  see also demons
Aurva, 74
Autour de la déesse hindoue, 1–8
  see also Biardeau, Madeleine
Avalokiteśvara, 145
avatāra, 59

Babb, LA, 9, 10, 210
Badami, 83, 107n, 109
Baghor (archaeological site), 26
Bailey, Greg, vii, ix, x, 17, 43, 44, 62, 210
Bālāsura (demon), 50
Bansuri/Bansapati (forest goddess), 26
Bapat, Jayant, vii, ix, 1, 16, 18, 79, 130, 189, 224
bards, 149, 152, 154, 156
Baubo (Egyptian goddess, typifying womb symbolism), 92, 93, 95, 96, 109
Bhagat, 170, 171, 174
Bhāgavatapurāṇa, 61, 62
Bhairava, 141
bhakti, 61
Bhṛgu, 71, 73, 74, 75, 76
Bhūdevī, 86, 88
Bhuwa Atta, 163, 164, 168, 169, 170, 171, 172, 173, 175, 176, 180, 181, 186
Bhuwi Ma, 163, 170, 171, 174, 176
Biardeau, Madeleine, 1–7, 210, 215
Brahmā (creator god), 48, 51, 74
Brahmāṇḍa Purāṇa, 69, 73, 74, 75
Brahmanism/Brāhmans, 1, 3, 4, 9, 10, 11–13, 15, 17, 18
  as orthodoxy 13, 17
  as rivals of Kṣatriyas 69

breast/breast mother, 10, 11, 37, 39, 47, 49, 51, 53, 54, 57, 58, 62, 92
Brooks, DR, 11, 210
Buddha, 31–33, 41, 196, 198, 213, 222
Buddhism, 32, 33
Bühnemann, G, 107

cakras, 128
Cakrasaṃvāra maṇḍala, 137
Caldwell, S, 7
Campbell, J, 106
Cāraṇa, 17, 15–7, 161, 162
Cāraṇi Devī, 156, 157, 158, 159, 160, 161
Chakrabarti, D, 24
Chapgar, Shri, 82, 94, 95, 107, 109
Chelāṇ, 164, 166, 172, 174, 175, 177, 178, 181, 182, 186
Citraratha, 66, 70
Courtright, P, 63
Cyavana, 74

ḍākiṇī, vii, 16, 17, 18, 130, 133–149, 223
Dakṣa, 74
Dalit, 19
Daniélou, A, 108n
darśan, 158, 163, 166, 167, 170, 173, 179
Dāsas, 25
De Sade, Marquis Donatien, 120
Dehejia, v, 22
demons, 52, 53, 58
  see also asuras; rākṣasas
Desai, D, 107
Desai, Rashmi, vii, ix, 15, 65
devadāsī, 35, 110, 120, 121
Devī, as consorts of gods 10, 11
  as concept developing in recent centuries 13
  as regional goddess 80
  as universal Great Goddess 13, 16, 19
  in modern perspectives 1
  in the Kula tradition 114, 115
  theories about, 1–7, 24, 25, 37, 38, 41
Devībhāgavatapurāṇa, 14
Devikoṣa (lexicon in Marathi), 85
Dexter, MR, 6, 212, 214
Devīkoṭṭā, 141, 142, 143
Devīputra, 156, 157
dhajā, 172, 173, 174, 175, 176, 177, 178, 180, 184
dharma, 119
Dhavalikar, MK, 95
Dhere, RC, 79–111, 212
Dhvanyālocana, 125
Di Castro, Angelo Andrea, vii, ix, 6, 15, 16, 21, 32, 130, 212
Doniger, W, 68, 87
Draupadī, 5
Ḍupuche, John, vii, ix, 16, 110, 113, 116, 117, 213
Durgā, 25, 27, 28, 41, 43, 80, 185, 195, 204, 207, 216

Earth Mother, 21
Eilberg–Schwartz, H, 87
Ekavirā Devī, 190
Ellammā/Allāmmā/Mariammā/Mūlā/Peri (goddess), 68, 86, 87, 97
Eller, C, 26, 40
Erndl, Kathleen, 10, 213

fecundity, 1, 80, 95
  see also Earth Mother

fisherfolk, 18, 189–203
five ignorances, 136
five transcendent wisdoms, 136
Fleet, JF, 82, 84, 85, 91
folk tradition, 4, 9, 11–12, 40
  see also Little Tradition
Foulston, Louise, 9, 11, 12, 213

Gandhāra, 98
Gandharvas, 68, 69
Gaṇeśa, 17, 18, 43–64, 109, 189, 195, 197, 217
Gaṇeśapurāṇa, 17, 43–64
Gaurī (a name of Pārvatī), 49, 50, 58, 81
George, Effy, vii, x, 18, 130, 163, 213
Gimbutas, M, 6, 22, 23, 25
Girijā (a name of Pārvatī), 57
Goddess, *see Devī*
Goldman, R, 59
Golphādevī, 190
Grāmadevatā (village deity) 33
Great and Little Traditions (anthropological concept), 3, 4, 9, 10, 11–12, 14, 28, 157
Guha, R, 65, 66

Harbādevī, 190
Harcourt, Max, vii, x, 17, 149, 214
harlots, 107
Harper, EB, 9
Hawley, JS, 22
Herukā, 140
Hiltebeitel, A, 5
Hindu fundamentalism, 18, 202
Hindutva, 18
Hirādevī, 190
Huligamma (Tiger goddess), 28
Humes, Cynthia Anne, 8, 14, 215

Inamgaon (archaeological site), 28, 29
Indo–Aryan (language), 24
Indus religion/civilization, 21–28, 35, 38, 39, 40, 211, 212, 216, 217, 219, 223
Insoll, T, 38

Jālandharipa, 136
Jamadagni, 66, 67, 68, 70, 71, 74, 86
Janssen, F, 81, 83, 89, 107
Jari–Mari, 193, 194, 195, 196, 205
Jayaratha, 118, 120, 125, 130
Joguḷāmbā, 110, 111

Kakar, Sudhir, 5, 198, 216
Kālaratri, 141
Kalaś, 164, 166, 174, 177, 178, 182
Kālī 7, 11, 18, 43, 196, 211, 215, 218, 223
Kaṃsa, 62
Kāñcīpuram Purāṇa 65
Kannada (language), 107
Kāpālikas (Śaivite sect), 113, 114
Karṇi Mātā, 159, 160
Kārtavīrya, 68, 72, 73, 77
Kashmir Śaivism, 16, 113
Kaśyapa 44, 72
Kaula tradition, 113, 114
Khāḍādevī, vii, 18, 189–201, 205–207
Khan Avatāra Sagats, 157, 158, 160
Khyāti, 74
Kolaba, 18
Koḷī, vii, 18, 189–207
Kramrisch, S, 80, 93, 94, 98
Kṛṣṇa, 62, 198

Kṛṣṇācarita, 61
Kṛṣṇācārya, 136–144
Krūra (demon), 49
Kṣatriyas, in relation to Brāhmans, 69, 71, 72, 75, 76
Kṣema, (demon) 48
Kula (tantric ritual practice), 113–131
Kurtz, S, 5
Kuśala (demon), 48
Kushan, 37

Lajjāgauri/Lañjāgaurī, vii, xi, 16, 18, 79–111, 130, 212, 215, 218
  meaning of name 81
Lakṣmī/Śrī, 88, 97, 197
Lañjīśvara/Lañjigeśvara (town), 83
Lele–Trymbakkar, Pandit Ganeshashastri, 82, 85, 91
liberation, 53
  see also mokṣa
liṅga (of Śiva), 16, 82, 85, 98, 109, 141
Lion Herders, 149–162
Little Tradition, 4, 9, 10, 11–12
lotus symbolism, 88, 96
Lumbinī (Buddha's reputed birthplace), 31, 32, 41

Mabbett, Ian, vii
mādh, 163, 164, 166, 167, 169, 170, 172–174, 176–179, 181–183, 185, 186
Mahābhārata, 15, 41, 59, 65–77, 222, 223
Mahādevī, 5, 13, 19
Mahākūṭeśvara Temple, 82, 85
Mahiṣāsura (buffalo demon), 18
maithuna, 118, 119, 124, 128, 129
Mālinī (type of *mantra*), 121, 122, 127
Mammai Mātāji, vii, 18, 163–166, 168–170, 172, 179, 182, 185
Mānava Dharma Śāstra, 36
maṇḍala, 116, 128, 133, 135, 137, 139, 140, 144, 145, 147
maṅgalasūtra (necklace), 107
māntā, 164, 166, 170, 175, 177, 178, 182
mantra, 121
Mariammā, 68
Mariatale, 68
Marshall, John, 21, 24–28, 35, 41, 217
Maruti, 197
matriarchy, 3, 25, 26, 37, 40
matricide, 70
mātṛkās, as Kushan deities 37
  as set of phonemes in tantra 122
Matsyapurāṇa, 89, 96
Māyā, 46, 56, 58, 59, 60,170, 171, 182, 183, 185, 198
Māyādevī, 31, 33
Mehrgarh (archaeological site), 30
Meskell, L, 25, 26
Moffat, M, 68
mokṣa (liberation), 48, 53
mother goddess cults, 3, 37
  and Lajjāgaurī image, 94
  in theory of prehistoric cult 6, 15, 16, 23, 80
Mumbādevī (Mumbai deity), 18, 189, 190, 191, 194, 204
Mumbai, 18, 189–208, 224
Murray, MA, 92, 93
Mus, Paul, 6, 7, 217

Nagarjunakonda, 80, 98, 106
Nav Ratri, 172
Navdatoli (archaeological site), 28

Neolithic, 16, 30, 31, 39, 92, 216, 224
nudity, 80

Old Woman's island, 194
Orientalism, meaning of, 6

padhiyār, 174, 176, 179, 181
Padmasambhava, 134
Padminī (lotus woman), 84, 107
Paramabrahma, 60
Paraśurāma, 15, 65, 68, 69, 70–76
parāṭh, 168, 172, 173, 178, 185
Parātrīṃśikā, 121, 122
Parpola, A, 25, 36
Pārvatī (consort of Śiva), vii, 17, 28, 35, 43–63, 79–111, 130, 156, 186, 205, 219
pāṭ chadwu, 168
Piggott, S, 23, 24
Pintchman, T, 14
pīṭha (sacred site), 127
pornography, and the Lajjāgaurī image 91, 92, 109
Prasenajit, 74
Pṛthvī/Pṛthivī (earth, earth goddess), 89, 93
psychology, in theories of the Devī, 4, 5
Punj (Rabari festival), 18, 164, 166, 168, 169, 172–174, 177, 178, 180–183
Purāṇas, 17, 24, 44, 65, 212
Puraṇic, 23–24, 27, 43, 89, 96, 97, 157, 185, 210
Pūrṇa Avatāra Sagats, 157, 159, 160
Pūrṇakumbha ('full pot', iconographic feature), 80, 83, 84, 89

Rabari, 17–18, 163–166, 168–172, 174–186–214
Radcliffe–Bolon, C, 80, 83
Rādhā, 198
Raghunathji, 201, 204, 220
Rajasthan, vii, 17, 19, 84, 103, 106, 149–162, 214, 216, 221–224
Rajput, 149–156
rākṣasas, 53, 54
Rāma, 189
Ramanujan, AK, 10, 181, 220
Ratirahasya, 107
Ratnadāsa, 145
Ṛcīka, 72, 74, 75
Renfrew, C, 22, 23
Reṇukā, vii, 15, 65–77, 80, 85–87, 97, 99, 111
ringstones, 27, 33, 34
Rudra–śakti, 122

sādhaka, 145
Sai Baba, 197
Śaivism, 113
  see also Śiva
Śakambharī (fertility goddess), 95, 97
Śākambharī Māhātmya, 83
śakti, 1, 11, 15, 18, 25, 27, 28, 43, 115–129, 156–158, 172, 183, 186
  as female partner in tantra 116, 118, 119, 120
Śakti–bīja, 122
Śāktism, 25, 28, 35, 36, 95
samekhiyā, 172, 173, 174
Sanderson, A, 113, 114
Sankalia, HD, 82, 94
Śaṅkara, 75
Sanskritic Gods, 9, 11–14, 17
Sanskritisation, 4, 9, 13, 14, 18, 83, 190, 191, 201, 222, 206
sarju, 164, 171, 172, 173, 176, 184

Satyavatī, 71, 72, 74
Saurashtra, 163, 170
Sax, WS, 11
Schopen, G, 40
self–mutilation, 17
sexuality, 1, 87, 135–137, 211
Shiv Sena, 189, 190, 202
Shulman, David, 11
siddhas, 116, 131, 145
siddhi (supernatural power), 121, 122
Silburn, L, 113
Sindhu (demon), 47, 63
Śītalā, 30
Sitalāmātā, 195
Śivā (a name of Pārvatī), 48, 63
Śiva, 11, 15, 36, 43–63, 68, 80, 82–85, 87, 89, 91, 93, 96, 98, 108, 109 115, 117–119, 121, 122, 124, 125, 127–130, 141, 153, 156, 219, 220
  see also liṅga
Śivapurāṇa, 108
Skanda, 45
Srinivas, MN, 4, 13–14, 206, 222
Śrīsūkta, 88, 107, 108
Sukanyā, 74
Swat, 29
swayambhū 190, 194,

Tagarapura, 106
tantra/tantrism/tantric, 16, 95, 113, 114
Tantrāloka, 114–131
Tāranātha, 138
Templeman, David, vii, ix, ix, 16, 17, 133, 147, 222, 223
Thakur 154, 162
Three Ms (forbidden things), 123–125
Tiwari, SR, 79, 80, 96, 98, 110
tooth mother, 10
trāga, 17, 153, 154, 155, 156, 157, 162
Trika, 114, 123, 126, 127

Umā, 141
Urban, H, 113

Vadagaon, 98
van Buitenen, JAB, 66
Varuṇa, 74
Veda /Vedic, 3, 6, 24, 25, 27, 35, 36, 38–41, 43, 80, 94, 97, 113, 119, 210, 211
Verardi, G, 39
Verhoeven, M, 23
Vicziany, vii, ix, xii, xiii, 18, 189, 190, 224
vidyā (type of *mantra*), 121, 122
Vindhyavāsinī, 14
Viṣṇu, 58, 88, 89, 62
Viṣṇupurāṇa, 66
Viśvakarman, 46, 47, 62
Vrātyas, 36

Wadley, S, 11
White, DG, 96, 113
Wilson, HH, 66
womb symbolism, 109, 110
  see also yoni

yakṣas (local spirits), 28, 33, 35, 38, 90
yoginī, 96, 113, 114, 116, 117, 125
yoni, 87, 88, 92, 99, 106, 122, 128